Van Gogh and the Art of Living

Van Gogh and the Art of Living

The Gospel According to Vincent van Gogh

Anton Wessels

Translated by Henry Jansen

WIPF & STOCK · Eugene, Oregon

VAN GOGH AND THE ART OF LIVING
The Gospel According to Vincent van Gogh

Wipf & Stock
An Imprint of Wipf and Stock Publishers
199 W. 8th Ave., Suite 3
Eugene, OR 97401
www.wipfandstock.com

ISBN 13: 978-1-62564-109-0
Manufactured in the U.S.A.

The author is grateful to the following organizations
for their financial support of this translation:
VanCoeverden-Adriani Stichting,
which has a close relationship with
VU University Amsterdam, and
De Stichting Zonneweelde

For Matthea Adrianne Vera Verdaasdonk
In special friendship and closeness

Contents

Preface xv
Introduction xiii
An Overview of Vincent van Gogh's Life xix

CHAPTER ONE: LIFE AND SOURCES OF INSPIRATION 1

Vincent Willem
A Family of Ministers and Art Dealers
Teacher and Evangelist in England
In the Book Trade (Dordrecht in the Netherlands)
Modern Christians
Preacher-Poets and Art
An Honest Man
Evangelist in Belgium
The Christ of the Coal Mine
Painting the Borinage
Choosing the Life of a Painter
Two Kinds of Painters
Important Painters and Artists
Peasant Life
His Painter Friend Anthon van Rappard
Paul Gauguin
Travelling Companions: Vincent and Theo
The Inspiration of Literature
The Bible, Literature, and Art
A Bringer of Comfort
The Role and Meaning of Parables
The Marketability of his Work

Contents

CHAPTER TWO: SORROWFUL, YET ALWAYS REJOICING 35

Sorrow in Vincent's Life and Work
The Voice of Conscience: Anguish
The Poor Class
Having Regard for Sien
"Doodling"
Master of Humanity
The Constitution of the French Revolution: A "New Gospel"
"An inner and hidden revolution is coming" (Tolstoy)
Mammon or Money
Humanity, Compassion, and Neediness
Workers
The Last Supper
The Pietà
The Garden of the Poet
The Garden of Paradise
Gethsemane
Death and Transformation
Death: A Journey Past the Stars
The Raising of Lazarus
The Yearning for the Eternal
There is Nothing Sad in Death

CHAPTER THREE: FROM DARKNESS TO LIGHT 69

The White and Black Rays
The Eternal Poetry of Christmas Night
Miners, Darkness, and Light
Literature as Light in Darkness
Light and Dark (Chiaroscuro)
Painters of the Light
Self-Portrait
The Language of Nature
Ivy
Sunflowers
Trees

Japan: The South, Nature, and the Sun
The Four Evangelists: The Seasons and their Colors
Stars in the Night
Doctor Gachet

CHAPTER FOUR: THE ART OF LIVING 105

Living and the Task of Living
Born to Faith
Religions Disappear, but God Remains
Our Life is a Pilgrimage
Exile and Strangers on the Earth
Walkers on a Pilgrimage
Pilgrims Together on the Road
Plunging into the Open Sea of Reality
Collaboration with Other Artists
On Board my Little Yellow House
A Comforting Beacon on Dangerous Seas
Savior from the Fear of Death
Empty Chairs
The Struggle to Live
Working to Distraction
Christ the Greatest Artist
God as Light, Christ as Sun

Bibliography 145
Subject/Name Index 157
Index of Biblical Texts and Characters 171
List of Artists and Writers 173

Preface

Van Gogh was an exceptional artist. He did not think much of the hero worship surrounding artists, but even before he knew how to hold a brush, he was opposed to rules and raised personal expression to the highest good. He was against "routine," "convention," and *trucs d'atelier*, searching single-mindedly for art that was full of character. Not every artist possesses an authentic voice or is able to develop that voice, but what was unique about Van Gogh was that he found his voice quite early—to his own surprise as well. He did not yet have the technical skill to give full rein to that voice, but something unique lay hidden in his art, and that gave him confidence for the future. It is also remarkable that that voice did not disappear when Van Gogh changed his style during his period in Paris and made the achievements of (Neo–)Impressionism his own. Indeed, he felt he understood since then more and more what his own taste and artistic personality meant. But this development did not lead to a heterogenous, uniform style, and within the boundaries of his own possibilities he continued to search for interesting variations and innovations. This experimentation was in his blood and it cannot be viewed separately from his lack of public success. Each day he strove anew to make that one work that would make a difference.

That experimentation led, we now know, to accomplishments whose range he himself did not comprehend. His talent lay in his unusually vivid but always harmonious use of color, which we notice properly only if we view his work next to that of others. Just as special are his unusually quick and accurate way of painting with a lavish amount of paint, clear compositions that are immediately and indelibly impressed on one's retina, his daring striving for graphic painting executed like drawings, and the unprecedented short time in which he mastered the field and developed a whole new view of art.

However important his qualities with regard to painting and technique may be, we would do Van Gogh an injustice if we judged him only on that basis. However important form may have been for him, he was not an art-for-art's-sake artist. He is often characterized as a "religious realist," and there is some truth to that. As a young artist, he was impressed by the artistic-religious program of the English writer George Eliot. The latter found human nature "loveable" and held that one could learn something of "its deep pathos, its sublime mysteries" only by "living a great deal among people more or less commonplace and vulgar." She did not condemn the striving for classic beauty but argued in her *Adam Bede*:

> Let us love that other beauty too, which lies in no secret of proportion, but in the secret of deep human sympathy.... [D]o not impose on us any aesthetic rules which shall banish from the region of Art those old women scraping carrots with their work-worn hands, those heavy clowns taking holiday in a dingy pot-house, those rounded backs and stupid weather-beaten faces that have bent over the spade and done the rough work of the world—those homes with their tin pans, their brown pitchers, their rough curs, and their clusters of onions.

Van Gogh was faithful to this humanistically tinged realism his whole life. He preferred to paint things of everyday that life had run over and marked, to use an expression he himself used. He preferred old women to young ones as subjects for painting, and when he lived in Holland he also liked to paint musty birds' nests. He later chose to paint worn-out shoes and bloomed out sunflowers, but because he had already developed into a precise colorist at that time, he was pulled to the latter still lifes more through the form than the subject. That experience was even so strong that the motif can be seen as nothing more than an excuse to paint in a masterly fashion. This is understandable but does not do enough justice to Van Gogh. To restore the balance, we must point every now and then, via solid argumentation, to the religious, humanistically tinged side of his art, and it is from this fact that this book by Anton Wessels derives its *raison d'être* and its value. Wessels gives his own view—as he rightly should: Van Gogh's search for truth in art and life asks for an authentic response.

Louis van Tilborgh
Curator of Van Gogh Research at the Van Gogh Museum

Introduction

THE TITLE OF MY book on Vincent van Gogh as evangelist, published in 1990 in the Netherlands and in English in 2000, was *Een soort Bijbel* and *A Kind of Bible* respectively. "A kind of Bible" is the expression that Van Gogh himself used for the illustrations he saw and cut out of illustrated English magazines. These illustrations were depictions of the "hard times" (Charles Dickens) of nineteenth-century England. Van Gogh was very inspired by those images, and therefore this expression is also very applicable to much of his own work.

The countless illustrations of biblical stories that Rembrandt and Marc Chagall made were used to publish a Rembrandt Bible and a Chagall Bible. One cannot do anything similar with the works of Vincent van Gogh, since he produced only a few paintings that could be called biblical illustrations, such as *The Good Samaritan*, *The Raising of Lazarus*, and *The Pietà* (*Mary with the dead Jesus on her lap*), and, of course, a series of *Sowers*. But Van Gogh succeeded in doing something different from making illustrations of biblical events and that went beyond that kind of enterprise: he was interested in the idea behind those events. "It was not his intention to illustrate the Bible but to express the life of faith to which the Bible testifies."[1]

In this book I want to present "the Gospel according to Vincent van Gogh" via three themes borrowed from Van Gogh himself, the painter and writer (of letters): "rejoicing and sorrow," "darkness and light," and "the art of living."

To begin with the latter theme, does it not seem contradictory to speak about Van Gogh's art of living or *savoir-vivre*? Is he not known more for having gone mad, cutting off his ear, and committing suicide at a relatively young age? Be that as it may, he was also constantly occupied with art—and with the art of living precisely. According to him, one had to "learn to *read*, just as one had to learn to *see* and learn to *live*" (italics mine) (July 1880).[2]

---

1. Miedema, *Vincent van Gogh*, 73.

2. References are always to the Dutch edition of Van Gogh's letters (1990). Dates will be indicated in the text.

When he advised his sister Wilhelmien to read modern literature, she in turn recommended a book to him called *De zin van het leven* (The Meaning of Life), which described one man's successful search for happiness.[3] But Van Gogh was a bit put off by "the terrible title." In his view, the moral of this story was "that a man in certain cases ultimately chooses a life with a friendly, devoted wife and her child above a life in restaurants, on boulevards, and in pubs, a life he had previously led without all too much excesses." "That is, no doubt, very nice," he answered his sister somewhat ironically. But to his brother Theo he frankly confessed that this book taught him absolutely nothing about the meaning of life he could use. He then referred to other literature that he found more true to life. As a "testator of our Dutch culture"—who was characterized by Annie Romein-Verschoor as a "master of humanity"—Van Gogh conveyed a message in his work about the path that he himself followed that was "more true to life," the path that human beings walk in their turbulent existence, the pilgrimage along the various stages of the road of life. In this work he does not speak about the meaning of life but about the true art of living.

It is fascinating to see and read the moving way in which he wrestled with the deep human questions of the whence, why, and whither of life. He did not see himself doing this on his own but acknowledged kindred spirits and allies in preachers, preacher-poets, painters, writers, and other artists who also attempt to find their own way through life in a similar fashion, to point to it, and to actually follow it themselves. It is constantly apparent how much he was in conversation with and inspired by these "fellow pilgrims" on that path.

In the first chapter, "Life and Sources of Inspiration," we will look at how Van Gogh initially worked in the family's art business and then as teacher, (assistant) preacher, and evangelist in England and the mining district of the Borinage in Belgium before finally choosing a life as an artist. Various religious influences had an initial effect on him: the denomination to which his father, the preacher, belonged and in which life is more important than doctrine. Furthermore, he was influenced by the modern theological thinking of his uncle, also a minister, who sought to bring the figure of Jesus closer to modern people. Moreover, he was also inspired by the preacher-poets who attempted to connect art and faith in the tradition of emblem books, allegorical prints that were provided with rhyming captions. There was also, of course, the influence of artists from the past and

---

3. Édouard Sens, *La sens de la vie.*

present. He loved modern literature, especially English and French, and saw a close connection between faith, literature, and art.

In the second chapter the accent lies on the theme of "rejoicing and sorrow" that characterized Van Gogh's whole life and work. Having passed through "the universe of sorrow," he himself wanted to mitigate the needs of others in very concrete ways (in the Borinage, in The Hague, and in Paris). Although suffering was inevitable, in his view, one should not complain. He painted gardens: from the Garden of Eden, Paradise, the poet's garden, up to the garden on the Mount of Olives, where Jesus was before he was arrested and crucified, a symbol for the expression of fear. He considered Gethsemane more beautiful than the Garden of Paradise. For him, there was no sadness in death.

The focus in the third chapter is the theme of "light and darkness." Chiaroscuro played a dominating role in his life and work as art dealer, evangelist, and painter: light and darkness in the lives of the miners, "the bearers of burdens," on the way to the light. The dark nights were illuminated by the light of the stars.

The Dutch painters of light were his great inspiration: Rembrandt van Rijn, Johannes Vermeer of Delft, and Jan Hendrik Weissenbruch, a painter of the Hague school, but modern literature was also a source of inspiration, full of reality, the light that shone in the modern period. In addition, Van Gogh read and interpreted "the great book of nature." The four seasons for him recalled the four evangelists of the New Testament (Matthew, Mark, Luke, and John), who spoke to him of a reality above this reality, the *quelque chose la haut* (something above) and "the ray from above."

Finally, Van Gogh was aware like no other of his duty and task in life: his vocation as human being and artist. That means that he was well acquainted with loneliness, fear, and despair, including having suicidal tendencies. Nevertheless, he sees himself as cut out for faith, rather than resignation. Human beings follow their life's path, through storms and dangers, on land and on sea, where the "star of the sea" (the Virgin Mary) helps them and provides light. Van Gogh rejects the unhealthy, sickly forms of religion but continues to embrace authentic forms of piety.

Possessed, like so many other painters, by the madness of the artist he worked until he almost went mad so that he could testify to the light. As an artist like no other, he understood the art of living that is also the art of dying. Christ, whom he called sublime, was for him the greatest artist.

A general overview of Van Gogh's life precedes the four thematic chapters.

An Overview of Vincent van Gogh's Life

March 30, 1852	Birth and death of Vincent van Gogh, the first child of Rev. Theodorus van Gogh and Anna van Gogh-Corbentus
March 30, 1853	Birth of Vincent Willem van Gogh in Groot-Zundert (North Brabant)
May 1, 1857	Birth of his brother Theo
1861–1862	Attends village school in Zundert
1862–1864	Between January 1862 and February 1864 thirteen drawings that we know of (primarily copies)
1864–1866	Attends boarding school in Zevenbergen
1866	Student at the secondary school in Tilburg as of September 1866
1867	One drawing that we know of
March 1868	Vincent returns home to Zundert before finishing the second year
July 30, 1869	The youngest employee at the international art dealership Goupil & Cie. in The Hague under Herman Gijsbertus Tersteeg (1845–1917); confidant of the owner, his uncle Vincent (Cent) (1820–1888)
1871	Van Gogh family moves to Helvoirt
August 1872	Begins correspondence with his brother Theo
January 1873	Theo employed at Goupil branch in Brussels, originally owned by their uncle Hendrik (Hein) van Gogh (1814–1877)

May 19, 1873	Vincent starts work at the London branch of Goupil; he boards at the home of Mrs. Sarah Ursula Loyer
June 1874	Unrequited love for Eugenie (Ursula) Loyer
October 1874	Transfer to headquarters of Goupil & Cie. in Paris.
January 1875	Returns to London branch
May 15, 1875	Transferred again to Paris headquarters
October 18, 1875	Van Gogh family moves to Etten
March 1876	Resigns or is let go by the successors of Goupil & Cie., Boussod and Valadon, the art dealership for which Theo van Gogh later worked
April 16, 1876	Teacher in the English seaside resort Ramsgate; assistant at William Stokes' school
July 1876	Assistant pastor at Isleworth (near London) for Rev. Thomas Slade-Jones (1829–1883)
October 29, 1876	Vincent delivers his first sermon in the Methodist church in Richmond
December 1876	Visits the Netherlands at Christmas, where he stays in his parents' home in Etten
January–April 1877	Works at the bookshop Blussé & Van Braam in Dordrecht
May 9, 1877	Leaves for Amsterdam to study for the university entrance exams so he can study theology. His teacher is Mendes da Costa
July 1878	Resigns his studies, particularly Latin and Greek
August 1878	Begins training to be an evangelist in Laeken (near Brussels)
November 1878	Drops out of the training program
December 1878	Goes to Bergen (Mons) in the Borinage to do evangelization work
January 1879	Appointed as evangelist in Wasmes

Winter 1880	Visits the studio of the poet-painter Jules Breton in Courrière (France), but does not dare to enter
March 1880	Works as an evangelist in Cuesmes and begins to draw
July 1880	"Conversion letter" after eighteen months of silence
September 1880	Discovers his calling as a painter
October 1880	Enrolls in the Royal Academy of Art in Brussels
October 1880	Becomes acquainted with Anthon van Rappard (1858–1892)
April 1881	Leaves the Art Academy in Brussels and returns home to his parents in Etten
August 1, 1881	Falls in love with his cousin Kee Stricker (1846–1918), his senior by eight years, whose husband, Rev. Vos, died three years before; his proposal of marriage is rejected
December 1881	Leaves Etten after quarreling with his father about church attendance at Christmas; goes to The Hague
December 1881	Lives in The Hague with Clasina (Sien) Hoornik (1850–1904) and her young daughter
Winter 1882	His uncle by marriage, the painter Anton Mauve of the Hague school, supervises him in his first steps as a painter, but the two have a falling out
March 1882	First commission from Uncle Cornelis for twelve townscapes
June 1882	Hospitalized because of venereal disease
July 2, 1882	Sien gives birth to a child (not his)
August 7, 1882	Van Gogh family moves to Nuenen
September 11, 1882	Leaves Sien and her children
September 1883	Goes to Drenthe, wanders on the moors
December 5, 1883	Returns to his parents, stays in Nuenen

January 1884	His mother breaks a leg, he looks after her; works in Nuenen first in a "studio" behind the parsonage, then in a studio of his own as a "painter of peasants"; teaches three students; makes an agreement with Theo on collaboration (support by Theo)
Spring 1884	Neighbor Margot Begemann falls in love with him
August 1884	Suicide attempt by neighbor (Begemann)
March 27, 1885	Death of Vincent's father
April/May 1885	Paints *The Potato Eaters*
Second half of June 1885	Breaks with Anthon van Rappard
November 24, 1885	Moves to Antwerp
January 18, 1886	Enrols in the Royal Academy in Antwerp
February 1886	Leaves for Paris and moves in with Theo; works in Cormon's studio; meets painters like Émile Bernard (1868–1941) and works with Paul Signac (1863–1935) and Paul Gauguin (1848–1903); displays his first work in Café Brasserie du Tambourin, run by the Italian Agostina Segatori
February 20, 1888	Leaves for Arles in Provence (southern France)
July 1888	Paints in Saintes-Maries-de-la-Mer
September 1888	Moves into the Yellow House
October 23, 1888	Paul Gauguin (1848–1903) moves in with him in the Yellow House to start an art studio together
December 1888	Theo announces his engagement to Johanna Bonger
December 23, 1888	Tensions with Paul Gauguin reach a climax; Vincent has a nervous breakdown and cuts off a piece of his earlobe
December 24, 1888	After Gauguin discovers Vincent in the morning injured, he leaves hastily for Paris, requesting Joseph Roulin to keep him informed; Rev. F. Salles becomes concerned about Vincent's condition; admission to the hospital in Arles

December 31, 1888	Rev. Salles sends a report to Theo about improvements in Vincent's condition
January 7, 1889	Vincent leaves the hospital and returns to the Yellow House
February 9, 1889	Admitted to hospital again; stays until 17 April
February 27, 1889	By order of the police commissioner, Vincent is committed to hospital against his will and completely in his right mind; thirty of his neighbors signed a petition accusing him of abnormal behavior that puts their safety in danger
April 17, 1889	Marriage of Theo to Jo Bonger (1862–1925) in Amsterdam
May 8, 1889	Voluntarily admitted to Saint Paul de Mausole, an institution for the mentally ill in Saint Rémy de Provence; Rev. Salles accompanies him to his new destination
January 1890	First favorable review by art critic Albert Aurier in *Mercure de France*
January 31, 1890	Birth of Vincent (1890–1978), son of Theo and Jo
March 1890	Sale of his painting *The Red Vineyard* to Anna Boch for 400 francs
May 17, 1890	Leaves Saint Rémy, arrives in Paris
May 21, 1890	Arrives in Auvers-sur-Oise (near Paris); moves into the inn of Gustave Ravoux; meets Dr. Gachet
July 1890	Visits Theo and Toulouse Lautrec in Paris
July 27, 1890	Shoots himself in the chest
July 29, 1890	Vincent dies at the age of thirty-seven in Auvers, in Theo's presence
October 1890	Theo, suffering from syphilis and great stress, has a nervous breakdown and is admitted to a clinic in Auteil near Paris; via Dr. Frederik van Eeden he is admitted to a hospital for the mentally ill in Utrecht

January 25, 1891	Theo dies in Utrecht at the age of thirty-three of dementia paralytica
1914	Johanna van Gogh-Bonger has Theo's remains brought to Auvers to be buried next to Vincent
1978	Theo's son Vincent dies at the age of eighty-eight in Laren

CHAPTER ONE

LIFE AND SOURCES OF INSPIRATION

Vincent Willem

VINCENT WILLEM VAN GOGH was born on 30 March 1853 in Zundert, a small village in the Dutch province of North Brabant close to the Belgian border. His mother, Anna Cornelia Carbentus, was an energetic woman with a zest for life and a great love for nature who was very adept at putting her thoughts down on paper.[1] His father, Theodorus van Gogh, was a Dutch Reformed minister. They called their son Vincent Willem; the first name is the same as the one they gave to a child who had been born and died precisely a year earlier, on 30 March 1852. Vincent's namesake was buried right next to the church in Zundert: *Vincent van Gogh 1852.* Engraved on the flat stone is the following text (in Dutch): "Suffer the little children to come unto me, for it is to such that the kingdom of God belongs" (Luke18:16).[2] While his brother had been given only the one name,[3] Vincent himself was also given the name Willem and was thus named after both his grandfathers. On 1 May 1857 his brother Theodorus (Theo) was born, and four sisters and another brother were born in the years following.

1. Van Gogh and van Gogh-Bonger, *Verzamelde brieven,* 3.

2. Unless otherwise indicated, all translations from the Bible, including those within quotations, are my own.

3. Meyers, *De jonge Vincent,* 24–25.

A Family of Ministers and Art Dealers

Vincent's family included several ministers and art dealers. His father, The-odorus, studied theology in Utrecht and was called as a minister to Groot-Zundert in 1849, where he was ordained by his father. He would also later serve the congregations of Helvoirt, Etten, and Nuenen, all small towns in the province of Brabant. Vincent's uncle on his mother's side, Johannes Paulus Stricker, would be ordained as a minister in Amsterdam in 1855.[4]

Vincent was influenced by the piety of his father, who supported the "Groningen school." This school put *life* above *doctrine*, and their emotional piety went contrary to the dry dogmatics of the Dutch Reformed church of that time. The "Groningen school" rediscovered Thomas à Kempis's *Imitation of Christ* and emphasized this imitation through love, humility, and social service.[5]

Vincent did confession of faith at Easter 1871, when he was nineteen years old, in The Hague. Five years later, in England, he still remembered his catechism teacher, Johannes Hillen. He asked Theo, who worked in the art trade in The Hague, to look Hillen up so that he could tell him that Vincent was teaching school in England and, who knows, might later be able to get a position of some kind in a church (July 8, 1876).

Vincent had no less than three uncles who worked in the great inter-nationally renowned art store Goupil & Cie. His godfather, Vincent (Uncle Cent), had a great love for art and literature, and the two of them got along very well. His godfather sold the art shop in The Hague to the Parisian concern Goupil, which also had galleries in Brussels, Paris, and London. Uncle Johannes, who became director of the naval dockyard in 1877 and later vice-admiral, would put Vincent up when he was studying in Amster-dam. After a high school education that he, for reasons that remain unclear, never finished, Vincent worked in the art trade for six years. He was first employed in Goupil's shop in The Hague but left with a favorable recom-mendation in June 1873 for the London branch. There he wrote: "I have a rich life here, 'we have nothing but possess all things'" (2 Corinthians 6:10). While he was in London he began to believe he was becoming a cosmopoli-tan, i.e. "not a Dutchman, Englishman, or Frenchman, but simply a man" (February 9, 1874). He then worked at the Parisian branch, where he was let go, however, on 1 April 1876 because it was felt he "had no ambition for

4. Van Gogh and van Gogh-Bonger, *Verzamelde brieven*, 1–3.
5. Bailey, *Van Gogh in England*, 112, note 2; Druick and Zegers, *Van Gogh en Gauguin*, 11.

his profession." The reason he was dismissed was that he visited his parents in Etten for a few days during the busy Christmas season (July 22, 1878). But Vincent no longer felt happy in the trade and had already considered leaving. Ultimately, however, his work in the art trade gave him a knowledge of art, and artists became very important for him.

Teacher and Evangelist in England

Vincent's father was happy when he was able to get a position in the seaside resort town of Ramsgate in southeast England. He taught French, German, and maths in a small boys' boarding school in return for board and lodging (April 4, 1876). Vincent was going through an intense religious period in his life at that time and emphasized religious education in the work he did at that school.

At his request Theo sent him two engravings by Ary Scheffer, a painter from Dordrecht whom Vincent greatly admired: *Christus Consolator* (Christ the Comforter) and *Christus Remunerator* (Christ the Avenger). He called them "unforgettable paintings." His pious outpourings in his letters were even too much for his father. The latter wrote to Theo:

> Oh, if he would only learn to be simple like a child and not throw Bible texts around so excessively and wildly. The more he does it, the more concerned [Mother and I] become, and I fear that someday he will no longer be suited for practical life. It's a bitter shame .... If he wants to become a servant of the Gospel, then he should be willing to do the preparatory work and enroll in the necessary university program. Then I would be more confident about it.

Vincent's dream began to come true in October: he was required to teach until 1:00 p.m., but after that he was free to work as an assistant minister in a small church in Turnham Green.

The position Vincent sought was one "between preacher and missionary" among workers in the suburbs of London. He wanted very much to become a "London missionary," someone whose job it was "to go among the workers and poor to distribute the Bible and, as soon as one had gained some experience, to speak with foreigners who were seeking work." By way of recommending himself, he wrote to a minister there:

> Although I have not been educated for the church, my earlier life of travel, of living in different countries, dealing with various people,

> poor and rich, religious and not religious, of doing different kinds of work, days of manual labor in between the days of office work, and speaking different languages can partly make up for my lack of education. (June 17 and July 5, 1876)

After a few months of teaching at the boarding school, he went to work as an assistant minister in Isleworth. The Methodist minister he assisted paid him a salary, and they became friends (January 21, 1877). Toward the end of his stay in England he delivered his only completely transmitted sermon in the Methodist church in Richmond. He began his sermon with quoting Psalm 119:19, "I am a stranger on earth; do not hide your commandments from me."

> It is an old faith and it is a good faith that our life is a pilgrims' progress—that we are strangers in the earth, but that though this be so, yet we are not alone for our father is with us. We are pilgrims, our life is a long walk, a journey from earth to heaven. . . .
>
> Our life, we might compare it to a journey, we go from the place where we were born to a far off haven. Our earlier life might be compared to sailing on a river, but very soon the waves become higher, the wind more violent, we are at sea almost before we are aware of it—and the prayer from the heart ariseth to God: Protect me o God, for my bark is so small and Thy sea is so great. The heart of man is very much like the sea, it has its storms, it has its tides and in its depths it has its pearls too. The heart that seeks for God and for a Godly life has more storms than any other (October 31, 1876).[6]

In the Book Trade (Dordrecht in the Netherlands)

But Vincent did not feel happy in England any longer. He wanted to return to the home and family life he missed and looked forward to spending Christmas at home. We do not know what precisely happened around Christmas in 1876, but he made the decision at the end of December not to return to England.

From 1 January to the end of April 1877 he worked in the Blussé & Van Braam bookshop in Dordrecht, on Voorstraat, opposite Schefferplein. During that period he often visited the museum there, alone or with his father, which displayed many works by the painter Ary Scheffer who was

6. The English is Van Gogh's.

originally from Dordrecht. Vincent hung the Scheffer prints he brought from England in his room.[7]

He would come to work sleepy in the mornings because he had been reading the Bible deep into the night. It was in Dordrecht that he expressed a wish for the first time to become a minister, just like his father. He told this to his employer in Dordrecht, Frans Braat, who later remembered that Vincent had said: "I want to be a pastor, just like Dad." "But boy," Braat warned him, "don't you find it sad that, after so many years, your father never got any further than Etten and Leur?" That was the only time he saw Van Gogh angry: his father was where he should be, a true pastor![8]

Vincent himself wanted specifically to become "a sower of the Word":

> In our family . . . from generation to generation, there has always
> been someone who was a servant of the Gospel. Why should that
> voice not be heard in this and following generations as well?

It was his heartfelt desire to be "a Christian and a Christian laborer" (March 22, 1877).

Modern Christians

To achieve that dream of becoming a minister, he left for Amsterdam in May 1877, where he would live until 24 August 1878. He stayed in Amsterdam with his uncle Johannes at the Naval Dockyard where he attempted to study for the university entrance exams so he could train to be a minister. To be able to start theological studies, he first had to gain the necessary knowledge of Greek and Latin.

He found it difficult. Sometimes his mind was dull, his head often burning, and his thinking was confused. He did not know how he would be able to complete that difficult and comprehensive study. After the irregular life he had lived, it was not always easy for him to get used to simply working regular hours and to keep that up (May 30, 1877).

Reverend Johannes Paulus Stricker, Vincent's maternal uncle, counseled him during his studies in Amsterdam, giving him a class once or twice a week, and Vincent was glad his uncle could make time for him (February 10, 1878). He saw a nice portrait of John Calvin by Ary Scheffer at his uncle's (May 28, 1877). Scheffer did not like the strictness in Protestantism

---

7. Cf. Wesseling, "Ary Scheffer," 86–88.

8. Cossée, "Vincent van Gogh," 2.

and was an advocate of freedom and tolerance. He painted Calvin as a melancholy old man who also had moments of doubt. One of the founders of the "Groningen school" wished that Calvin had always been as "mild and gentle" as Scheffer had painted him![9] Vincent often heard his uncle preach in the Eilandskerk (Island Church) on the text, for example: "By Your light we see light" (Psalm 36:10) (December 9, 1877). He was very pleased with what his uncle said, saying that his uncle spoke with warmth and feeling (July 9, 1877). One Sunday morning he quoted Jean de la Fontaine's fable of "Death and the Woodman":

> A poor wood-chopper, with his fagot load,
>
> Whom weight of years, as well as load, oppressed,
> Sore groaning in his smoky hut to rest,
> Trudged wearily along his homeward road.
> At last his wood on the ground he throws,
> And sits him down to think over all his woes.
> To joy a stranger, since his hapless birth,
> What poorer wretch on this rolling earth?
> No bread sometimes, and never a moment's rest;
> Wife, children, soldiers, landlords, public tax,
> All wait the swinging of his old, worn axe,
> And paint the veriest picture of a man unblest.
> On Death he calls. Forthwith that monarch grim
> Appears, and asks what he should do for him.
> "Not much, indeed; a little help I lack—
> To put these fagots on my back."
> Death ready stands all ills to cure;
> But let us not his cure invite.
> THAN DIE, IT'S BETTER TO ENDURE,—
> Is both a manly maxim and a right. (August 18, 1877)

Vincent also became familiar with his uncle's scholarly works, finding the works he had written to be "very good and [testifying] to deep *feeling*" (November 23, 1881). Stricker was a liberal theologian who explored the relationship between faith and modernity in his works.[10] The explicit question in his work was: How does one preach Christianity for "modern people"?[11] Vincent had also read his *Jezus van Nazareth, volgens de historie geschetst* (Jesus of Nazareth: A Historical Sketch) (1868), which Stricker

9. Namely, Hofstede de Groot. Ewals, *Ary Scheffer*, 314–16.

10. Kôdera, *Vincent van Gogh*, 19; Berlage, "Levensbericht," 27–55.

11. Cossée, "De gehele godsdienst," 105.

himself had called a bold venture.[12] This book would reinforce Vincent's view that Christ was human and not a supernatural being, a "suffering servant of the Lord" (Isaiah 53) and a man of the people.[13]

His uncle made use of the work of the leading scholars in Germany at the time, such as Ludwig Feuerbach's *Das Wesen des Christentums (The Essence of Christianity)*, and David Friedrich Strauss's *Leben Jesus (The Life of Jesus)*, and sought support for his views in Ernst Renan's *La Vie de Jésus (The Life of Jesus)* as well. Renan was one of the greatest figures in French intellectual life in the second half of the nineteenth century.

A striking connection can be observed between Vincent's views, the modern insights of his uncle, and the thought of Ernest Renan. Renan is an example of a "modern Christian," who, confronted with modern Bible criticism and the hypocrisy of the church as an institute, left the church but remained a believer in Christ.

Vincent saw in Renan a kindred spirit, one who had indeed distanced himself from the institutional church but not from the faith. The first time he quoted Renan was in London:

> The people who want to spread a religious view (want to be a "missionary of a religious idea") have no other footing than that thought. Man is not only on earth to be happy, not even simply to be upright. He is on earth to achieve great things for society, to attain nobility, and to rise above the commonplace in which almost all people spend their existence. (May 8, 1875)

Ten years later Renan continued to influence him, and Van Gogh still believed in what Renan wrote about "universal sympathy":

> Whoever wants to achieve something good or useful should not count on the approval or appreciation of the public at large nor desire those things. Rather, such a person should not expect anything other than that only a few hearts—and that is only a maybe—will sympathize and join in.

Van Gogh places the "Christ" of Renan over against the institutionalized church: "Is the Christ of Renan not a thousand times more comforting than so many Christ figures of paper maché?" (April 25-28, 1889).

---

12. Van 't Hooft, "Johannes Paulus Stricker," 364; Liagre, "Een veelkleurig bestaan," 211.

13. Cf. Greer, "'Een man van smerten,'" 35.

Preacher-Poets and Art

During his study period in Amsterdam he also often heard Jan Lodewijk I. Ten Kate and Eliza Laurillard preach, both of whom were ministers in Amsterdam like his uncle (July 9, 1877). In the Eilandskerk he listened to Ten Kate, the "poet of Creation," one of the most famous of the "preacher-poets" in his time and one of the most prolific Dutch writers of the nineteenth century (August 5, 1877). His name is usually mentioned in connection with the typical "minister culture" in the Netherlands of the nineteenth century, when almost 80 percent of all students studied theology and ministers had an influential position not only in the church but also in culture (literature and poetry). If Ten Kate preached or spoke somewhere, Vincent said, "people [stood] in line to hear him because he [was] a truly gifted speaker who [spoke] directly to the hearts of people in fluent and ornate language" (November 19, 1877). Ten Kate also wrote about artworks such as *Christus Remunerator*, the well-known painting by Ary Scheffer.

Vincent heard the preacher-poet Eliza Laurillard preach different times in the Oudezijds Kapel (Old Side Chapel) (August 18, 1877; March 3 1878). Laurillard was enormously popular, dedicating himself to the care of prisoners and neglected children, and advocated the abolishment of the death penalty. His skill as a speaker was characterized by an edifying and humorous style.[14] Laurillard was known for "his clear presentation and silver voice." According to Vincent, he had a splendid gift, coming up with constantly new views and everything full of life and spirit: "There is something unique, something 'evergreen,' something of the imperishable, an always youthful and fiery passion," that he also found in his father (December 4, 1877). Laurillard's book *Met Jezus in de natuur* (With Jesus in Nature) contained many of the subjects that would later become themes in Vincent's painting, such as the ploughman, the sower, the grain, the sun and the rain, darkness and light.

> Many and varied are the beauties of nature, wonderful in all its parts. Its labor is magnificent, its peace sweet, its visual imagery rich, its polyphonic song uplifting and enchanting . . . . In all generations there have always been many who "heard the Lord walking in the garden in the cool of the evening" (Genesis 3:8) when they walked outside and who also had the gift to decipher in

---

14. Liagre, "De jonge Vincent," 212–13.

delight the hieroglyphics written by God, to understand the symbolism of nature signed by God.[15]

An Honest Man

It can be seen from Vincent's letters from that time in Amsterdam how much he wanted to be an "honest man" and to become even more honest. He thought that the "inner and spiritual man" could be developed by knowledge of history in general and of specific people in particular: from biblical history until that of the French Revolution, and from the *Odyssey* of Homer to the books of Charles Dickens. He cites in particular the French writer, historian, and social philosopher Jules Michelet, the hero of the poor and oppressed, a critic of the official church and its leaders.[16] During his study he found that

> a good minister must be someone who has the authority to say what can be good and useful in the world, and it is perhaps good that I have had a relatively long period for preparation in that. (April 3, 1878)

Vincent always wanted to know more about what was useful and to gain more experience.

> *Weemoed* [melancholy] is a good thing to have, if it is written in two words. *Wee* [woe] is in every person, everybody has reason enough for that, but *moed* [courage] must also be present, the more the better, and it is good to be someone who never despairs. (April 3, 1878)

Little actually came of his original purpose for going to Amsterdam. Vincent once asked his teacher:

> "Mendes, do you actually believe that such horrors—learning Latin and Greek—are necessary for someone who wants what I want: to give poor creatures peace with their earthly existence?"
> And I [Mendes], who, as his teacher, could not say he was right, but deep down in my soul I thought that he—note well, I say, he, Vincent van Gogh—was completely right, I did the best I could, but it didn't yield anything. (October 1876)

---

15. Laurillard, *Met Jezus in de natuur*, 1–2. Kôdera, *Vincent van Gogh*, 22–23.
16. Callow, *Vincent van Gogh*, 53.

He did not pass his university entrance exams. While working in the Borinage (Belgium) after a short preparatory training for evangelist, he would call this whole educational undertaking, however well intentioned, "daft" and "grossly foolish" (August 15, 1879). He called it the worst time he had ever had, whereby the very difficult and troubling time he had in the Borinage, in those uncivilized surroundings, appears desirable and attractive in comparison with his time in Amsterdam. It was not because he lacked the capacity that he was unable to finish his education. He later explained to a friend that he, who did learn other languages, could have mastered that wretched bit of Latin and other languages. It was just an excuse because he did not want to admit that he viewed the theological faculty as an unutterable mess, "a breeding ground for Pharisees." He attempted to prove that it was not a question of (lack of) nerve precisely by going to the Borinage, where it was certainly more difficult for him than as a student of theology (September 22, 1883).

Evangelist in Belgium

After quitting his studies in Amsterdam, he went with his father to Belgium for two days and visited the Committee of Evangelization of the Flemish-speaking evangelist training school in Laeken, close to Brussels.[17] Mr. Jones, the head of the school, who was from Isleworth and had come from England especially for this purpose, accompanied them on this visit. An evangelist from that school was expected to be able to hold easy, cordial, and popular talks or speeches, better short and to the point than scholarly and long. Extensive knowledge of the classical languages was less important than suitability for the practical side and a natural faith (July 22, 1878).

The program lasted three years, but Vincent quit after a trial period of three months (November 15, 1878).[18] He was not given an appointment as an evangelist, but his heart did go out to the French-speaking population in the mining region of the Borinage, and Rev. Van der Wayen Pieterszen promised to see to it that he could work there in that capacity.[19] He was allowed to work on a trial basis as an evangelist in the mining district of Bergen (Mons), among the miners, a "job" without any social prestige. From

17. Lutjeharms, "Abraham Van der Wayen Pieterszen," 141; Liagre, "De jonge Vincent," 211–16.

18. Cf. Hulsker, *Van Gogh in Close-up*, 118, 122.

19. Liagre, "Een veelkleurig bestaan," 205, 216, 220.

late 1878 until July 1879, he lived and worked in the villages of Pâturages, Wasmes, and Cuesmes.

In his work in these villages he made frequent use of a small French booklet of seventy psalms set to music, in which he underlined a number of texts, as we can see in his personal copy that has been preserved. We can determine something of his attitude from the notes and underlining he added.[20] At the beginning of the section on brotherly love, he writes: "charity, 1 Corinthians 13"—Paul's famous text on love: "thus these three remain: faith, hope, and love, but the greatest of these is love." And above the heading on the brevity of life he said, "a little time." He underlined the lines in Psalm 77, "My God himself amazed me" and "My troubled soul is dismayed." Several horizontal and vertical lines are found with Psalm 86:

> In my unparalleled pain
> see the misery that envelops me
> and lessen my cares.
> My God, protect my life,
> for I want nothing more than to serve you.
> Save your servant, O God,
> who is sure of your favor.

His trust in someone who goes "through the darkness to the light" can be seen in the underscoring in Psalm 138:

> No, in the gloomy days of
> the painful march, never, O never,
> are you alone here below.[21]

During his time in the Borinage, Vincent took as his example the apostle Paul, who, after all, spent three years in Arabia before going to preach and beginning his great missionary journeys (Galatians 1:17).

> If I could only work for three years or so in such a region in peace.
> If it please God and he spares my life, I would be ready when I
> would be around thirty. (August 1878)

It was customary to hold Bible readings in workers' homes, and Vincent spoke on such occasions about, among other things, the parable of the mustard seed (Luke 13:18, 19), on which he wrote a twenty-seven-page essay, and he hoped that there was something good in it. At Christmas, he

20. Hammacher, *Van Gogh*, 64.
21. Liagre, "Een veelkleurig bestaan," 217.

spoke, of course, of the stable in Bethlehem and "peace on earth" (Luke 2) (December 26, 1878).

The Christ of the Coal Mine

He saw true poverty in the Borinage. In Wasmes he initially lived with a baker, Jean-Baptiste Denis, and his wife, Esther. But, because he felt he was being spoiled there, he moved to a dirty cattle shed "where he slept on straw like an animal." When Esther asked him why he went so far, he said: "Esther, we have to do as the good God does; once in a while we have to live among His equals."[22]

He wanted to imitate Christ quite literally. He took the Gospel so seriously that he identified with the poverty and misery of the miners. After one mining disaster, he literally gave the sheets from his bed and the shirt off his back in caring for the injured. If he spoke of an artist painting a scene of striking charcoal burners, he could say that he had experienced that situation down to the smallest detail (October 10, 1182).

For the official church authorities, however, Vincent's activity was too much of a good thing. He was let go and "failed" as an evangelist. But none of the miners who knew him could ever forget the man they called the "Christ of the coal mine." Mme. Bonte, the wife of the pastor, recalled that, when he called on them to say good-bye, he looked pale and said in a sad tone: "No one understood me." Then he walked away barefoot, with his "cross" on his shoulder. While he walked away, some mean young boys from the village called after him, "He's crazy, he's crazy!"[23] An older minister in the Borinage would later say:

> His religious feelings were very fervent, and he wanted to obey the words of Jesus Christ in the most absolute way. He felt compelled to imitate the first Christians.[24]

The "evangelism committee" evaluated him as follows:

> In his care of the sick and injured Mr. van Gogh has given proof of having admirable qualities. He has testified many times to devotion and self-denial by sacrificing his nightly rest for those who were in distress and by even giving up the best part of his clothes

22. Tralbaut, 1969, quoted by Callow, *Vincent van Gogh*, 99.
23. Callow, *Vincent van Gogh*, 114.
24. Quoted by Maurer, *The Pursuit of Spiritual Wisdom*, 2.

and linen for them. If he also had a gift for speaking, which is indispensable for someone placed at the head of a faith community, he would certainly have been a perfect evangelist.[25]

What was the problem? He could not preach extemporaneously.

Painting the Borinage

Van Gogh called the Borinage region unique, remarkable, and picturesque:

> There is something simple and good-hearted about the people. Those who leave are homesick for their country, just as, conversely, strangers who suffer from homesickness feel at home here. (March, 1879)

Later in The Hague he played for two months with the idea of returning to the mines of the Borinage—though only to paint. But he could not afford it (November 26, 27 1882). Still, many years later in Arles, he thought back on his time in the Borinage when he wrote that one could easily tell where his friend, the Belgian painter Eugène G. Boch, came from. "In how he speaks and what he does I can very much recognize the accent of his country, the shyness of the miners, whom I still think about quite often." Boch thought seriously about—if he went back—painting the miners in the Borinage. Indeed, he would be able to work in an area where, Vincent felt, one could spend one's whole life. The women miners, especially in their miners' rags, were beautiful. He asked Boch to tell a certain farmer and miner for him when he arrived in Petites-Wasmes that he never forgot the Borinage and that he would like to return. That somber country would remain in his memory forever. That was when he finally worked according to nature for the first time. He was moved by the idea that all those spots would in the end be painted.[26]

After his dismissal as evangelist and already before he decided to become a painter, he had shown some interest in drawing and painting. As a boy, he had already made some small sketches (February 2, 1881)! "Did I not stand and draw along the wharf of the Thames in London when I went home in the evening from Southampton Station?" (October 12, 1883). A small room in the home of the mining family, where he had to

25. Van Gogh and Van Gogh-Bonger, *Verzamelde Brieven*, 1973, 127–28.
26. October 1888.

share sleeping quarters with the children, would also be his first "studio."[27] He began with the first drawing of miners going to their work in the early morning. It was not until the winter of 1879, however, that he made the definitive decision to become a painter.

His brother Theo sent him etchings so he could train himself in drawing and painting. Vincent read books on anatomy and perspective and informed Theo that he was working hard, even though there were no results to be seen yet. But he did have strong hopes that "the thorn-bushes would bear white blossoms when it was time" and that these apparently fruitless struggles were nothing more than labor pains: "first the pain, then the joy." He hoped that Theo would see him as a laborer, although he did not know in advance what he would be able to produce. Nonetheless, he hoped he would be able "to produce some doodlings that might contain something human" (September 7, 1880).

Choosing the Life of a Painter

A long letter from the summer of 1880 marks the beginning of his life as a painter and reads like a program of action.

> So I think . . . that everything that is truly good and beautiful, the inner, moral, spiritual, and exalted beauty in people and in their works, that all this comes from God, and that everything that is evil and bad in the works of people and in people, that that is not of God and that God does not approve of it either.

He was inclined to believe that the best way to know God was to love: loving with an exalted and genuine inner sympathy, with surrender, with intelligence; loving and attempting to understand more of it—that is what, in his view, led to God, to an unshakable faith.

One person loves Rembrandt—he knows very well that God exists. Another studies the history of the French Revolution—but such a person would not be an unbeliever either. He would also see that there is a sovereign power present within great things that manifests itself. Again, another has recently been attending the free lessons at the great "university of sorrow," has paid attention to the things that he sees with his eyes and hears with his ears and has pondered them. He will ultimately believe and learns perhaps more about them than he can say. Whoever attempts to understand

27. Van Gogh and van Gogh-Bonger, *Verzamelde brieven*, 14.

the essence of what the great artists, the serious masters, say in their master works, will find God in them.

> One person wrote or said it in a book, another in a painting. Just read the Bible and the Gospel, which makes you think . . . and think about all the things, think about that everything that raises thought, despite yourself, above the level of the everyday. For we *can* read, *let* us then read!

For Vincent, his move to being a painter meant

> choosing art as the way to reach God and to witness to God, beyond the way of the religious apostolate that had been followed until then. (July 1880)

Indeed, he did give up certain religious ideas, such as the "mysticism" that had confused him earlier (March 1, 1884). If he had any regrets later, it was that he allowed himself to be confused for a time by mystical profundities and as a result retreated too much into himself (December 21, 1881). He slowly emerged again. For him, it was not a question of a conventional faith[28] but one of acting humanely toward the prostitute Sien (June 3, 1883), for instance, whom he took pity on. It was more a matter of human compassion than decent goodness. He called prostitutes like Sien "infinitely pitiful"; he felt they possessed a certain passion and warmth that was so human about it that decent people could learn something from them (September 22, 1883).

A book like Victor Hugo's *Les Misérables* primarily kept his feelings and disposition both to love of neighbor and to a faith in and awareness of something higher alive. He called this something above, a *quelque chose la haut*" (something on high)—an expression he borrowed from Jean François Millet (March 30; April 1, 1883).

> Love of mankind is something one should be able to assume in every man as being the basis of almost everything. But some people feel there are better foundations.

Vincent was not very curious about those "better" foundations. The old and—for so many centuries—tried and apparently good foundation was enough for him (April 11, 1883).

---

28. Scherer, *Religiöse Motive*, 121.

Two Kinds of Painters

To indicate what kind of painter he would like to be, Vincent drew a comparison between two sorts. A drawing of two ministers depicts one as a city minister, glorious, broad, and imposing, and the other as somewhat shabby, an insignificant village pastor, apparently the father of a large family. To Vincent, many illustrators among painters belonged to the village pastor group, while others were the city minister type. Vincent included himself among the village pastors (December 2/3, 1882).

He spoke once about this choice with Theo while they were taking a walk in The Hague. Theo said that he wanted to remain an art dealer and did not want to become a painter. That entailed a choice for a certain status or affluence. But Vincent said, "I'll be a dog, a rough shepherd's dog" (December 2/3, 1883). He felt that the future would probably make him uglier and rougher, and he saw a certain poverty as his lot. But he would be a painter and, man or dog, a creature with feeling. He deliberately chose the path of the dog (December 17, 1883). With respect to painting he was not concerned so much with technique, impeccable drawing and painting but with something that made one feel and think. When he saw the "masterly works" *Alleen op de wereld* (Alone in the World) and *Langs moeders graf* (Along Mother's Grave) by Jozef Israëls in Amsterdam, he wrote:

> Let people shoot the bull about technique as much as they want with pharisaical, hollow, hypocritical words—true painters are led by conscience, which people call sentiment. (May 4/5, 1883)

It is striking that, when he talked about his work as a painter in The Hague, he thought he would last only six to ten years:

> The world concerns me only to the extent that I have, as it were, a certain debt and duty, because I have been wandering around on this earth for thirty years, to leave behind out of gratitude a kind of souvenir in the form of drawings and paintings—not done to please this or that school but in which one expresses a sincere human feeling. (August 4–8, 1883)

It would be seven years!

Important Painters and Artists

In a letter from London in January 1874, Vincent had already made a list of more than fifty painters he particularly liked. The Dutch painters he found outstandingly exceptional and inspiring for him were Rembrandt, and painters from The Hague School like Jozef Israëls and Anton Mauve, an uncle by marriage. This uncle would support him during his first steps toward becoming a painter. When Mauve died early in 1888, Vincent dedicated the painting *Pink Peach Tree in Blossom* to him: "In Memory of Mauve," a painting that obviously symbolizes his feelings for the artist who had encouraged him seven years before to "blossom." It is conceivable that the blossoming trees were intended as a sign of his own birth as an artist.[29]

The artists working in black and white and painters of the English illustrated magazines like *The Graphic* and *The Illustrated London News* were a major source of inspiration for Vincent's life and work, especially in the years 1881–1883. That converged with the period he lived in The Hague, where he drew the dirty streets of Geest and Slijkeinde with their toiling and destitute populations.[30] The illustrations of the hardships under which the people in Victorian Great Britain bowed and the portrayals of the working class appealed greatly to his conscience.[31] For him, these artists were "what Charles Dickens [was] in the field of literature" (September 18/19, 1882). Vincent discovered these illustrations during his first stay in London. Every week he would go past the printer's to see the weekly issues in the shop windows. The impressions he received stayed with him more than ten years later (February 4, 1883). He developed a passion for these "social realists": Luke Fildes, Frank Holl, and Hubert von Herkomer. These were the three most important artists who worked for *The Graphic*, and their work would inspire him to draw the dregs of society.[32]

No winter would go by without *The Graphic* doing something to keep sympathy for the poor alive. Vincent saw it as his task to do that as well (November 1, 1883). He also thought the woodcuts by the French illustrator Auguste André Lançon were beautiful: *A Rag Picker's Tavern in Paris*, *The Paris Poor*, *Soup Distribution*, and *A Gang of Snow Shovellers* (September 9, 1882). He liked his gray sketch of a few ragmen eating their soup while it

---

29. De Leeuw et al., *De Haagse School*, 139.
30. Boime, "Van Gogh, Thomas Nast," 75.
31. Bailey, *Van Gogh in England*, 74–75. Cf. Treuherz, *Dante Gabriel Rossetti*, 53–64.
32. Bailey, *Van Gogh in England*, 39; Treuherz, *Dante Gabriel Rossetti*, 90.

was snowing and raining outside. Fildes's *Houseless and Hungry*, which he himself owned, depicts a group of poor men, women, and children waiting for shelter for the night. Thanks to a law for the homeless and hungry, they have gathered at a police station and are waiting for a ticket to be admitted to a section of a workhouse. On the far right is a respectable policeman from the country visiting his criminal son to whom he had given all his money; next to him is a woman with a baby and scruffy-looking children, evicted from their home after her husband was arrested for assaulting her; a child who had grown up in the gutter huddles on the ground; and in the center is a drunk who sacrificed his health and position to alcohol.[33]

In *The Last Muster* Von Herkomer shows British soldiers whose faces are marked by age and adversity. One feels the pulse of an old man who has just died during the morning church service (January 25-29, 1883).

Holl presents a lonely young girl and a soldier in *Leaving Home*. Both are waiting outside the third-class waiting room, waiting. The girl is sitting on one end of the bench with "her purse lighter than her heart." On the other end is the soldier who has been visiting his village while on leave and is now saying good-bye to his father and mother. In *Deserted—The Foundling* a couple of policemen have found a child abandoned by a poverty-stricken mother on a wharf by the river Thames. There are a few curious onlookers, and the gray silhouette of the city can be seen in the background through the mist. *Her Firstborn* shows the funeral of a child, whose coffin is being borne by four girls while the grieving father, mother, grandfather, and a child follow behind (January 25-29, 1883).[34]

In The Hague Vincent became an ardent collector of these illustrations and had the complete volumes of *The Graphic* from 1870–1880 (January 15, 1883). He cut out reproductions and saved them, collecting about 1400 pages, drawn from real life (February 18-22, 1883). When he was unable to sleep at night, he would rummage about in the woodcuts with renewed pleasure (September 9, 1882), especially because he himself could make similar sketches of what interested him in particular on the street, in the third-class waiting room, on the beach, or in a hospital (September 12-14, 1882). He would like ordinary workers to hang such prints in their rooms or workplaces (November 16, 1882). He was thinking of doing a series of worker types: a sower, digger, woodman, ploughman, and washing woman,

33. According to the description of the *Graphic*. Cf. Treuherz, *Dante Gabriel Rossetti*, 92.

34. Bailey, *Van Gogh in England*, 39, 42, 54,135, 139, 240.

and a cradle or old man from an orphanage. What he wanted to express in a figure or a landscape was not something sentimental, something melancholic, but serious pain (December 1, 1882).

These illustrators influenced him both in his *choice* of subjects and in his style.[35] *The Poor and Money*,[36] made in The Hague, and *The Potato Eaters* from Nuenen are examples of that. Thus, it was not surprising that he gave his first successful drawings English titles: *Worn Out, At Eternity's Gate, Sorrow*, and *The Great Lady*.[37] The miners' wives carrying bags of coal he called *The Bearers of the Burden* (April 12, 1881). It shows how much he was affected by the life and work of ordinary people (May 15, 1883). These illustrations were intended to invoke compassion for the hard lives these people led. In his view, these sheets constituted "a kind of Bible" (February 9, 1883).

Peasant Life

"Barbizon" is the name of a group of French landscape painters who had an almost mystical love of nature. This group included Charles F. Daubigny, Camille J.B. Corot, and Jean-Francois Millet. Following them, Vincent sought inspiration in peasant life (October 13, 1883). That is why he saw communion with nature as a goal, a "walking with God" that stood opposed to "life in the business of the big cities" (October 29–November 15, 1883). The Barbizon artists also knew, according to Vincent, that the city was no good, and that was why they sought renewal in nature and in peasant life. Vincent even imagined that Theo was also an artist deep down, and he envisioned himself and Theo working the peat country of Drenthe (October 13, 1883). He thus wanted Theo to leave the art trade in the city of Paris:

> Theo, become a painter, break out and come to Drenthe. C'mon man, paint with me on the moor, the potato field, just walk behind the plough and the shepherd—come look into the fire with me—let the cobwebs get blown away by the storm blowing over the moor, break out. (October 13, 1883)

35. Bailey, *Van Gogh in England*, 43.

36. Leeman and Sillevis, *De Haagse school*, 131; Bailey, *Van Gogh in England*, 76, 142.

37. Bailey, *Van Gogh in England*, 73–83; Collins, *Van Gogh and Gauguin*, 15.

He felt that the best life was one that consisted of communion with nature outdoors over a number of years and with something that transcended nature—ineffable, enormous, unnamable (for no name for it could be found) (October 29–November 13). Vincent spent the last months of his life in Auvers, a place that was discovered by the Barbizon painters in the 1840s.[38]

The peasant painter J.F. Millet was a counselor and guide for Vincent in everything. Through him "one [could] best learn to look, perhaps receive 'a faith'" (January 24, 1885). He saw in him an essential modern painter who opened up horizons for many and was "the painter of humanity" more than anyone else (March 5, 1883).

For him, Millet was the painter of peasant life, the believer who fled the terrors of the city to live and work in the country.[39] It struck Vincent that Millet knew that the public was indifferent to his work: "That would have been bad if Millet needed nice shoes and a gentleman's life. But because he wore wooden shoes, he pulled through." Vincent also therefore felt that he should not forget to wear wooden shoes, "to be satisfied with respect to food, drink, clothing, and sleep, with what the peasants are satisfied with" (April 13, 1885).

Millet taught him the poetry of country life. He saw painting the peasant life as something serious and thought that he should paint the peasants as one of them, thinking and feeling as they did (April 13, 30, 1885). That was how he set about his work in Nuenen:

> The more I work at it, the more peasant life absorbs me . . . . To live in those huts day in day out, to sit in the fields just like the peasants—to endure the heat of the sun in the summer, the snow and frost in the winter, not indoors but outside, and not for a walk, but day in day out like the farmers themselves. . . . No motifs in painting are as difficult as these ordinary people!

Vincent held that the painters of the old Dutch school did not make the digger or sower a "worker." The figures in the old paintings do not work. "A peasant has to be a peasant and a digger has to dig. That is what is essentially modern" (July 1885).

38. Van der Avert and Van Ketwick Verschuur, *Stad & land*, 2.
39. Pollock, *Vincent van Gogh*, 93–94.

His Painter Friend Anthon van Rappard

Vincent met the painter Anthon van Rappard for the first time in Brussels (1880) (October 22–29, 1882) and they were friends for five years; actually, it was the only friendship he made in the Netherlands. They shared an enthusiasm for the illustrations in *The Graphic*,[40] which he spoke about often in his correspondence and sent examples of. He gave him the doubles of copies he possessed. It was precisely because Van Rappard had an eye for and was passionate about them that Vincent esteemed this friendship so highly and said it would be difficult to do without it (February 9, 1883).

In the second half of June 1885, however, the two friends became estranged over a difference in appreciation of *The Potato Eaters* (May 24, 1885), Vincent received such a high-handed letter full of insults that he was certain he had lost a friend forever (second half of June 1885). Vincent saw their quarrel as a dispute between two devout ministers on the geography of the road to eternal happiness (July 21, 1885). The dispute became so intense that, at a certain moment, they quarreled heatedly. There were a few letters afterwards, and one could therefore conclude that the break seemed to have been repaired. Vincent did want to remain friends, for he saw in Van Rappard a striving that he esteemed highly (second half of August 1885).

After Vincent's death, Van Rappard wrote to Vincent's mother:

> Whoever saw that toiling, struggling, and suffering existence would not have felt any sympathy for the man who asked so much of himself that he destroyed himself body and soul. He belonged to that race from which great artists are born. . . . Although Vincent and I had become estranged in recent years because of a misunderstanding that I have often regretted—I have not thought about him and our contact in any other way than with a great deal of friendship. . . . If I think henceforth about that time—and it is always a pleasure for me to think about the past—then the characteristic figure of Vincent that will appear to me in a melancholy but nonetheless clear light: the toiling and struggling fanatically gloomy Vincent, who could often be so enthusiastic and intense but who also always deserved friendship and admiration for his noble feelings and high artistic abilities.[41]

40. Bailey, *Van Gogh in England*, 73.

41. Van Gogh and van Gogh-Bonger, *Verzamelde brieven*, 14–15.

Paul Gauguin

After leaving Nuenen and a short stay in Antwerp, Vincent went to live with his brother Theo in Paris. There he became acquainted with the painter Paul Gauguin who was five years older. This son of a Breton father and Creole mother went to sea as a cabin boy, worked in a banker's office, and initially painted only in his free time. After his marriage he devoted himself entirely to his painting. Vincent and he would live and work together for a few months in southern France in the "Yellow House" in Arles, even though their collaboration and sharing of accommodations would not last long.[42]

In a letter dated the day of the crisis between them, 23 December 1888, Vincent wrote to Theo that he thought that Gauguin "[was] a bit disappointed in the good city of Arles and especially in me. There are serious difficulties here for both him and me that we have to conquer." In complete resignation, he was willing to wait to see if Gauguin was going to stay or leave (December 23, 1888).

On that Sunday evening, 23 December, he chased and threatened Gauguin with a razor. That is, at least, the later version (in his memoires of 1903) that Gauguin gave of the events. He made no mention of a razor immediately afterwards in a letter to their mutual friend Émile Bernard. Did Gauguin later exaggerate the aggressiveness of his friend in order to better justify the fact that he abandoned him at a critical moment? After the episode, Gauguin left the "Yellow House" for a hotel.[43] When Vincent came home, he cut off part of his left ear lobe and at 11:30 in the evening brought it to a prostitute called Rachel with the words: "You will remember me; I assure you" (cf. 1 Corinthians 11:24) (January 22, 1889).[44] Later, when he was better, Vincent looked her up, the girl "to whom he had gone in his stupidity. They told me there that such things were not at all unusual in that neighborhood. It made a deep impression on her, and she had fainted. But she had calmed down" (February 3, 1889).

Only on the morning of the next day did Gauguin hear from the police what had happened. He telegraphed Theo in Paris, and he came immediately to Arles. The first days in the hospital were so critical that Theo feared for Vincent's life. But on New Year's Eve, Vincent was feeling better and on 7 January he was discharged from hospital.

---

42. Van Gogh and van Gogh-Bonger, *Verzamelde brieven*, 14–15, 28–29.

43. Hulsker, *Lotgenoten*, 476.

44. Émile Bernard wrote to Albert Aurier. Cf. Collins, *Van Gogh and Gauguin*, 164.

After the scene in the brothel, his friend the postman Joseph Roulin brought him home, bandaged him, put him in bed, and looked after him when he got out of the hospital.[45]

As far as the relationship between Vincent and Gauguin was concerned, Vincent had already scribbled a message to Gauguin on 14 January 1889 on the back of a letter to Theo: "Now that I am out of the hospital for the first time, I am taking the opportunity to write a few words of quite sincere and deep friendship to you" (January 4, 1889). A few days later he thought that they were both sufficiently in tune with each other to begin again together. He also felt remorse when he thought of the suffering he had caused Gauguin, however unintentionally. He stated that, despite the estrangement between them that had possibly arisen, he and Gauguin would always remain friends. They would never meet again (January 19, 1889).

Traveling Companions: Vincent and Theo

Throughout his life, Vincent was continually searching for friendship. He was very grateful that Theo visited him in the Borinage, even though it had been a long time since they had seen each other or even corresponded. When they walked together, he experienced the same feeling he used to have and felt more cheerful and livelier. If one lives with others and is connected to them by feelings of affection, one is aware of a reason to live. Like everyone else, Vincent needed friendship, affection, and intimacy; people need one another and journey together as *compagnons de voyage* (August 15, 1879).

His brother Theo, in many respects his companion in adversity, was especially and, more than others, his most loyal friend to the end (February 12, 1883). Vincent did not actually have any other friends and, when he felt miserable, he always thought about him (July 22, 1883). When, in Nuenen, his relationship with both his father and, for a time, Theo was strained, he nevertheless saw Theo as the one who saved his life. There were mutual misunderstandings, but they never led to a final separation or break between them (beginning of February 1885).

Vincent did not allow what began as friendship with mutual respect to degenerate into patronage (March 21, 1883). He passed on becoming Theo's protégé, which increasingly became a danger. He asked Theo not to view his "painting business" as ballast. At the time he was the ship and Theo was taking Vincent in tow, and that could appear to him as ballast.

---

45. Maurer, *The Pursuit of Spiritual Wisdom*, 85.

That could be fixed by cutting the towing rope, but he wanted the boat to be caulked and supplied so that it could be of service in time of need (August 7, 1885). When Vincent and he had lived together in Paris for about two years—the first half of which was not without tension—they became so attached that Theo could write to his sister Wil:

> When he came here two years ago, I did not think that we would become so attached to each other, for the apartment is certainly empty now that I am alone again. He knows so much, and he has such a clear view of the world. That is why I am sure that if he's still alive in a few years, he will make a name for himself. Because of him I have come into contact with many painters, among whom he himself was esteemed. He is one of the advocates of new ideas. Moreover, he has such a generous heart that he is always looking to do something for others. (February 24–26, 1888)[46]

Years later, in June 1888, Vincent went on a five-hour coach trip from Arles through the Camargue to the fishing village of Les Saintes-Maries-de-la-Mer on the Mediterranean Sea. This place had been the destination of pilgrimages of a sort since the Middle Ages: tradition has it that relics of both Mary Magdalene and Jesus's mother had been found there. According to an early Christian legend, they had come to the French coast by boat from Palestine and, with that spot as their basis, had converted Provence to Christianity. One of the boats in his painting *Fishing Boats on the Beach at Les Saintes-Maries-de-la-Mer* is called "Friendship."[47]

How deeply he and Theo were connected by a deep friendship became apparent at crucial moments of their lives. After Vincent's death, Theo wrote to his mother, "O mother, he was so very much my brother."[48]

The Inspiration of Literature

From childhood on Vincent read a great deal. When he was young he copied the texts that were "formative for him" and made albums of them for his friends. Victor Hugo's book on William Shakespeare[49] played an important

---

46. Hammacher, *Van Gogh*, 128.

47. On May 30 188. Van Kooten and Rijnders, *De schilderijen*, 221. Cf. Amiel, *Vincent Van Gogh*, 11–13.

48. Van Gogh and van Gogh-Bonger, *Verzamelde brieven*, 38.

49. Hugo, *William Shakespeare*.

role in his decision to become an artist: "the man who reads is the man who knows" (September 24, 1880).

Vincent viewed the reader of literature as "the prototype of the contemporary modern human being."[50] He referred to more than 150 different writers—including more than fifty English ones—about 800 times in his letters. He showed immeasurable admiration for "naturalist" writers like Émile Zola and Guy de Maupassant, who made life in the modern city accessible for him (September 19, 1889).

He found reading well-written books "a comfort in life" (October 14, 1875). Vincent had a more or less irresistible passion for books, and his need to continually reeducate himself was the same as his need to eat. Gauguin defined him once as "a Dutchman whose brains were branded by Alphonse Daudet, De Goncourts, and the Bible." Aside from the Bible, he also studied "more or less serious" books by Michelet, Shakespeare, Hugo, Dickens, Thomas Carlyle, Harriet Beecher Stowe, Aeschylus, Honoré de Balzac, and George Eliot (July 1880; December 21, 1881). When, during his illness in March 1889, he went out for a while in Arles with his painter friend Paul Signac, he immediately took advantage of the opportunity to buy a book, devouring two chapters right away. Reading meant a great deal to him and also contributed to his healing (March 24, 1889). Vincent read because writers looked at things more broadly, gently, with more love, and had a better understanding of reality. He could learn something from them (December 21, 1881). He considered the love for books as sacred as that for painters: the two complemented each other. His favorites in the literary and artistic areas were those in whom he saw the soul at work the most (March 1884).

Vincent had great admiration for novels by George Eliot (Mary Ann Evans's pseudonym), whom he read when he was barely twenty. He found Eliot's work to be masterful in its workmanship and admired her realism and religious views. Something of Vincent's own life was reflected in her views and the changes in her life.

George Eliot was the daughter of a strict Methodist, and her *Scenes of Clerical Life* are often described as a nostalgic tribute to the evangelical past that formed her. She suggests that church life, as experienced by women, can differ considerably from the church history written by men. She compares her own art to that of a painter, and many references to painters and paintings can be found in her *Scenes of Clerical Life*.[51]

50. Dorn, *Vincent van Gogh*, 72.
51. Carpenter, *George Eliot*, 30.

Van Gogh and the Art of Living

Eliot's decision to stop attending church caused a painful break with her church-going father. The Bible, she wrote to him, no longer seemed to her to be the divinely inspired truth and had instead become "stories consisting of truth mixed with fiction."[52] The moral teaching that she continued to appreciate in Christianity found a new form, a "religion of humankind," that did not seek divinity in the supernatural but in what was most noble in human nature itself.[53] Through the influence of a skeptic,[54] whom she became acquainted with after 1841, she gave up her faith and broke with the church, the "miserable dolmen of dogmas." She escaped the "pernicious influence" of evangelicals through literature![55]

In 1842 Shakespeare's plays became "the book of books" for her. The evangelical fire was replaced by the wish to serve humankind. She took up the cause of social reform and rejoiced in the French revolution of 1848. Eliot introduced a new awareness; in the end all partial truths fall away to reveal the true essence of faith, the truth of feeling. She could now say that any faith that was the expression of human sorrow and the desire for justice met with her approval.[56]

Scenes of Clerical Life consists of three stories, of which primarily the last, "Janet's Repentance," struck Vincent. "Janet's Repentance," the final story in George Eliot's *Scenes of Clerical Life*, is about a minister who lives with the inhabitants of the dirty streets of a city. His study looks out on gardens with cabbage stalks and the red roofs and smoking chimneys of poor homes. His lunch usually consists of poorly cooked mutton and watery potatoes, and he is nursed during his long illness by a woman who used to drink but has overcome her habit through his words and leaning, as it were, on him, and has found peace for her soul. The minister dies at the age of twenty-four and the passage read at his funeral was the one containing the words: "I am the resurrection and the life; whoever believes in me will live, even though he dies" (John 11:25) (February 19, 1876; cf. August 18, 1876). Reading this story of the minister who was like Christ would certainly have stimulated Vincent's own work as an assistant minister when he was in Ramsgate.[57]

52. Eliot, *Scenes of Clerical Life*, chapter 11.
53. Eliot, *Scenes of Clerical Life*, chapter 12.
54. C. Bray, author of *The Philosophy of Necessity*.
55. Eliot, *Silas Marner*, 227, chapter 24.
56. Eliot, *Silas Marner*, 233.
57. Eliot, *Scenes of Clerical Life*, chapter 20, 30; Meyers, *De jonge Vincent*, 202.

For Vincent, there was a close affinity between what writers do and what artists do. He found George Eliot and Honoré de Balzac surprisingly "expressive" in their descriptions, and there was, according to him, no writer who is so much painter and writer as Dickens (March 5, 1883), who himself sometimes said about his work: "I sketched" (May 28, 1882).[58]

He was enthusiastic about the books by Émile Zola and his *Le Ventre de Paris* (*The Belly of Paris*), which led him to exclaim: "How those markets have been *painted*" (July 26, 1882). He cited the work of the French historian Michelet and envied his style. Vincent found that some of Michelet's books had something of the rough sketch of a painter: (November 19, 1881);

> He feels intensely and what he feels he spreads on thick. Michelet
> has indeed been called a visionary of the past. (July 6, 1882)

According to Vincent, Michelet wanted to write in such a way that the past of France (January 3, 1890), of Joan of Arc (March 6, 1875), and the French Revolution came to life for the reader (July 1880). His philosophical books deal with nature; the desire for autumn (October 1873), the sea (March 6 1875), and birds (April 3, 1878).

Vincent once said that if he ever found he was going nowhere with his painting he would either go into business or become a writer (October 22, 1888). He did do the latter, in fact, in the form of his letters.

> There are so many people, especially among our friends, who think
> that words do not mean anything—quite the contrary, isn't it? Isn't
> it just as interesting and difficult to say something well as to paint
> something? There is the art of lines and colors, but what there is
> also and will always be is the art of the word. (April 21, 1888)

Literature was always a source of inspiration for Vincent's work as painter: George Eliot's *Silas Marner* about a weaver and Zola's *Germinal* about miners were direct sources of inspiration. Dostoyevsky's *Notes from Underground* led him to resume a major study of a madhouse he started in Arles (October 20–22, 1889).

58. He mentioned a series of personages: Mrs. Sarah Camp, Little Dorrit, Sikes, Nancy, Sidney Carton.

The Bible, Literature, and Art

For Vincent, it was neither a question of the Bible or literature nor of the Bible or art but one of the Bible *and* literature, the Bible *and* art. He wrote in Amsterdam

> One can do no better than to keep thinking about God in all things and to attempt to learn more about him under all circumstances, in all places, and at all times. That can be done via the Bible or other things. It is very good to be versed in the things that are hidden from the wise and the learned but revealed naturally to the poor and simple, women and children (cf. Matthew 11:25). For what can one learn that is better than what God has given by nature into every human soul, than what lives in the basis of every soul, and loves, hopes, and believes, unless one intentionally destroys it? (April 3, 1878)

From 1879 to 1880, before he took up painting, his guide was Thomas à Kempis's *Imitation of Christ*. Reading Renan's *La Vie de Jésus* became a bridge between his life as an evangelist/minister and his life as a painter. He saw a kindred spirit in Renan who had rejected the institutional church but not the faith.[59]

Years later he still spoke in Arles of his enormous need for religion (September 29, 1888). In certain respects, he reminds one of the Remonstrant minister-poet Petrus A. de Genestet, whom he read at his father's encouragement (May 21, 1877). He quoted his poem, "Toen ik een knaap was" ("When I was a boy"), which begins:

> When I was a boy, living carefree
> I followed whatever seemed best
> Free to go, search, and strive as I pleased
> free in my dreams, my travels, my rest.

He then ends with the first verse of some poem by De Genestet ("Peinzens-moede"; "Courage to Reflect"):

> He is beyond the priest's power to explain
> But no person on earth searches in vain.
> Though no Elijah am I, I also saw
> the Lord pass by in storm and awe. (February 18, 1877)

Vincent never cared much for the dogmatic forms of church and faith, and was never raised in them.

59. Erickson, *At Eternity's Gate*, 80, 82.

> I do see God in every church and, if the minister preaches or the
> priest, it's all the same to me. It's not a question of dogma but the
> spirit of the Gospel, and I find that spirit in all churches.[60]

That the Bible remained important for him is apparent from both his earliest letters and his later correspondence with his painter friend Émile Bernard, whom he met for the first time in 1886 in Paris in the shop owned by the art dealer Julien Tanguy ("Father" Tanguy). He became a mentor of sorts for Bernard, who was eighteen at the time. On one of the few photos that exist of Van Gogh, from early in 1887, they are sitting together on a bench by the Seine, near the railway bridge in Asnières where Bernard came from.[61] But Vincent's back is to the camera, and he is wearing a hat. He would say later that he found photos disagreeable and did not want to have any, certainly not of people he knew and loved.

> To begin with, such pictures fade sooner than we do, whereas the
> painted portrait lasts for generations. A painted portrait is, by the
> way, something that is keenly felt, that is made with love or with
> respect for that which it depicts: What remains of the old Dutch
> painters other than the portraits? (September 19, 1889)

He wrote to Bernard that he would do well to read the Bible (June 23, 1888):

> The Bible, that is, Christ, for the Old Testament leads to the climax. Paul and the evangelists are on the opposite slope of the same
> holy mountain. But the comfort of the often sorrowful-sounding
> Bible, which awakens our despair and indignation, that hurts us
> deeply, completely confuses us through its narrow-mindedness
> and infectious foolishness—the comfort that it contains, like the
> pit surrounded by a hard shell and bitter flesh, that is Christ. (June
> 23, 1888)

In his view, only the heart of the Bible, Christ, is superior from an artistic viewpoint.

> Well, I say again, this Christ is more of an artist than artists themselves. He works with living spirit and living flesh; he makes (fashions) people instead of images. (June 24, 1888)

---

60. Tralbaut, *Over godsdienstige richtingen*, 103–8, Letter A 7; Kôdera, "Van Gogh and the Dutch Theological Culture," 118, 128, note 13.

61. Hammacher, *Van Gogh*, 146; Zemel, *Van Gogh's Progress*, 145.

A Bringer of Comfort

It was characteristic of what Van Gogh did, as an (assistant) minister in England, as an evangelist in the mining district in the Borinage, or later as artist, that he constantly wanted to bring people comfort. For him, painters are bringers of comfort, just like the evangelist Luke who, according to the classical tradition, was also a painter.

For him, the portrait of a human being, of a painter like Rembrandt, gains something inexpressibly radiant and comforting: "an art that offers comfort to sorrowful hearts!" (January 22, 1889).

He also wanted to say something comforting in a painting, like music does (September 3, 1888). He compared what he had in mind with the personal interpretation of someone who performs a musical composition by Ludwig von Beethoven. His brush moves between his fingers like the bow over a violin. In music, and especially in song, the interpretation of a composer is one, but it does not have to be only the composer who can play his music (September 19, 1889).

Vincent, therefore, does not see copying one's favorite masters to be merely a matter of imitation. During his illness he used, for example, a work by the French painter, Eugène Delacroix, a master of Romanticism, as a motif for a study in black and white. He then improvised on it with color and thus gave it his own interpretation (September 19, 1889). When Van Gogh speaks about color, he speaks of tones, by which he means hues or tints, but one can also hear the imagery of music here. He also uses the term harmonists rather than colorists for painters and speaks of the "harmony of color," "the symphony of the yellow," (second half of October 1885) and "the harmony of tones" (July 6, 1889). In a certain painting he sees an attempt at a melody in colors. Technique in some artists (like Lançon) reminds him of violin music, and in others (like Paul Gavarni, a French artist, illustrator, and graphic artist) of piano music. According to him, someone like Millet makes one think perhaps of solemn organ music (December 31, 1882; January 2, 1883).

When he was in Drenthe, he said, he once walked past an old church in Zweeloo that a shepherd was taking his flock past. "That return of the flock in the evening twilight was the finale of the symphony—Beethoven's sixth symphony, the Pastoral![62]—that I heard yesterday."

---

62. Dijk and Van der Sluis, *De Drentste tijd*, 231, note 439.

The day had passed like a dream for him. He had been so caught up in music the whole day that he even forgot to eat and drink. He had a slice from a loaf of farmer's bread and cup of coffee in the inn where he drew the spinning wheel.

> The day was over and I had lost myself in the symphony from the early light of dawn until the evening twilight. (November 16, 1883)

The Role and Meaning of Parables

Vincent gave Thomas à Kempis's *Imitation of Christ* as a present to Maurits Benjamin Mendes da Costa, one of his Jewish teachers in Latin and Greek. Mendes lived in an upstairs apartment on Jonas Daniel Meyerplein in the Jewish district. Vincent did not give him the book with the intention of converting him but, according to Mendes, to acquaint him with the human aspect in it.[63] He was more concerned with a Christianity of deed, of the gospels and the parables, than with one of dogmas (summer, autumn 1887). During his study Vincent arranged all the parables in order of importance (August 18, 1877). The number of allusions to the parables in his references to the Bible in his letters is striking. In a Methodist church in Petersham, a village on the Thames where he worked for a while, he spoke of the parable of the lost son and the parable of the unmerciful servant (Matthew 18:21–35) (November 25, 1876). He and his English friend Harry Gladwell (August 18, 1876), with whom he had earlier lived in Paris and who also worked at the Goupil art shop, read many parables in Amsterdam (September 7, 1877). The parable of the sower (Mark 4:1–27)—of the man who sowed seed in the field and then sleeps and gets up, day and night, and the seed germinates and grows without his knowing how—was important to him, and he referred to this parable often in word and image (June 12, 1877). Vincent also referred to Sir John Everett Millais, one of the so-called pre-Raphaelites, who had once painted the parable of the lost coin—a young woman searching early in the morning for

63. Van Gogh and van Gogh-Bonger, *Verzamelde brieven*, I, 170. Cf. December 9, 1877.

the coin she lost (Luke 15:8–10) (July 15, 1877). When he was working as an evangelist in the mining district of the Borinage, he preached about the parables of the mustard seed (Matthew 13:31–32; Luke 13:19) (December 26, 1878) and the fig tree that bore no fruit (Luke 13:1–9) (November 15, 1878; December 26, 1878). He referred to the parable the prophet Nathan tells King David (2 Samuel 12), of the rich man who steals a poor man's ewe lamb, to show him that he was like the rich man in sending his army commander Uriah to be killed so he could marry his wife Bathsheba (June 2/3, 1882). Vincent would also paint the parable of the Good Samaritan (Luke 10:25–37). (September 19, 1889)

The Marketability of his Work

Throughout his entire life, Vincent's work seemed to be unmarketable. In The Hague he said he had no other pretentions with regard to the market value of his work than that it would surprise him if his work would not be sold over time like others (August 1, 1882). A few months later he expressed regret at the fact that he was not successful in making a marketable drawing. He had no idea what the problem was (December 28–30, 1882).

When Theo told him a year later that it would be difficult to keep supporting him financially and that he should hope for better times, Vincent replied he kept hope alive by throwing himself energetically into his work at present. He asked Theo to have sympathy at least for his work, marketable or not, (July 22, 1883) even though he continued to wonder if he could go on (July 23, 1883). He was happy to note that this did not change anything in their friendship and that Theo saw progress in his work (July 24/25, 1883). In Nuenen, after Theo had sent him some money, he expressed the hope that he could consider the money he received from Theo as well deserved (April 1, 1884). Toward the end of the month, painting became a burden for him because the work cost so much and he was not selling any of it. That would, in his view, not always be the case, for he worked too hard and too much not to get to the point where he would be able to pay for his expenses from his work without getting into a position of dependence (January 24, 1885)

His fellow painter Gauguin said that Vincent had once gone without food for days in Paris. To be able to buy something to eat, he sold some small works for five francs.[64] But when he came out of the shop, he saw a girl begging who reminded him of Elisa a French novel,[65] and there went his franks. In the fall of 1886 he wrote from Paris: "even with respect to the price, the public will pay for them in the long run" (August/October, 1886). He did continue to reproach himself that his painting did not yield what it cost (May 28, 1888). He found that terrible and feared that it would ultimately lead to a shortage of funds for household expenses for both his brother and himself. The money painting cost gave him a crushing sense of guilt and cowardice. He even thought of joining the French Legion for five years (May 1, 1889).[66]

While he was in Saint Rémy, he said that the more he was able to think clearly the more he considered painting, which cost so much and did not even let him break even, to be a foolish pursuit, something that was completely insane (October 25, 1889).

He managed to sell only a few of his works at a reasonable price during his lifetime.[67] His hope that the public would pay over time was not fulfilled while he lived. The painting *The Irises*, for which he never saw a penny, was sold about a hundred years after his death for 53.9 million dollars.[68]

64. Gauguin, *Avant en Après*, 44. Sund, *True to Temperament*, 136, 292, note 93. Takashina, "Vincent van Gogh," 409.

65. Edmond de Goncourt, *La fille Elisa* (Paris: 1877).

66. May 2, 1889 (letter from Theo). Cf. May 3, 1889.

67. With the exception of *The Red Vineyard*. Bought by Anna Boch, sister of his Belgian painter and friend E.G. Boch. Hammacher, *Van Gogh*, 202.

68. *Time Magazine*, November 27, 1989.

CHAPTER TWO

SORROWFUL, YET ALWAYS REJOICING

[A]s sorrowful, yet always rejoicing; as poor, yet making many rich; as having nothing, and yet possessing all things. (2 Corinthians 6:10; KJV)

FROM 1876 TO 1878 Vincent repeatedly referred to himself as "sorrowful, yet always rejoicing," seeing this as a kind of motto for his life. He also came up with that idea by reading John Bunyan's *Pilgrim's Progress* several times, a book that describes Christian's journey to heaven.[1] This double mood of sorrow and rejoicing would follow him to the end of his life.

Sorrow in Vincent's Life and Work

On 21 January 1877, on the first Sunday evening of his stay in Dordrecht, Vincent heard a minister preach on the following text:

> Now we see through a glass darkly, but then face to face. Now I know in part but then I will know completely just as I am known. (1 Corinthians 13:12) (January 21, 1877)

At the end of his life he referred again to the same text, in a letter to his mother: "Through a glass darkly . . . . That is how it has remained; life and the why of departing and going away and the unrest that remains." Vincent thought that his life could remain a lonely one. He did not look at those to whom he was most attached in any other way than "through a glass darkly" (June 12 1890).

---

1. Erickson, "Testimony to Theo," 211.

It was in that spirit that he observed and drew people around him with the mixture of sorrow and joy. Here he was inspired by the illustrations in *The Graphic* and *The Illustrated London News*, as well as by illustrators of Charles Dickens's novels. He made drawings that vaguely resemble English woodcuts (January 1881), including one of a man in front of a hearth. In Etten he drew an old, sick peasant sitting on a chair by the hearth in which the fire has gone out, his head in his hands and his elbows on his knees. Vincent took the title, *Worn Out* (October 15, 1881), which he used for his drawing, from the Scottish illustrator Thomas Faed,[2] who sketched an exhausted father after a wakeful night at his young daughter's sickbed.[3] This illustrator advised his students at an art school to paint only what they saw with their own eyes: it was better to paint the children from the gutter in London than Helen of Troy, Agamemnon, or Achilles.[4] While in The Hague Vincent drew this subject of an old man again and called it *Old Man, Head in Hands* (February 25, 1882; November 26, 1882; April 2, 1888).[5] Here he was inspired by an illustration in Charles Dickens's *Hard Times*, where a father sits with his head in his hands after learning that his son is a bank robber.[6] An illustration in Dickens's Christmas story "The Cricket on the Hearth" depicts a desperate figure with his head in his hands. This theme made Vincent think of Jozef Israëls's painting *Lezende boer bij haardvuur* (Reading Farmer at a Hearth), a painting of an old man sitting in a corner by the fire, in which a small piece of peat is still glowing in the twilight. It is a dark hut, with a small window and a white curtain; his dog, which has grown old with him, sits next to him. Both old creatures, the man and the dog, stare into each other's eyes. Meanwhile, the man takes a tobacco box from his trouser pocket and fills his pipe in the twilight.

> Otherwise nothing—that twilight, that silence, that loneliness of those two old creatures, man and dog, that knowledge they have of each other, that reflection the old man is doing—what is he thinking of—I don't know, I can't say—but it must be a deep and long thought, something, but I don't know what, from a distant past

2. It took him time before he appreciated him. November 5, 1882. Cf. Bailey, *Van Gogh in England*, 43.

3. Leeman and Sillevis, *De Haagse school*, 123–24. Treuherz, *Dante Gabriel Rossetti*, 44.

4. Treuherz, *Dante Gabriel Rossetti*, 45.

5. *The Christmas Books*, Volume 2, 90. McChesney Alhadeff, "Van Gogh's 'Worship of Sorrow,'" 58, 60.

6. Bailey, *Van Gogh in England*, 146; Treuherz, *Dante Gabriel Rossetti*, 21.

that has surfaced perhaps produces that expression on that face: melancholic, satisfied, subdued. (March 11, 1882)[7]

In 1889 Vincent was admitted to Saint Paul de Mausole, a psychiatric asylum in Saint Rémy. Shortly before he went there he produced yet another version of the old bowed man, but this time it was a painting. The man is close to death and on the point of leaving his chair (April 29/30, 1890).[8] The title *At Eternity's Gate*, instead of *Worn Out*, is said to be borrowed from John Bunyan's *Pilgrim's Progress*, which speaks of the "Gate to the Celestial City" that allows poor, plodding earthly mortals to enter the promised paradise.[9]

Vincent held that it is the painter's duty to express an idea in his work, although he "cannot express it as beautifully, as strikingly as the reality, of which it is only a weak reflection 'in a glass darkly.'" He also held that one of the strongest proofs for the existence of "something on high" (*quelque chose la haut*), the existence of God and eternity, was the inexpressible, stirring quality of the expression of an old man like this, sitting so quietly in the corner by his fire, "and that this is also something majestic, something noble, that it cannot be destined for worms" (November 26/27, 1882).

The Voice of Conscience: Anguish

Already as a student in Amsterdam, Vincent thought deeply about life. He believed that it was good to go into the world often and mix with people, "but for whoever would actually rather work quietly alone and have very few friends, it would be safest out among people and into the world." We should find it strange if we did not encounter any difficulties or worries; we should not make it too easy for ourselves. In the most civilized circles and the best circumstances, something of the original character of a natural human being like Robinson Crusoe was always to be preserved—for without that we have no root in ourselves. We should never let the fire in the human souls go out but keep it going (April 3, 1878).

Vincent was convinced that whoever experienced poverty and loved had a great treasure and would always hear the voice of his conscience

---

7. Cf. De Leeuw et al., *De Haagse School*, 305.
8. Two letters of the same date. Bailey, *Van Gogh in England*, 126.
9. Van Kooten and Rijnders, *De schilderijen*, 353.

clearly. If we follow that voice we hear deep within, we will find a friend and would never be alone. The conscience was the compass of a man:

> Whoever has retained faith in God will sometime hear the gentle voice of conscience, whereby it is good perhaps to follow it with the naiveté of a child. (January 11, 1883)

Vincent considered the conscience to be the supreme intellectual power, reason within reason. If people follow it, they can sometimes think they have acted wrongly or foolishly, especially when other, more superficial people take pride in the fact that they are so much wiser and think they are much more successful in life. That is difficult sometimes, and if situations arise in which people are faced with a spring flood of difficulties they tend to be much less conscientious (July 27, 1883).

Vincent did not want to fall into an impenetrable "blackness" but wanted even more to avoid the "white" of a whitewashed tomb[10] that represents hypocrisy and pharisaism (Matthew 23:27). His own conscience was the compass pointing him in the right direction, although he did not know if it would work properly (October 28, 1883).

How his conscience influenced him can be seen in a drawing he made in connection with the poem "The Lady's Dream" by Thomas Hood, a British poet and publisher of various English illustrated magazines. Hood, who was appreciated for his humorous poetry, explored social abuses in his serious poetry. Vincent referred to Hood's poem about a dignified lady who cannot sleep at night because during the day she had gone out to buy a dress and saw the poor pale, consumptive-looking and haggard seamstresses working in cramped quarters (beginning of April 1882).[11]

The Lady's Dream

> The lady lay in her bed,
> Her couch so warm and soft,
> But her sleep was restless and broken still;
> For, turning often and oft
> From side to side, she muttered and moaned,
> And tossed her arms aloft.
>
> At last she startled up,

10. Cf. A white churchwall. December 21, 1881.
11. Soth, "Van Gogh's Images," 107.

. . .

And, O! those maidens young,
Who wrought in that dreary room,
With figures drooping and specters thin,
And cheeks without a bloom;—
And the voice that cried, "For the pomp of pride,
We haste to an early tomb!"

Alas! I have walked through life
Too heedless where I trod;
Nay, helping to trample my fellow-worm,
And fill the burial sod—
Forgetting that even the sparrow falls
Not unmarked of God!

. . .

She clasped her fervent hands,
And the tears began to stream
Large, and bitter, and fast they fell,
Remorse was so extreme;
And yet, O, yet, that many a dame
Would dream the Lady's Dream![12]

The Poor Class

Van Gogh painted his *The Great Lady* in April 1882 in The Hague on the basis of the above poem. It was completely in line with the mood of the illustrators of *The Graphic* of the "hard times" (Charles Dickens) in England that Vincent himself saw and experienced.

He had already earlier, in March 1877, when working in a bookshop in Dordrecht (the Netherlands), come to understand how difficult peasant life in Brabant was. He was thinking about a peasant and his family in Zundert whom he knew and wondered where such people drew their strength and support in life from. He attributed it to their faith and thought of the wonderful attraction that Christ held as depicted by the painter William Holman Hunt in his *Light of the World*, which hung in many living rooms at that time (March 16, 1877).

12. Van Gogh mixes up two poems by Thomas Hood: "The Lady's Dream" and "The Song of the Shirt" (*The Poetical Works of Thomas Hood* [London: Little Brown and Company, 1854], 625–26).

When he read in a letter from his father that a certain peasant in Zundert was dying, his own heart was so drawn to Brabant that he took the last train from Dordrecht. He walked to Zundert from the station in Oudenbosch late at night. It was still quite early the following morning when he arrived in the village and went to the churchyard where his brother was buried. He looked at all the old places and paths, waiting for the sun to rise. Everything in that quiet churchyard on that morning reminded him of the story of the resurrection. When he arrived at the peasant's family, he heard that the latter had died during the night. They were very sad, and he felt sorry for them, for he was fond of the man. That noble head lying on the pillow was unforgettable: next to the signs of suffering the impression of peace and something holy could be seen. "O, it was so beautiful! I would say it expressed all the peculiarity of this country and the life of the people of Brabant" (April 8, 1877).

When he walked through the Jewish quarter and other old districts of Amsterdam, he had to think of the work of the Belgian painter Charles de Groux. There he encountered the woodcutters and carpenters, grocery shops, chemists, and smiths that would have elated De Groux (September 4, 1877).

De Groux was one of the painters whom Vincent liked very much, and he was disappointed that this artist was not appreciated as much he should have been. De Groux painted portraits, and religious and historical subjects, but his primary theme was scenes from daily life. He wanted to move the public with social realistic themes in which he focused people's attention on the miserable circumstances in which the rural population and workers lived and depicted that hopeless misery. His works show processions and pilgrims in search of healing, good weather for the crops, or protection for their livestock. Such a realistic perspective spoke to Vincent (March 4, 1883).[13]

When his uncle Cor, the art dealer in Amsterdam, asked him if he liked the beautiful *Phryne before the Areopagus* by the French painter, Jean-Léon Gérôme, he replied that he would much rather see an ugly woman by Jozef Israëls or Jean-François Millet, or an old woman by Edouard Frère, such as *The Seamstresses*, which he hung in his room in Paris (July 6, 1875; August 23, 1875). "Animals have beautiful bodies as well, but they do not have a soul like those other painters who paint them." When his uncle then asked if he felt nothing for a beautiful woman, he answered that he:

13. Bailey, *Van Gogh in England*, 124.

[had] more feelings for and would rather have to do with someone
who was ugly or old or poor or unfortunate in one way or another
and has acquired a soul though experience or acquaintance with
life, through sadness or wisdom. (January 9, 1878)

He lived up to this idea in a very concrete way in The Hague in both dealing
with and depicting the prostitute Sien, her children, and family.

Having Regard for Sien

Vincent met the prostitute Christine Clasina (Sien) Hoornik on the streets
of The Hague in the winter. She was four months pregnant at the time,
abandoned by the man whose child she was carrying, and looked ill. She
had to earn her bread "you know how," he wrote to Theo. He wondered
what was more civilized, more sensitive: "to abandon a woman or to be
concerned about the lot of someone who has been abandoned." He decided
to pay her rent himself and to share his bread with her (May 3–12, 1882).
He understood that if she was left alone, she would probably not survive.

> After all a woman should not be alone in a society and in a time
> like the one we are living in now, which does not spare the weak
> but tramples a weak creature underfoot and rides over her when
> she falls. (May 12/13, 1882)

That is why he was very suspicious of what was called progress and
civilization. He believed only in a civilization that was based on actual love
of one's fellow creatures (May 12/13, 1882). According to him, this was
expressed in a drawing by Frank Holl: "her Poverty, not her Will, consents
[with prostitution]."

After a difficult birth in hospital, he invited Sien to move in with him
and to allow him to do what he could for her. "Anyone with a heart in his
body should feel up to taking in someone like Sien, who also has another
sickly and neglected child; otherwise, he's not worth his life." For him, the
baby was a light in his home throughout the whole dark winter. He was
happy with Sien as his model, and it made no difference to him that people
gossiped about the situation. Whatever others might say about her, he
found her beautiful:

> Life had run over her and pain and adversity had marked her. If
> the ground isn't ploughed, you can't do anything with it. She has
> been ploughed—thus, I find more in her than in a whole group of
> unploughed people. (May 28, 1882)

Although Vincent's father saw this relationship with a woman of lower social status as immoral, Vincent himself thought his father was wrong because he did not see any connection between status and morality. "Status is something the world is concerned about; morality something God is concerned about." Vincent was convinced that one can attain a great inner peace by becoming involved in a relationship and being in harmony with nature, and that one would go contrary to eternal moral laws in trying to withdraw from the consequences of a relationship. Despite the fact that his father was opposed to his living with her, he did send Sien a warm overcoat for the winter. "For such a deed I would gladly take three sacks of words [from my father] lying down" (June 5/6, 1883). Thus, Vincent's father did practice charity, and in that sense he was faithful to the Groningen school: life was more important than doctrine.

When Vincent saw that the only way to rescue her from her harsh circumstances was to marry her he expected that Theo would disapprove of his actions and withdraw his financial support (September 6/7, 1883).

He drew Sien at different times and in different ways, even in the form of a landscape

> rooted, as it were, desperately and passionately in the earth and yet half pulled out by storms.[14]

He wanted to express something of the struggle of life in both that white, slender female figure and black grumpy, gnarled roots (May 1, 1882).

He did not depict Sien in his drawings as a sinner but primarily as a lonely and desperate woman who could barely keep her head above water in her naked struggle to survive. The etching of Sien does not show a fallen woman but indicts the vision of prostitution in his time. Under one of the etchings he writes in English: "Sorrow."[15] It is sorrow he hears in the voices of the Bible (September 4, 1877) and hymns, which he cites, as well as in the poems of Henry Wadsworth Longfellow (October 3, 1876).[16] He quotes Thomas Carlyle, who thought that the temple of "the worship of sorrow," built some 1800 years before, was now a ruin. "Nevertheless, its holy flame still burns" (June 22, 1883).

14. *Study of a Tree;* late in April 1882.

15. Appreciated by the painter J.H. Weissenbruch to Vincent's pleasure. May 1, 1882.

16. Like *"Oft in sorrow and in woe/Onwards, Christians, onward go;/Fight the fight, maintain the strife,/Strenthen'd with the bread of life/Of Let not sorrow dim your eye, Soon shall ev'ry tear be dry;/Let not fear your course impede,/Great your strength, if great your need!"*

Under the second version of the drawing of Sien he wrote the words by the French historian Jules Michelet, *La Femme (The Woman)*: "How can there be a woman alone on earth—abandoned?" (June 22, 1883). He had read the book in which this sentence appears already in 1874, and it made a great impression on him. To him, Michelet was a "humane man," an apostle who stood up for the woman as a victim of modern society. According to Michelet, the mission of men is to liberate such women from oppression through misery, despair, and abandonment (April 10, 1882).

Vincent takes these words to heart when he attempts to save this "fallen" pregnant woman like a Mary Magdalene. He was moved to tears when, to his great joy, her son was born six weeks later (July 2, 1882).[17] In one of the versions of *Sorrow* there are snowdrops and lilies of the valley, heralds of spring and symbols of innocence and purity. These are the specific attributes of the Madonna and the immaculate conception, and they symbolize the coming of Christ.[18]

But before Vincent could carry out his plan to marry Sien, they had a serious falling out, and in September 1883, under Theo's advice (September 27, 1883, December 25–28, 1883), they separated (September 6/7, 1883): he decided to move to Drenthe without her (September 15, 1883). Nevertheless, he remained concerned about her and spoke regularly about her in his letters. In Drenthe he was overcome by a feeling of great concern, despondency, and despair:

> In every life some rain must fall
> And days be dark and dreary.
> —Longfellow

"It was in fact so, it could not be otherwise. But can't the number of dark and dreary days become too many sometimes?" (September 26, 1883) When he saw a poor woman in a field with a child on her arm or nursing a child, his eyes would become misty. This was so even though he came to realize in the meantime that Sien was not good and that he had good reason to do what he did, that he could not stay with her or take her with him and that what he did was even wise and for the best (September 15, 1883). He had done everything he could to help her out of her situation and now that he had failed, he felt a "kind of melancholy about life." He drew serenity "from the worship of sorrow" (September 6/7, 1883). In his mind he

---

17. Cf. Werness, "The Symbolism," 45.
18. Cooper, 1982, 98, referred to by Werness, "The Symbolism," 44.

understood the prejudices and rejection that women like her face in society. But the judgment of men does not always coincide with the judgment of God: "Who is so pure that he wants to play judge? Far from it. Ultimately, it is God's mercy that is able to understand her" (September 22, 1883).

"Doodling"

Vincent "doodled" regularly in the public soup kitchen or in third-class waiting rooms or similar places in The Hague. He attempted to master drawing by drawing a third-class waiting room, a rainy day in a poverty-stricken neighborhood, or a home for poor old men, a pub, or soup kitchen (September 26, 1883). In Saint Rémy, the room where he had to stay on rainy days made him think of a kind of third-class waiting room in a sleepy village somewhere, all the more because there were respectable fools present who always had a hat, a pair of glasses, a walking stick, and traveling clothes with them and who intended to represent travelers in that room (May 22, 1889).

His *Public Soup Kitchen* depicts poor people who had to live on charity. He remembered how, one time in Brussels in winter, he saw the opening of a soup kitchen where broth was served free in the morning to poor people and wanted to depict not so much the right type as the sense of the whole, whether it was a "free soup occasion in Brussels, London, or The Hague" (October 22–29, 1882).

In order to save on expenses, Vincent himself also often made use of a public soup kitchen and made different drawings of a public soup kitchen where soup was sold (January 12–16, 1882). He used Sien's family (her mother and younger sister) and a boy from the neighborhood as his models. They posed for the painting, together with his housemates (March 3, 1882). He wanted to make a sketch true to life, scenes from the everyday life of ordinary people. His drawing portrays Sien and her six-year-old daughter Maria, who is walking away on the right with a bowl of soup. Her younger sister is having her bowl filled, and her mother is holding baby Willem in her arms. He felt at home with these people (May 4–12, 1882).

Master of Humanity

Vincent looked on his fellow human beings with compassion. He showed that in word and deed as a teacher and as an assistant minister in England, as an evangelist in the Borinage, and as a painter as well. He knew that for his work as an artist and painter he needed to have a warm feeling of sympathy for people, "actually for all, otherwise drawings remained cold and weak" (October 31, 1882).

A few times he also experienced the sympathy of others. One such time was in The Hague when a young girl he had asked to be his model canceled but then showed up anyway: "I didn't come to be drawn; I came to see if you have enough food." She had a serving of French beans and potatoes with her (March 11, 1882).

Among Vincent's earliest drawings of his fellow human beings are those of a sower, a large old fellow, a long, dark silhouette against a dark background. A second sower type is very different, with a fringe of beard, wide shoulders, and is somewhat thickset. Vincent sketched him with a light-brown fustian jacket and pants, which appear light against the black field bounded by a row of pollard willows at the end. He did not want to draw any figures at rest but only those at work, for he agreed with his friend Anthon van Rappard who remarked that Vincent's *Sower* is not a man sowing but someone posing as a sower (October 15, 1881). Vincent saw the worker and depicted him or her with the lines of pain and suffering and fatigue in his or her face, for "his looks were not striking, and he lacked all beauty" (Isaiah 53:2). That was how he saw the workers with whom he lived and worked in the Borinage and spoke about them (April 13, 1885).

In May 1889, shortly before he was discharged from the asylum in Saint Rémy, he painted *The Good Samaritan*, someone who lifts the victim of a robbery onto his own mount. He hung a copy of *The Good Samaritan* by the painter Eugène Delacroix in his room in the hospital in Arles (May 3, 1889). It is possible to view his own *Good Samaritan* as a self-portrait,[19] for Vincent identified with the Good Samaritan various times, such as when he cited his affinity with Madame François from a novel by Émile Zola, *Le Vente de Paris (The Belly of Paris)*. Madame François picks up a poor man, Florent, who has fainted in the middle of the road where the vegetable carts are being driven and takes him with her, even though the other vegetable farmers call out: "Let him lie there, the drunk! We don't have time to pick up men who lie in the gutter." Vincent saw true humanity in the attitude shown by Madame François. He thought that what he did with Sien was the same as what Madame François would have done. Humanity for him was the salt of life; without it, he would not have any interest in life. He also once

19. Miedema, 1948, 75.

nursed a poor, burned miner for six to eight weeks and shared his food with him for a whole winter. He did not see that as foolish or bad but so natural and a matter of course that he did not understand how people could be so indifferent toward one another. He still believed that "Love your neighbor as yourself" was not going too far (July 23, 1882).

The Constitution of the French Revolution: A "New Gospel"

Vincent was aware that he was living in the last quarter of the nineteenth century, which, in his view, would end in a colossal revolution. He felt instinctively that a lot was changing and there were more changes coming. He saw himself, together with Theo, standing toward the end of their lives at the beginning of that revelation: they themselves would not witness the better times of clear skies and the renewal of society as a whole but would live through the dark and oppressive hours that came before the thunderstorm. The history of the past century shows how terribly revolutions end—however nobly they may begin (middle of February 1886)

On one of his many walks from Voorburg to Leidsendam, Vincent saw a tragedy played out in the storm-swept trees, which reminded him of society. This society appears as a large, gloomy silhouette, seen against the light of renewal (September 22, 1883).

In Amsterdam he was reminded of an indescribably beautiful and unforgettable painting by Jules Goupil on the French Revolution, *A Young Citizen of the Year V*: eyes that had seen the spectacle of the terrible guillotine, a mind that had survived all the events of the revolution; he is almost surprised that he was still alive after so many disasters (October 21, 1877).

Vincent called the French Revolution the absolutely greatest modern event, around which everything else revolved. Everything had changed since then (May 25, 1883). The French Revolution was the greatest step forward the human species had taken since the coming of Christ. The French Revolution *and* the meaning of Christ's coming in year 1 were comparable events in his view (May 21, 1883). Michelet compared the constitution of 1789 with the virgin birth in Bethlehem and called it a "new gospel."[20] Van Gogh also referred to Charles Dickens's *A Tale of Two Cities*, which was about the French Revolution. The opening passage reads:

20. Sund, *True to Temperament*, 42.

It was the best of times, it was the worst of times, it was the age of wisdom, it was the age of foolishness, it was the epoch of belief, it was the epoch of incredulity, it was the season of Light, it was the season of Darkness . . . .

For Dickens, the French Revolution was a monster, a nightmare—his own as well. That monster was to be fought, in his view, not by hanging even more people or putting them in prison but only by acknowledging and easing the conditions that lead to revolution. Dickens himself tried to understand the serious social grievances and help rectify them by writing about them in his work (October 21, 1877).

In *A Tale of Two Cities* Vincent found something of the spirit of "the Resurrection and the Life." He referred to the characters in the drama of self-denial and resurrection that Dickens describes as those who are resurrected. Sidney Carton, a licentious lawyer who wastes his talents (July 1880),[21] takes the place of a condemned man and dies in his place by guillotine. Just before life washes everything away like an immense wave, he hears in his mind the words from the funeral liturgy: "I am the resurrection and the life" (John 11:25).[22]

"An inner and hidden revolution is coming" (Tolstoy)

In his ambition to become a painter of peasant life, Vincent was also inspired by Leo Tolstoy, who also wanted to live like a peasant. When Vincent was thirty and walking around Nuenen, his thoughts turned to Tolstoy who described himself as "ugly, clumsy, sloppy, and undeveloped socially."

Toward the end of his life, Vincent referred approvingly to Tolstoy's *My Religion* (September 19, 1889), in which Tolstoy was looking for what was still eternally true in the Christian religion and for what all religions had in common. "An inner and hidden revolution is coming, from which a new religion will emerge or, rather, something completely new, which will be nameless but will have the same effect of comfort as the Christian faith had before."

That book seemed to be very interesting to Vincent. Over time people began to have enough of cynicism, skepticism, mockery, and a more musical life was sought.

---

21. Sund, *True to Temperament*, 34.
22. Dickens, *A Tale of Two Cities*, Introduction; Davis, *Charles Dickens A to Z*, 373–81.

> How will that happen and what will be discovered? It would be strange if we could predict it. It is better to anticipate it than only see disasters in the future that will, by the way, strike the modern world and civilization any way, just like so many terrible flashes of lightning. (September 24, 1888)

Tolstoy did not appear to believe in a resurrection, neither that of the body nor that of the soul. He especially did not seem to believe in heaven. But he did think it of great importance to do what one does well because it is the only thing one has. Tolstoy appears to believe in what is equated with the resurrection: the continuation of life, the development of humankind, the human being, and work, which will almost certainly be continued by the next generation. Although born an aristocrat, Tolstoy became a laborer. He could make boots, repair stoves, plough the soil, and turn over the ground. Vincent appreciated the human spirit that was energetic enough to transform itself.

> Tolstoy believed in a non-violent revolution that flowed from the need for love and faith and would present itself to people as a reaction to skepticism and the suffering that makes people desperate. (September 29, 1888)

Mammon or Money

Vincent called avarice a very ugly word and greed a devil that does not leave anyone alone. It would not surprise him if greed had even tempered him and Theo to such an extent that they were inclined to say: "Money is the boss, money can do everything, money is number 1"—not that they in effect bowed to and served "Lord Mammon" but in the sense that it made life surprisingly difficult for them both. There were temptations to bow to the demon of money, but Vincent trusted that they were not inclined to become the prey of mammon in too radical a way (November 23, 1881).

For Vincent, the city was associated with the economy of money,[23] and the latter played an impudent role in society (November 17, 1883). He drew a comparison with sheep and wolves: it is better to be a sheep than a wolf, better yet to be the one that is killed than the one that kills—thus, better to be Abel than Cain (Genesis 4). He knew he was no wolf. If Theo and he were truly sheep in society, it would be best if they were consumed by rather

23. Pollock, *Vincent van Gogh*, 90.

hungry and false wolves. Although that was not particularly pleasant, it was nevertheless better to be destroyed than to destroy another. Vincent did not envy the wolves (December 5, 1883). He often felt he was rich—not in money but because he found his work, because he had something he could live for with heart and soul that gave inspiration and meaning to life (March 11, 1883).

In a letter from Nuenen at the beginning of 1884 Vincent relates an old legend. According to this legend, the human race descended from two brothers. Both could choose what they wanted. The one chose gold and the other a book. Everything went fine with the former, while the latter had a difficult time. The legend relates how the man with the book is banned to a cold, miserable, and isolated country. Nonetheless, he begins to read the book in his misery and learns things from it so that he can make his life more bearable. He invents various things to relieve his difficult circumstances and finally acquires some power through work and struggle. While the one with the book becomes stronger, the one with the money becomes weaker and learns that not everything revolves around gold. For Vincent, "the book" not only represented all books or literature but also stood for the conscience, reason, and art. Thus, in his view, "gold" is not only money but also a symbol for many other things (January 2, 1884).

The Poor and Money is what Vincent called his painting of the poor wretches who were hoping in vain to draw the winning ticket at the state lottery in The Hague.[24] One day he saw a group of these "wretches" standing at the top of Spuistraat in The Hague at the state lottery office. He came there on a rainy morning when a crowd of people were standing there waiting to get their lottery tickets. Most of them were old women of whom it was impossible to tell what they did or how they lived but apparently managed to scrape through and struggle along, people who apparently had great interest in the "Drawing today" ("Heden trekking"). Their expression of waiting struck him, but while he was making the painting, that expression acquired a greater and deeper meaning for him than at first. Curiosity and illusion about the lottery may have looked childish to Theo and him, but

> it became serious when it was remembered that these wretches imagine themselves to be saved by buying lottery tickets out of desperation with the pennies they saved by not eating. (October 1, 1882)

24. Cf. Pollock, "Stark Encounters," 349–50.

Humanity, Compassion, and Neediness

When he was in The Hague Vincent drew a whole series of old men and women from the Dutch Reformed Home for Poor Old Men and Women, the so-called *diaconiemannetjes* ("diaconate men") (June 3, 1883). They posed for him regularly for a meager fee of a few coins for an afternoon or morning. It was his ideal to work with more and more models all the time,

> a whole herd of poor people for whom the studio could be a kind of refuge on cold days or when they had no work or were in need, knowing where they could find warmth, food, drink and where they could earn a few coins. (October 10, 1882)

He thought that Theo would understand what he wanted and intended with his drawings of old men from this home for poor old men and women.

> A figure's expression does not lie so much in the features of a face as in the whole appearance: an impoverished couple arm in arm at the beech hedge, the type of man and woman who have grown old together and where there is still love and faithfulness.

The "master of humanity" (Annie Romein-Verschoor) managed to give poor old men an air of humanity, compassion, and neediness.[25]

Workers

Through his own observation and experience, as well as through literature, Vincent became acquainted with the lot and poor living conditions of workers. Early in 1880 he undertook a punishing walk (140 kilometers!) from the Borinage to visit the studio of the poet-painter Jules Breton in Courrières in northern France (September 24, 1880). He went there and back, from Mons to Valenciennes by foot, with less than two francs in his pocket, walking for three days and three nights at the beginning of March, in rain and wind with no shelter. It was an exhausting journey. He arrived at the studio but did not dare go inside (September 24, 1880), even though he had once met the poet-painter with his wife and two daughters in Paris (May 31, 1875).

Along the way, however, he saw weavers' villages. Just like the mineworkers, the weavers constituted a people apart, compared with other workers and craftsmen. He felt great sympathy for them and wanted to draw them, which he did in Nuenen in the first months of 1884 (September 24, 1880).

25. Romein-Verschoor, "Meester der menselijkheid," 817.

In 1881 Vincent had read Charlotte Brontë's novel *Shirley* on the difficult living conditions under which the unemployed poor in Yorkshire lived.[26] The book revolves around the workers and the role of women. Vincent undoubtedly recognized his own views in what she wrote on religion. Brontë was, after all, the daughter of a minister and depicted the clergy in her books as stubborn, oppressive, and sometimes even cruel. She advocated a substantial reform of organized religion.[27]

When Vincent dreamed of rural Brabant (May 15, 1884), he imagined Drenthe to be like the North Brabant of his youth, about twenty years prior. He remembered the heath and the small farms, the looms, the spinning wheels, etc.—a Brabant landscape that had been greatly changed by exploitation and industrialism (August 13, 1882). He found George Eliot's description of the time of transition after the industrial revolution in her *Felix Holt, The Radical*, a book he reread when he was in Nuenen (second half of March 1884),[28] to be a good one. The words "The Radical" are in reference to both politics and religion. Felix stands up for the rights of the workers and is a member of a movement of "dissenters," Protestants who did not belong to the established church. Felix is a kind of "secular saint" who puts Christian values into practice.[29] Eliot's book spoke to Vincent's imagination because the main character chose, just like Vincent himself, a sober life among workers above a job in the family business (the art dealers).[30]

During the winter of 1884 in Nuenen, he said it was depressing and gloomy outside on the dark winter days. That darkness was in harmony with the appearance of farmers and weavers. The latter did not complain, he said, even though life was hard.

> A weaver who works steadily makes sixty yards of material in a week. While he weaves, a woman has to sit spooling (winding spools of yarn), thus there are two who work and must live from the work. He earns about four and a half guilders a week for such a length—and when he brings it to the factory owner, he is often told that he can bring a new length in eight or fourteen days. Thus, not only the wage but work as well is minimal. Therefore, there is often something flustered and uneasy about those people.

26. Brontë, *Shirley*, 20.

27. Sund, *True to Temperament*, 43.

28. Cf. Zemel, *Van Gogh's Progress*, 63; Hammacher, *Van Gogh*, 112.

29. So Sund, *True to Temperament*, 24, 25 with references.

30. Stolwijk et al., *De Keuze van Vincent*, 90.

The mood of the weavers was different from that of the mineworkers: they were quiet, and Vincent heard nothing that seemed like rebellious talk. They seemed as cheerless as the carriage horses or sheep that were transported to England by steamboat (January 20, 1885).

Vincent drew and painted many weavers in 1884. A lament could be heard coming from out of the looms in which the weaver was shackled, but "the miner is the man in the depths, in the abyss, *de profundis*" (Psalm 130). The weaver is the man with the dreamy gaze, sunk in reverie, almost sleepwalking (September 24, 1880). Vincent did not want to draw a loom as such but wanted people to think about those who worked it (half of March 1884). He saw a kind of poetry in the weavers' life like that articulated in Michelet's *The People*, which describes how the textile industry was responsible for the rise of a "miserable, misformed type of machine people who could only lead a half-life" (February 1, 1883).[31] According to him, the weavers were indeed poor, but they were not as bad off as the modern factory workers in their textile factories. The weavers could at least dream during their monotonous work,

> [humming] their pious laments in a low voice, like a woman rocking a child. The poor recluse always feels small, always a child, and he sings a comforting rocking song to himself to soothe the restlessness and whining will to power to sleep, next to God.[32]

His depictions of weavers were undoubtedly inspired by George Eliot's *Silas Marner, The Weaver of Raveloe*. He read this novel in 1876 while in England and again in Amsterdam in 1878 (May 12, 1876; March 3, 1878). This work invoked comparisons for Vincent with his own life and influenced his depictions. In *Silas Marner, The Weaver of Raveloe* (March 3, 1878)[33] Eliot describes the life of factory workers who have organized themselves into a small congregation and hold religious services in a chapel in Lantern Yard (May 12, 1876). When Silas Marner is wrongly found guilty of theft through the casting of lots, he blasphemes a God of lies who witnesses against an innocent man. He leaves Lantern Yard and goes to live in Raveloe alone, in bitterness. Silas's absolute trust in the divine is now replaced by materialism, and his trust in the miraculous by the mechanical.

31. De Leeuw, *De brieven*, 58.
32. Quoted by Uitert et al., *Schilderijen*, 38–39.
33. Vincent is convinced that Theo will not regret reading it.

When the money is stolen, however, and an orphan child finds her way to his house, Silas is given the chance to transform his life.[34]

Vincent described his work as a poor painter as like that of a peasant worker or a factory worker who had to organize his daily life (August 18, 1883). In the final phase of his life, long after he painted (mine)workers, he drew a comparison between his own work and that of the miner who constantly lives with danger and has to hurry up with what he is doing (October 8, 1889).

The Last Supper

The Potato Eaters, the painting that, years later, Vincent still considered his best (summer, autumn 1887), can be viewed as a summary of his work from his Dutch period. It is a true peasant painting (June 1, 1885). Here he wanted to paint peasants in their own surroundings. He sought the motif for this study in the heart of the people, and he wanted to draw that motif as it really was (second half of August 1885). Through *The Potato Eaters* he wanted to lead people to

> the idea that these small people, who eat their potatoes by the light of their lamp, with the hands that they stick into the bowl, have turned the soil themselves, thus it speaks of their manual labor and that they earned their food so honestly. (April 30, 1885)

He wanted it to make people imagine an entirely different and better way of life than that of civilized people. A peasant girl is more beautiful in her dusty and patched blue skirt and jacket than a lady in her finery. Weather, wind, and sun give her the finest nuances. If she were to put on a lady's costume, she would no longer be authentic. He thought a peasant in the field in his fustian clothes to be finer than when he went to church on Sunday in a gentleman's suit. If a peasant painting smelled of bacon, smoke, potato vapors—that was fine, it was not unhealthy. It was good in the way it was good when a stable smelled of manure—that was what a stable was for. If a field gave off an air of ripe grain or potatoes or of guano and manure— that was in fact healthy, especially for city people.

> A painting of peasants should not be perfumed. One should paint peasants like one of them, feeling and thinking like them. (April 30, 1885)

34. Eliot, *Silas Marner*, Introduction, chapter 18, 122.

The solemnity of the figures in *The Potato Eaters* and the solemn character of their gestures allow the painting to be seen as a "Last Supper."[35] There is a special emphasis on "the peculiar lighting of the dirty hut: a gray interior, lighted by a lamp, the walls gray with smoke, the dusty bonnets that the women wore when working in the fields" (beginning of May and second half of August 1885).

The child in the foreground of the painting is, as it were, transformed into someone who reveals herself to her disciples: a Christ figure. The steam from the potatoes creates a halo around her. She is standing almost directly under the gaslamp, the only source of light. This lamp is a miraculous beacon. An older man is holding his cup as reverently as if he were holding a chalice. This religious allusion is reinforced by a print on the upper left, behind a younger man, of the crucifixion of Christ with Mary and John, a so-called house blessing, which refers to the Catholic faith of the inhabitants.[36] The table is their altar and the food a sacrament for everyone who is weary. The details are striking: the cup with its gray shadows, the potatoes on the plate, and the beautiful cups. The eyes of both figures on the left are radiant, and the shadows on their faces are more marks of their characters than the result of darkness. "I would rather paint peoples' eyes than cathedrals," Vincent wrote shortly afterwords (December 19, 1885).[37]

When he was once asked to paint a "Last Supper" for a dining room in Eindhoven, he asked in turn if scenes of local peasant life would not quicken the appetite of those sitting at table more than a mystical "Last Supper" would. He proposed six motifs from peasant life: sower, ploughman, harvest, potato planters, shepherd, and winter with an oxcart (August 1884).

The Pietà

In the visual arts, a pietà (from Italian *pietà*: compassion) is a representation of Mary in intense sorrow, with the body of the just deceased Christ on her knees or at her feet. Michelangelo's pietà in St. Peter's in Rome, which he produced at a young age, is the most famous example.

---

35. De Mooij, "Devotionalia en volkskunst," 147–48; Van Tilborgh, *The Potato Eaters*, 37; Van Tilborgh, *Vincent van Gogh*, 138–39.

36. De Mooij, "Devotionalia en volkskunst," 147–48.

37. Schapiro, *Vincent van Gogh*, 30, 38.

Vincent hung Delacroix' *Pietà* in his room in Saint Rémy. He felt that the features of the *mater dolorosa* in Delacroix' painting were not like those on Roman statues but more in line with the main character of the novel by Edmond and Jules de Goncourt, *Germinie Lacerteux* (one of his favorite books) (September 19, 1889), which told of the sad life of their own maid.[38] The De Goncourts described Germinie's temperament as passive and slow, the classic lymphatic type that could be seen in the color of her skin, i.e. "whiteness, at once *unhealthy and angelic*, of flesh in which there is no life."[39]

During Vincent's illness, a lithograph of Delacroix' *Pietà* fell into some oil and paint and was damaged, to his regret. He then decided to paint that scene himself. His reproduction showed Christ lying at the entrance to a cave, bent forward over his left side, his hands stretched out in front of him, and Mary behind him. It is evening after a storm, and this extremely somber figure clothed in blue stands out against a sky of purple clouds with gold edges. In a grand desperate gesture she stretches her arms in front of her, and her hands are the good, solid hands of a working woman. Her blowing clothes make her almost as wide as she is tall. Because the face of the dead Christ is lying in shadow, the woman's own pale face stands out clearly against a cloud—a contrast that makes these two heads remind one of two flowers, one dark and one light, painted deliberately in that way to make them prominent in the painting. The pale face, the distraught and vague look of someone who has been exhausted by fear, weeping, and watching is more like a Germinie Lacerteux figure (September 19, 1889).

The Garden of the Poet

By painting part of the public park in Arles, *The Garden of the Poet* and *Weeping Tree on a Lawn* (September 16, 1888). Vincent wanted to allude to the time of the early Renaissance (fourteenth century), the time of the Italian poet Petrarch (Francesco Petrarca). He felt connected to Petrarch by the experience of the landscape of Provence that he shared with him: these gardens are thus given a loaded meaning. Vincent was aware that Petrarch had lived nearby, in Avignon, and had seen the same cypresses and oleanders he was seeing now. Petrarch's younger friend and protégé

---

38. Hammacher, *Van Gogh*, 118.
39. Quoted by Sund, *True to Temperament*, 136.

Giovanni Boccaccio was known primarily for his *Decameron*, in which the love stories are told in the garden of an estate.[40]

Vincent asked Theo if he did not think that the style of the painting of this park was a funny one, leading the observer to imagine that the poets of the Renaissance were parading about with flowers between the shrubs on this lawn. The friendship between Petrarch and Boccaccio was nourished by their shared conviction concerning the exalted position of the poet and their belief in the revelatory power of poetry.[41]

Vincent associated his plans for a renaissance of art in "the South" (southern France) to this earlier Renaissance, which was achieved at that time by the friendship and collaboration between Petrarch and Boccaccio (February 10/11, 1890). In his imagination he saw the rich beauty of the gardens and parks from the *The Garden of the Poet* and the shades of Petrarch and Boccaccio wandering around (September 17, 1888). A place where such important artists lived and their work blossomed—impressionism could do that too! October 1888). He saw himself in the role of the younger Boccaccio over against the latter's older and more established friend Petrarch—the role of Gauguin (October 3, 1888).[42]

The Garden of Paradise

Once, in the summer of 1888, Vincent was in Montmajour with a friend Paul E. Milliet, a second lieutenant in the Swiss Guards, to whom he gave drawing lessons (June 18, 1888). Montmajour is a place northeast of Arles, where there was a former Benedictine abbey, once a much visited destination for pilgrimage. They explored the old garden there together and stole delicious figs. One of the farms in the area was called "La Paradou," the Provençal word for paradise.[43] Vincent thought that if the garden had been bigger it would have reminded him of the Paradou in Zola's novel, *La Faute de l'Abbé Mouret* (*Abbe Mouret's Transgression*):

> long reed stems, clusters of grapes, ivy, fig trees, olive trees, pomegranate trees with fleshy, very bright orange flowers, hundred-year-old cypresses, ash trees, willows, holly oaks, half-dilapidated steps, collapsed arched windows, blocks of white rocks, covered

40. Cf. Druick and Zegers, *Van Gogh en Gauguin*, 366, note 212.

41. Druick and Zegers, *Van Gogh en Gauguin*, 142, 366, note 212.

42. Druick and Zegers, *Van Gogh en Gauguin*, 151.

43. Gayford, *The Yellow House*, 213.

with lichens and collapsed walls scattered here and there in the grass. (July 9, 1888)

In his *Abbe Mouret's Transgression*, Zola describes the life of a twenty-five-year-old village priest, Serge Mouret, who is characterized by devotion to duty and a strong devotion to Mary. When his love for the sixteen-year-old Albine while working as a priest leads him into a crisis, he seeks refuge with Mary. He contracts a fever and becomes unconscious. A doctor knows of no better place for his recovery than, remarkably, Paradou, a Paradise-like park about five kilometers from the village, where he brings him in secret. There the priest "falls" because he is taken care of by Albine, who lives there together with her guardian. The garden, which he did not know about the day before, is now a source of unprecedented pleasure for him. After reaching the pinnacle of happiness, they discover one day that they are naked. Now Serge begins to be ashamed. Through a hole in the wall of the garden he sees his village in the golden beams of the setting sun. He begins to shake. Everything surfaces again. The past is revived. Although Serge experiences the greatest happiness in Albine's arms, he tortures himself because of the passions he now rejects. At their last meeting in Paradou, Serge mumbles, "The garden is dead." The evening falls, and the garden is now only a large, dark grave, for Paradou will teach Albine to die, just it had taught her earlier to love. In the end Albine, pregnant with Serge's child, kills herself.[44]

Vincent took a drawing of Montmajour home, although it was not one of the garden.

When he painted *Peat Diggers in the Dunes* in The Hague, with a small church tower in the middle, his intention was that it be a counter to "Paradou" in Zola's novel (August 19, 1882). He wrote that he was happy that Theo was enjoying himself at the time, alluding to the good time he had with a girlfriend: "Paradou [paradise] will have been real" (January 13, 1883). [45] He suggested that he could paint Theo and his girlfriend in para-dise but would still rather see diggers and finds it nicer outside Paradise, i.e.

44. Zola, *Abbe Mouret's Transgression*.
45. Hulsker, *Lotgenoten*, 273.

where one thinks more of the more severe "By the sweat of your brow you will eat your bread" (Genesis 3:19). He finds that the one becomes nicer precisely over against the other. A drawing of a digger with a bald head bent over the black earth makes him think of that that laboring in the sweat of one's brow as depicted in Genesis 3:19 (May 21, 1883). The *Peat Diggers* shows a different landscape than that of Paradou, and yet it still gives him a "Paradou" feeling (May 30, 1883). When Vincent felt unhappy after his break with Sien, he went outside to commune with nature. Seeing one gigantic cloud chasing another high above the pastures, he saw a tragedy in every tree. To him, the tragedy of the storm in nature was the tragedy of sorrow in nature. "A paradou [paradise] is nice, but Gethsemane is still nicer" (September 4, 1883). For the Garden of Paradise does symbolize an idyllic and utopian life, but Gethsemane represents the tragedy of sorrow, with the diggers as the symbol of the tragic lot of humankind, banished from Paradise.[46]

Gethsemane

Vincent never actually wanted to draw or paint Christ directly. In September 1888 he did, however, attempt to paint *Christ in the Garden of Gethsemane* in Arles.

> A Garden of Olives with a Christ figure in blue and orange, a yellow angel, a red piece of land, green and blue hills, olive trees with violet and carmine red trunks with gray and blue-green leaves, and lemon-yellow sky.

He did two studies of this.

> I can't, or rather don't want to, paint without models, but I have it in my head in color, the starry night, the figure of Christ in blue—the most powerful blue hues—and the angel in off-yellow. And in the landscape all violet hues from blood-red purple to ash. (September 22, 1888)

Starry Night, which he would paint a year later, was interpreted as his depiction of the "death struggle in the garden."[47]

He disagreed very much with Gauguin and Bernard regarding their depiction of this theme. Gauguin sent him a sketch of *Christ in the Garden of*

46. Kôdera, "In het zweet," 76.
47. Soth, "Van Gogh's Agony," 301, 313.

Olives, which he thought Vincent would like (November 8, 1889). Gauguin painted himself into it as Christ, "a purple Christ with red hair, with a yellow angel" (October 20, 1889; November 8, 1889). Vincent talked about religious paintings that Bernard had made, such as *The Adoration of the Magi* (November 20, 1889), *Christ in the Garden of Olives* (November 17, 1889; November 21, 1889), and *Christ Carrying the Cross*. He did not want to have anything to do with their interpretations but wanted to produce a different work based on the Bible. Both artists distance themselves, in his view, from reality. He assumed that Bernard had never seen an olive tree for real (September 7/8, 1889), whereas he himself had seen women picking and gathering olives at that time. He found Bernard's biblical paintings hopeless: his *Christ in the Garden of Olives* made him despondent, and he thought his *Christ Carrying the Cross* horrible, a nightmare. (November 20, 1889).

He also considered how other great artists dealt with depictions of Jesus. With respect to depicting the scene in Gethsemane he did agree with how Delacroix had done it because Delacroix had first studied actual olive orchards (September, 6/7, 1889).

.Millet, who grew up with the Bible and did nothing else but read that book (like Vincent himself), never or almost never produced any depictions of biblical stories. The French painter Gustave Courbet, one of the greatest realistic artists, once advised against painting Christ unless one knew him personally (July 1885).[48]

Rembrandt was the only Dutch painter to paint Christ, and his work scarcely resembles that of other religious painters. Only Delacroix and Rembrandt painted the figure of Christ in the way Van Gogh felt was authentic. Millet painted the *teaching* of Jesus, Rembrandt worked with *values*, Delacroix with *colors*. There is a world of difference between the method used by Delacroix and Rembrandt and that used by all other religious painters (July 21, 1888). In his etching *Jesus in Gethsemane* Rembrandt brought the agony of death to expression (Luke 22:43–44). Jesus wrestles with his fears. Peter and the two sons of Zebedee are lying asleep under the rock on which Jesus is kneeling. In the distance one can see the band of men coming to arrest Jesus. Jesus has turned his gaze inward and conducts a desperate struggle with himself in which an angel comforts him.[49] According to Van Gogh,

48. Druick and Zegers, *Van Gogh en Gauguin*, 144.
49. Hoekstra, *Rembrandt en de Bijbel*, Vol. 3, 10, 11.

Rembrandt, did not make up anything and "that angel and that remarkable Christ—that was because he knew them, felt them there" (July 23, 1888).

In Saint Rémy he would not attempt to paint Christ himself in the garden of olives, but he would paint picking the olives in his depiction of the asylum garden. This painting included one corner of the asylum and the garden with a large, sawed-off tree, the first tree. It had an enormous trunk but had been struck by lightning and had been cut off. A side branch, however, still went up quite high, and a rain of dark green needles is falling.

> This gloomy giant, its pride offended, to give it a human trait, stands in contrast with the faded smile of a last rose on the almost flowered out rose bush across from it.

Under the trees are empty stone benches and dark box trees; the sky is reflected (yellow) in a puddle after the rain. The combination of red ochre, green that has turned dark with gray, and black stripes that indicate contours arouse the feeling of fear that some of his fellow painters suffer from. This can be expressed without referring immediately to the historical Gethsemane (November 20, 1889).

Death and Transformation

When Vincent was making sketches in pen in Arles of an immense flat landscape with vineyards and mown fields of grain, as viewed from a bird's eye view on top of a hill, one of his painter friends said to him, "It seems boring to paint that." Vincent said nothing but found the scene so impressive he did not even have the strength to "tell the idiot" off. Again and again he went to the fields. When a soldier passed by on another occasion when he was drawing, he asked him, "Do you think it strange that I find this as beautiful as the *sea*?" "No, it doesn't surprise me," the soldier said, "that you find this as beautiful as the sea, but I find it even more beautiful than the ocean, for it is, after all, inhabited." Which of the spectators was the best artist, the painter or the soldier? (July 15, 1888).

When he arrived for the first time in Arles, Vincent immediately took advantage of the fact the trees were in blossom to make his first studies of spring. He went to work like a man possessed; the trees were, after all, in blossom for only a short time and he wanted to turn a Provençal orchard into a mad joyousness (April 2, 1888). One of his first studies was *Blossoming Almond Branch in a Glass*, which he did for his sister Wil (March 30,

1888). Almond trees are the heralds of spring, symbolizing fertility, and are ancient symbols of divine approval and favor.[50]

In this same spring Vincent received news of the death of his uncle Anton Mauve, who had been very important for his formative period as a painter in The Hague. Mauve's death was a heavy blow. He heard the news when he was working in an orchard on a canvas of a ploughed piece of land—a reed fence, two peach trees against a radiant sky in blue and white. It made a deep impression on him and he choked with emotion. He wrote the dedication on the painting "Souvenir de Mauve. Vincent & Theo," and proposed to Theo that he send this painting to Anton's wife. It seemed to him that something done in memory of Mauve should be tender and very joyful and not a more serious gamut of colors.

> Do not think the dead are dead;
> as long as there are people living,
> the dead will live,
> the dead will live.
> That's how I see it, not more sadly. (March 30, 1888)

Two years later, again in the spring, he received news of the birth of Theo and Jo's child. Already before the child was born they had asked him to be their son's godfather, "whereas it could be a girl, couldn't it?" Under those conditions, he would have thought it more logical to name it after their father and thought that their mother would appreciate that (July 6, 1889). For that matter, he said in a following letter, there was reason enough to feel a bit like living again when he remembered that he would be an uncle of a boy Theo's wife brought into the world. He hoped that the child's soul would be less restless than his own, which was being destroyed by that restlessness (July 6, 1889).

When a son was indeed born, it was named after him. He wrote to his mother:

> I would much rather that he had called his boy after Dad, whom
> I think about so often these days, than me. But, anyway, now that
> the situation is what it is, I have actually begun a painting for him
> to hang in his bedroom. Large branches of white almond blossoms
> against a blue sky. (February 20, 1890)

---

50. Werness, "The Symbolism," 48, note 17.

He considered *Almond Blossom* the best he had done perhaps, with the most patience, painted in calm, and with greater accuracy in wielding the brush. Theo's wife Jo sent Vincent a birthday letter on behalf of his godson:

> He always looks at Uncle Vincent's paintings with a great deal of interest—the flowering tree that hangs above our bed especially fascinates him very much. (March 29, 1890)

Death: A Journey Past the Stars

He saw death, the great journey to the other hemisphere of life, as a journey past the stars.[51] How simple it would be if life had a second hemisphere where we would be after death! (July 31, 1888). Vincent related the following parable in a letter from Arles in June 1888 to his friend Émile Bernard:

> Look, it was once thought the earth was flat. That is still true today, from Paris to Asnières, for example. But that does not take away from the fact that science has shown the earth is round, which cannot be disputed by anyone today. Despite that, it is still thought today that life is flat and runs from birth to death. But life is probably round as well and, with respect to dimensions and possibilities, is probably much greater than the hemisphere we now know. Future generations will probably be able to clarify this very interesting topic to us; and then science itself—with all respect—can come to conclusions that correspond more or less with what Christ said about the other half of existence. (June 23, 1888)

He finds it strange that all artists, poets, musicians, painters are worriers, from a material point of view—including the happy ones. That raises the eternal question: "Is life visible to us in its entirety or do we know only one hemisphere of it before death?" Painters speak, when they are dead and buried, to new or different generations via their work. Is that everything or is there even more yet? In the life of the painter, death is perhaps not the most difficult thing.

Although he held that he knew nothing about it, the sight of the stars always set him to dreaming, just as easily as if he were set to dreaming by the black dots on a map that represent cities and villages. Why, he thought

---

51. In connection with *Starry Night*, Sund, "The Sower," 673, note 70, refers to Zola's *Joi de Vivre*: "The Joy of a new beginning under the stars, a new existence with family and friends."

then, should the lighted points of the firmament be less accessible to us than black dots on the map of France? If we take the train to Tarascon or Rouen, then we take death to a star. Something in this reasoning that does make sense is that we cannot go to a star during our lives any more than we can take a train after our death. Vincent did not think it impossible, however, for cholera, kidney stones, tuberculosis, and cancer to be heavenly means of transport like steamboats, omnibuses, and trains on earth. "Dying peacefully of old age is thus going there by foot" (July 8, 1888).

The Raising of Lazarus

In the weeks prior to his departure for Auvers in May 1890, he thanked Theo for Rembrandt's etching *The Raising of Lazarus* (John 11:1–5, 23–25, 38–44), where the emphasis lies on the reaction of Lazarus's sisters, Mary and Martha, who respond emotionally to their brother being raised.

> Three figures are standing in the background of the etching: the dead Lazarus and his two sisters, Mary and Martha. The cave and the dead body are violet. The woman who removes the shroud from the face of the individual who has been raised is wearing green garments and has orange hair; the other has black hair and is wearing green and pink striped clothing. Behind them is a landscape of blue hills and a rising orange sun. (May 3, 1890)

When Vincent "translates" Rembrandt's etching into color, these colors express the same, as such, as the chiaroscuro of the etching itself (May 3, 1890).[52] It depicts the contrast between life and death—that is the meaning of Rembrandt's use of light and dark. The models for the women in the painting were Madame Roulin, wife of the postal carrier (*La Berceuse*, *The Rocker*), and Madame Ginoux of the Café de la Gare, where he lived temporarily (*The Arlésienne*). He saw both of them very much as mother figures in their care for him during his illness (May 3, 1890).[53]

Vincent's own facial features can be seen in Lazarus's face, which appear to ask for healing and resurrection.[54] Perhaps he also painted his own hope of resurrection in *The Raising of Lazarus*, just as his endless sowers testify perhaps to that hope of the resurrection. One notices immediately

52. Hecht, *Vincent van Gogh*, 54 with reference to what, in Charles Blanc's *L'ouvre complete de Rembrandt*, is said about Lazarus.

53. Cf. Uitert et al., *Schilderijen*, 247.

54. Cf. Dorn et al., *Van Gogh*, 197–98.

that the figure of Christ that dominates Rembrandt's etching has been omitted from Van Gogh's painting. Instead of that, the warm, yellow light of the sun is central. He did not, however, replace Jesus by the sun; rather, the sun becomes the symbol for Christ and for God, as it did for the church in the early centuries, when Christians saw Christ as the "sun of righteousness" (Malachi 4:2). The sun translates the raised hand of Christ in Rembrandt's etching that woke the "dead" to life (May 3, 1890).[55]

The Yearning for the Eternal

When looking at nature, Vincent noticed that many flowers were trampled, frozen, or scorched.

> Not every kernel of grain goes back to the earth after ripening in order to germinate and become a stalk. Most kernels by far do not end up there but go to the mills. People can be compared with kernels of grain. Germinative power is found in every person who is healthy and natural, and natural life is like germination. What the germinative power is to grain love is to us. (summer, autumn, 1887)

Vincent was impressed very early by Jacob Jan van der Maaten's *Funeral in the Cornfield* (June 12, 1877). Copies of it hung in his father's study and in his own room in Paris (June 29, and July 6, 1875) and Amsterdam (May 19, 1877). He gave a copy of it to his teacher in Greek and Latin, Mendes da Costa, with poetry and Bible quotations on both sides, as well as quotes from the Bible on the promise of the resurrection. This is an example of margin poetry (*bijschrift poëzie*) for which J.J.L. ten Kate was well known.[56] Early one Sunday morning Vincent was influenced by an early morning sermon by the preacher-poet Laurillard in which the latter spoke about the parable of the sower. "At that time Jesus was walking through the cornfields on the Sabbath" (Matthew 12:1). In that sermon Laurillard referred to Van der Maaten's painting, just as his father had at a funeral. Vincent's father also used texts here such as "Truly, I say to you, unless a kernel of grain falls into the earth and dies, it will remain a seed. But if it dies, it will bear much fruit" (John 12:24) (June 12, 1877).

55. Wessels, *"A Kind of Bible,"* 104–6.
56. Stolwijk et al., *De Keuze van Vincent*, 68; Kôdera, *Vincent van Gogh*, 18.

In the first months of 1889 during his illness in Arles, he spoke of "inexpressible inner fears," although he found it best to accept the extremely gloomy reality. He showed that he was quite impressed by an old epitaph that he had read about Thebe (Telhui), a priestess of Osiris, who had never complained about anybody (March 29, 1889). In Saint Rémy he painted *Mask of an Egyptian Mummy*, characterized by melancholy and a smile that brought his early motto to mind: "sorrowful, yet always rejoicing" (2 Corinthians 6:10).[57]

> Is the extraordinary thing of Egyptian art not those serene, calm, wise, gentle, patient, and good kings that gave the impression of not being able to be anything but farmers worshipping the sun eternally? (June 9, 1889)

When one of his uncles died in September 1888, Vincent thought about his own purpose in life and about a future life. How is it, he wondered, that the face of the dead person is calm, serene, and serious whereas the uncle was never that during his life, neither when he was young nor when he was old. He then compared life to a simple ride in the train: we go fast, but we are unable to distinguish any single object close by and, what is more, we do not see the engine (August 6, 1888).

> Learning to suffer without complaint, learning to face sorrow without acquiring an aversion for it, it is precisely then you run the risk of becoming dizzy and yet you even see the vague probability that beyond this life we will learn to know the meaning of pain that, viewed from this perspective, sometimes so governs our horizon that it becomes as large as a terrible deluge. We know very little about that size, and it is better to look at a field of grain, even in the form of a painting. (July 2, 1889)

His painting *Field under a Stormy Sky* has often been called his image of the "gospel of nature." It reveals the invisible power of the "something above": the way of human labor, germinating earth, and the cycle of the seasons that bring us the harvest again.[58] Fragments of memories from earlier, the yearning for the eternal, of which the sower and the sheaf of grain are the symbols, still made him rapturous. He mentioned the sower and the sheaf in one breath: the sower stands at the beginning of the grain harvest and symbolizes the new life; the sheaf (just like the reaper) represents the final stage and

57. Maurer, *The Pursuit of Spiritual Wisdom*, 90.
58. Edwards, *The Shoes of Van Gogh*, 116.

stands for the end of life. The yearly cycle of nature gave him a sense of the "eternal."[59] Vincent once saw a sower who did not set one foot on soil ready for sowing without first throwing a handful of grain into the air in the form of a cross, and when he did step onto the field, he spoke incomprehensible texts in a low voice that sounded like a prayer (June 18, 1888).[60]

In the fall of 1888 he again painted a sower to mark the season of planting. He did yet another study of a sower, the figure small and vague, and still another of a ploughed field with the trunk of an old yew tree, (October 28, 1888) which since antiquity has been the symbol of immortality.

He thought about Millet's *The Sower* (June 18, 1888). Vincent wanted to be a sower of the Word (March 22, 1877) and one of his first activities in drawing was, in fact, copying Millet's work. In Millet he found "the precious pearl, the human soul expressed in a still more and better way, in a nobler, worthier, and, if I may be permitted, more evangelical tone" (September 24, 1880). This work continued to impress Vincent throughout his life as a painter. The trunk of the great large tree forms a parallel with the striding sower and produces new shoots as the living witness to the cycle of nature. The religious meaning was expressed by the great sun that is present like a natural "halo." The yellow beaming sun is precisely in the center and almost has the effect of an altarpiece.[61]

Once, in June 1888, in Arles he worked for a week very intensely and long in a grainfield, in the blazing sunshine, making studies of grainfields, landscapes, and a sketch of a sower.

> On an unploughed piece of land, a large piece of land with violet clods of earth, leading to the horizon—a sower in blue and white. On the horizon a field with low ripe grain. Above all of this was a yellow sky with a yellow sun. (June 21, 1888)

Regardless of whether he would be successful, he nevertheless believed that the work he did would be continued.

> Not immediately, but we are not the only ones who believe in things that are truly real. And what does your person matter? He feels that the history of the human being is like the history of the grain; if you are not sown into the earth to germinate, what does it matter? You are milled so you can be turned into bread. (September 19, 1889)

59. Van Heugten, *Vincent van Gogh*, 256.

60. Druick and Zegers, *Van Gogh en Gauguin*, 114–16.

61. Rosenblum and Janson, *Art*, 413.

There is Nothing Sad in Death

In November 1878, when he was about to go to work in the Borinage as an evangelist, he described a work called *The Life of a Horse*.

> The plate presents an old white horse, thin and emaciated and knackered to death by a long life of hard labor and much and difficult work. The poor animal stands there, indescribably lonely and abandoned, on a plain covered with scanty, dry grass with here and there a twisted tree, bowed and broken by the gale wind. A skull is lying on the ground, and in the distance in the background is a bleached skeleton of a horse lying next to a hut, where a man who kills the horses lives. Above everything hangs a stormy sky, it is an inclement and bleak day, gloomy and dark weather . . . .
>
> It is a sad and deeply melancholic stage that will strike everyone who knows and feels that we also must go through what we call dying, and the end of human life consists of tears and gray hairs. What still lies behind it is the great hiddenness that God alone knows. He, however, has revealed irrefutably in his Word to us that there is a resurrection from the dead. (November 15, 1878)

In the last paintings he did in Auvers of the expansive grainfields, "boundless like the sea," he attempted to express the sadness and loneliness that he experienced as characteristic for his own time (July 10–14, 1890). Few people worked around Saint Rémy, thus he was struck when he looked through the bars of his cell at the walled field behind the asylum where he was being treated and saw a peasant mowing with a sickle. What else can we do than look at the grainfields when we think about all the things whose background we do not understand?

> Their story is ours, for we who live from bread—are we not largely grain ourselves? Do we not at least have to accept that we grow like a plant, unable to move as our imagination inspires us and that, when we are ripe, we are mowed down like grain? (July 2, 1889)

He sees the image of death in that reaper, a vague figure who labors in the blazing heat like a horse to finish his work , in the sense that humanity represents the grain that is cut down. To Theo he expressed the hope that the family would be for him (Theo) what nature was for himself (Vincent):

> the clods of earth, the grass, the yellow grain, the peasant, that is, that you not only draw courage from your love for people in order to work but also to comfort yourself and to gain strength

> when you need it (September 5/6, 1889) . . . Nevertheless, there
> is nothing sad in death. It takes place in full light, in a sun that
> drenches everything in a fine, golden light. . . . It is a presentation
> of death as talked about in the great book of nature—but what I
> have attempted to achieve is death "almost with a smile." (September, 1885)

Is it not said of Eugène Delacroix—the great source of inspiration for Vincent, particularly because of his discovery of color—that he died "almost smiling" (Vincent took this quote from Théophile Silvestre's biography of Delacroix)?[62]

62. Cf. Uitert et al., *Schilderijen*, 220–21.

CHAPTER THREE

FROM DARKNESS TO LIGHT

The White and Black Rays

VINCENT USED THE IMAGE of the white and black rays several times when characterizing artists, writers, or even his father. This image was borrowed from Victor Hugo's novel *Ninety-Three* (referring to 1793) on the French Revolution (July 1880).[1] There are two people in this novel who each represent one pole of the truth: the one has been given "the white ray," the other "the black" (October/November 1883).[2] Vincent used this analogy for various people: Millet had the white ray like no other, as did Camille J.B. Corot, the best landscape painter of the nineteenth century. In Vincent's eyes, his father had more of the black ray. He felt that the prejudices that had guided his father with precision throughout his whole life deserved a better cause. His father's light is black and conventional compared to "Father" Millet and Corot (November 23, 1881).

Vincent viewed Theo's and his own youth as somber, cold, sterile, and cruel under the influence of the black ray, and he invited Theo to search from that moment on for the gentle light for which he knew no other name than the white ray (December 17, 1883).

Even though, in his view, his father had more of the black ray and the painter Corot the white ray, both had a "ray from above." The ray from above does not always appear and is hidden behind the clouds. Following

---

1. *Quatrevingt-treize* (Paris: 1957).

2. Hugo, second volume, chapter 4; Cf. Paris edition of 1957. In an earlier novel by Hugo, *L'homme qui rit*, in connection with the hero Gwyynplaine. (Thanks to Serge Adamovicz for this information).

Hugo, Vincent says: "God is a lighthouse whose light is eclipsed every now and then," and states, "We are now, without question, in the middle of such an eclipse" (September 29, 1888).

The Eternal Poetry of Christmas Night

Christmas was celebrated solemnly in Vincent's childhood home. The house was decorated with pine branches and a pine tree was placed in the austere church. Even after having left home years ago, Theo and he still returned at Christmas, something that Vincent looked forward to with longing. When he was working as an evangelist in the Borinage, he preached at Christmas on the stable in Bethlehem and on peace on earth (December 26, 1878). On her birthday he gave his sister Willemien the children's book by Louis Bungener, *Het Kerstfeest aan de Pool of God overall* (*Christmas at the Pole; Or, God Everywhere*; published originally in French as: *Noël au Pôle; ou, Dieu partout; quelques pages pour les enfants*) (March 16, 1877).[3]

Vincent's letters contain many references to Charles Dickens's Christmas stories and in March 1883 he said that he had just bought a new edition of those stories. "There are such profound things in it that you often have to read them twice." His interest in these stories continued until the end of his life. On 29 March 1889 he still said that he had reread these stories extremely attentively (March 27, 1889; April 30, 1889; April 12–15, 1889).

In the most well known of them, "A Christmas Carol," the miserly Scrooge represents the selfishness and indifference of the prosperous classes with respect to the poor. Scrooge thinks he has fulfilled his social obligations when he pays his taxes. But then Scrooge is visited by the ghosts of Christmas past, present, and future, and through this series of visits he is reborn as someone who responds in loving helpfulness to people in need. Such contrasts led Vincent to compare Dickens's most characteristic and accessible works with a wonderful light and dark (chiaroscuro) painting.[4]

Vincent reread other Christmas stories numerous times, almost every year, such as Dickens's "The Haunted Man," about a popular chemistry professor whose life is limited to the "intellect." Grief eclipses his life and, instead of being an enlightened man, he is surrounded by darkness and wallows in desperation and self-pity. When the darkness of the Christmas

3. He reads it in Amsterdam (September 7, 1877).

4. Smiley, *Charles Dickens*, 212. See *David Copperfield*; *Great Expectations*; *Dombey and Son*; *A Tale of Two Cities* and *Our Mutual Friend*.

feast descends, his depression deepens and it ultimately dawns on him how his denial of emotion paralyzes him and prevents him from acting positively or in a loving way (beginning of September 1876).[5] Vincent saw a great deal of truth in Dickens's "The Haunted Man." Although he did not exactly see himself in that character—to the contrary, almost—he became very aroused when he read it (February 7, 1883).

Christmas, "the feast of light," played an important role in Vincent's life from the beginning. Crisis periods coincide several times with Christmas, such as the well-known disagreement with Paul Gauguin (1888). In 1881, he had a quite heated exchange with his father during Christmas in Etten that went so far that his father said it would be better if he left the house. He did so the same day.

The reason for their argument was that he did not attend church on Christmas Day (!) (December 30, 1883) and also declared that if attendance was compulsory he would certainly not go, even as a courtesy. Actually, there was a lot more behind it, namely, what had happened that summer between him and Kee Vos-Stricker, his niece and sister-in-law who had lost her child and was widowed in 1878. She had come to stay in the parsonage with her four-year-old son Johannes. Seven years older than Vincent, he fell in love with her and wanted to marry her, an idea she completely rejected.

> I don't remember ever having been so angry, and I said frankly to Dad that I found the whole system of religion abhorrent, precisely because during a miserable time of my life I studied those things too much and no longer want to have anything to do with them and have to be on guard against it as if guarding myself against something deadly. (December 29, 1881)

Back in The Hague Vincent made, among others, two drawings: one of an old man reading a book, *Old Man with Head in his Hands*, and another of a man praying before his midday meal on the table in front of him, *Prayer Before the Meal*. According to him, they both evince what could be called old-fashioned sentiment. With these two drawings he intended

> to express the peculiar mood of Christmas and New Year's. In Holland and in England, it is always something religious, actually, it is religious everywhere, at least in Bretagne and in Alsace as well. Aside from the question if people are precisely in agreement in

---

5. Wilson, *De begrafenis*, 176–77. Davis, *Charles Dickens A to Z*, s.v., Redlaw, Swidger Family.

> form, it is something that is respected because it is sincere. (December 12–18, 1882)

He shared this feeling completely, and even needed it, at least in the sense that he had as much feeling for it as such an old fellow might have and believed in "something on high," even though he did not know precisely what that something was or what it would be. One of the things "that [would] not pass away" was the "something on high" and faith in God, even if the forms change: "change is just as necessary as the rejuvenation of green in the spring" (December 12–18, 1882).

He described the interior of his room in The Hague where he lived with Sien: "a small iron cradle with green cradle covering." He could not look at the latter without emotion:

> for it is a strong and powerful emotion that grips a person when one has sat next to the woman one loves with a child in the cradle. And although she was lying in hospital and I was sitting with her, it is always that eternal poetry of the Christmas night with the child in the manger, as the old Dutch painters depicted it . . . that light in the darkness, brightness in the midst of a dark night.

He hung the large etching of *The Holy Family in the Evening* by Rembrandt there: two women at the cradle (July 6, 1882), one of whom is reading from the Bible by the light of a candle while the shadows place the whole room in deep chiaroscuro. He sees it as a Christmas scene: "A child in the cradle also has . . . infinity in his eyes" (August 6, 1888).

Vincent did not think it was enough to simply feel the "Christmas feeling"; he had to put it into his work (December 21, 1882). Thus, in December 1882 he was working on two large heads of an old man with a white beard and an old-fashioned, old high hat. "This guy has the kind of funny face that people want at a cozy Christmas fire" (December 21, 1882).

He learned from models in a drawing by Arthur Boyd Houghton,[6] who depicted a hallway where some invalids (one on crutches, one blind, and a boy from the streets) come to visit a painter on Christmas day. A few months later he said, however, that it was a hallway in the offices of *The Graphic* at Christmas. The artist's models come to say "Merry Christmas" and certainly to receive a tip as well. Most of them were invalids:

> a man on crutches walks in front, a blind man holding on to his coat-tails, and the blind man carrying another person on his back

6. See cover of Dickens's *Hard Times*. Bailey, *Van Gogh in England*, 89.

who can't walk at all, and whose coat-tails are in turn held by a second blind man who is followed by an injured man with a bandage
on his head, followed by several more figures who come slouching
along. (March 21, 1883)

In the first half of 1884 he observed weavers in Nuenen one evening working
by lamplight, and this sight, in his view, produced very Rembrandtesque effects. One of the weavers gave him a lamp whose light they used to work by
and is depicted in Rembrandt's *Evening* (April 30, 1884). Such a lamp in *The
Potato Eaters*, which is shining down on the table, is striking (April 21, 1885).[7]

When Theo's wife Jo was expecting a child, he painted *Evening:
The Watch (after Millet)* for his pregnant sister-in-law, which evokes the
Christmas atmosphere and makes one think of the cradle in his studio in
The Hague (July 6, 1882). In this work he wanted to produce the feeling
of Christmas night with the child in the stable and hoped that Jo Bonger
would see this in *Evening* (November 2, 1889). Theo liked this work the
most of those Vincent sent.

Vincent appreciated Theo's compliment (January 12–15, 1890). The
more he thought about it the more he felt it would be good to attempt to
copy Millet's work. But, instead of copying, it was more a matter of translat-
ing chiaroscuro effects in black and white into a different language, that of
colors. *Evening* is a spectrum from soft purple and lilac hues with the pale
lemon yellow lamplight and the orange glow of the fire and the man in red
ochre (November 2, 1889).

That the Christmas theme continued to influence his work later becomes clear in the *The Arlésienne*, the portrait of Madame Marie Ginoux,
where the book of Dickens's Christmas stories is lying on the table. Together
with her husband, Madame Ginoux ran the Café de la Gare on the Place
Lamartine in Arles, where Vincent would live from May to September 1888
before moving into the "Yellow House." Although he saw her every day
for months on end, it was obviously Gauguin who managed to convince
her to pose as a model for both of them. She did that at the beginning of
November 1888 for both artists in the "Yellow House." The painting shows
her sitting in the chair Vincent had specially made for Gauguin.[8]

Months later, after Gauguin's departure, Vincent returned to the subject and made a number of paintings of her after a drawing by Gauguin.

---

7. There he spoke of painting darkness while it is color. Cf. Van Tilborgh, *Van Gogh
& Millet*, 110.

8. Druick and Zegers, *Van Gogh en Gauguin*, 186.

He thought back wistfully on the time he and Gauguin were comrades and saw his painting now as a symbol of the months of their collaboration (June 17, 1890).

Vincent and Madame Ginoux became real friends. He approvingly quoted her statement, "If you are friends, you are that for a long time" (December 30/31, 1889). During his own sickness he felt a bond with her because she suffered from nervous attacks, a sickness that was characteristic of the modern period (February 2, 1890).[9]

When he saw her again in the middle of January 1890, he was a little worried because she was still sick. He found her so changed: she was still suffering from nervous attacks, made worse by early menopause, and thought she looked like an old grandpa. He wrote her and her husband that he found it remarkable that they were both sick at the same time a year ago and that this was the case again that Christmas.

Vincent believed that the adversity one met in life could do as much good as bad. What made someone sick one day and brought him or her to the brink of despair could give that same person energy the next day to get up and want to get better. A year before that, Vincent had not wanted to get better. He often said that he would rather that his life be over.

> But indeed, we do not have any authority over our existence and, apparently, we have to learn to have the will to continue on, even in our suffering. . . . Afterward, we go back to our daily work less afraid of adversity and provided with a new dose of serenity. (December 30 /31, 1889)

Sometimes, when the waves of despair smashed against the rocks, he wanted to express a "tumultuous desire to embrace something, a woman of the stout, domestic type." At such times Vincent thought of Marie Ginoux. Although it did bother him later that the women who took care of him in Saint Rémy believed in the holy Virgin of Lourdes, he portrayed Madame Ginoux in *The Arlésienne* as "the modern equivalent of the Virgin of Lourdes."[10] In addition to the copy of *Contes de Noël*, the French translation of Dickens's "A Christmas Carol,"[11] Harriet Beecher Stowe's *Uncle Tom's Cabin* is also in the painting, helping to depict Madame Ginoux as a modern woman, a reader of modern literature. Both books were among Vincent's favorites and he had just reread them (April 30, 1889).

9. Uitert et al., *Schilderijen*, 247.

10. Soth, "Van Gogh's Images," 160–62.

11. Dorn et al., *Van Gogh*, 123.

Miners, Darkness, and Light

On 15 November 1878, when Vincent was being trained as an evangelist in Laeken, close to Brussels, he read a French book about the Borinage that related how the inhabitants of that region were occupied exclusively with mining coal. He saw the open coal mines at 300 meters below ground as an impressive spectacle. The workers who went down into the mines everyday deserved, in his view, respect and sympathy.

> The miner is a type peculiar to the Borinage; day does not exist for him. Aside from Sunday, he can hardly ever enjoy the sun. He works hard by the light of a lamp that shines pale and dull in a small passageway, his body bent double; sometimes he even has to crawl. From the depths of the earth he brings up the mineral whose usefulness we know. . . .
>
> When he goes into the mine, with a lamp on his cap to show him the way through the darkness, he trusts in God who sees his labor and protects him, his wife, and his children. His clothing consists of a cap made of cardboard, a cotton jacket and pants. (November 15, 1878)

Vincent worked as an evangelist in Borinage among the miners and their difficult living conditions. He read about these conditions in Dickens's *Hard Times,*[12] in which he saw a parallel with his own surroundings at the time (March 5, 1883). This novel is about England in the middle of the nineteenth century after the industrial revolution. The social oppression that Vincent witnessed with his own eyes in England he encountered in the flesh in the Borinage (March 5, 1883).

He went down a mine in Marcasse, one of the oldest and most dangerous in the area, one time for a period of six hours. This mine had a bad name because many died in the descent into the mine or the ascent to the surface as a result of the stifling heat, gas explosions, flooding, or cave-ins in old shafts. It was a gloomy spot and, at first glance, everything in the area had something dreary and dead about it. The workers were usually skinny and pale because of fever and look tired and gaunt, weather-beaten, and prematurely aged, the women drab and withered. Surrounding the mine were the poor dwellings of the workers, with a few dead, smoke-blackened trees, thorn hedges, dunghills, and mountains of unusable coal. Some of the people

12. Dickens dedicated the book to Thomas Carlyle. Cf. Bailey, *Van Gogh in England,* 87. Vincent had a nearly complete edition of Dickens's works in French translation. His friend Van Rappard told Vincent that Dickens's English was difficult - particularly the dialect of the miners in *Hard Times.* Cf. March 5, 1883.

worked on maintenance, others loaded the extracted coal into small carts that were transported via rails like a tram. It was primarily children who did this, girls as well as boys. And seven hundred meters below the ground was also a stable with six or seven old horses that transported large quantities of coal and brought them to where the miners were taken to the surface.

Just as all sailors are homesick for the sea, despite the dangers and difficulties that threaten, so all miners would rather be underground than above. The villages seemed quiet, abandoned, and desolate because life there was all below the surface instead of above it. He described the people as

> very unlearned and ignorant, most of whom cannot read, but at the same time wise and quick in their difficult work, courageous, small of posture, but square-shouldered and with deep-set eyes. Very nervous disposition, not weak but sensitive, they have a deep-rooted and deep-seated hatred and a profound distrust of everyone who wants to lord it over them. With the coal-burners, you have to have the character of a coal-burner and no pretensions, pride or bossiness, otherwise you cannot get along with them and you will never win their trust.
>
> There are many sickly and bedridden people, gaunt in their beds, weak and miserable. Everyone in one house is sick with fever and they have little or no help so the sick have to look after the sick. "Here are the sick who look after the sick," the wife says, "just as the poor man is the friend of the poor man." (April 1879)

Vincent relates what a peculiar sight it is when the miners return home at twilight.

> The people are completely black when they emerge from the dark mines into the daylight again and look like chimney sweeps. Their homes are usually small and could sooner be called huts. Here and there one still sees moss-covered roofs, and the light shines welcomingly at night from the windows with their small panes. (December 28, 1878)

In October 1880, when he was in Brussels, Vincent hoped to return to the Borinage, "the black country," the country of miners and weavers, as soon as he had mastered painting in watercolors and etching, so that he would be able to paint more according to nature than he had done until now. Nine years later he regretted not returning to the Borinage to paint when he learned that Constantin E. Meunier, a Belgian sculptor, painter, and graphic artist, painted the women of the Borinage who towed the coal— the procession of people on their way to the mine, and the factories, their red roofs and black chimneys against a fine gray light. This was something he once dreamed of doing himself. Meunier is known for his paintings on the topic of the "industrial landscape with miners" and depicted "heroes of labor" in life-size forms (October 8, 1889). In one of his first drawings, in a letter dated November 1878, Vincent depicted the indescribably hard and impoverished existence of the miners and the social oppression under which they suffered (*The "Au Charbonnage" Café*).[13] He found Émile Zola's book *Germinal* (1885), on which he worked while Vincent was in the Borinage (May 11; May 15; June 15, 1885),[14] very helpful in this respect. In this connection as well literature was thus constantly important for him and became a part of 'us' Theo and himself (August 11, 1888).

At the beginning of the 1880s, Émile Zola traveled to northern France to visit the mining region because of a general strike. There he spoke with many who were involved in the strike and used this material for his novel. Zola depicted the mine in *Germinal* as a man-eating monster, its dark passages resembled a labyrinth in which the people underwent hellish torments. Above the ground they form an animal herd that is bowed down under hunger and cold. A strike, which for a time provides hope of a better life, is broken with brute force. *Germinal* (seed month) was the new name for March, the first month of spring, in revolutionary France. It symbolized the unanswered idealistic expectations of social renewal. In his evocations of the social unrest and the uprising by the miners, Zola also uses images of sowing and harvest borrowed from the well-known parable of "the sower" (Matthew 13; Mark 4).[15]

When Zola died, miners traveled from northern France to Paris for his funeral. They walked behind his coffin to the cemetery in Montmartre and chanted in a show of respect: "Germinal! Germinal!"[16]

13. Gayford, *The Yellow House*, 89.

14. He refers to the figure of Hennebeau in *Germinal* (second half of June 1885).

15. Chapter 3 of Volume 3 and chapter 7 of Volume 4; quoted by Sund, *True to Temperament*, 280, note 41.

16. De Ayala and Guéno, *Belles Lettres*, 122.

For Vincent, Zola's *Germinal* called up memories of his own experiences in the Borinage, and as soon as he had received and read the book in Nuenen, he wrote "if everything goes well—if I earn more—so that I can travel, well, I will go, I hope, to paint the heads of the miners as well" (May 15, 1885).[17] He also sent Theo "a head," *Peasant Woman in a Green Shawl*, which he painted spontaneously in June 1885 after reading *Germinal* (June 1, 1885).

In the Borinage Vincent drew women who were bowed down under their burdens: *The Bearers of the Burden* (miners' wives carrying bags of coal). This drawing with an English title seemed to be inspired by a passage in *Germinal* in which the work of miners is described after their strike was broken:

> Everywhere, in the morning mist, along the shadowy roads, the trampling herd could be seen, lines of men plodding along with their noses to the ground like cattle being driven to the slaughterhouse. They were shivering in their thin cotton clothes, their arms folded for warmth, shambling and hunched up so that the *briquette*, held between shirt and coat, looked like a deformity. But behind this mass return to work, these silent dark shapes with never a smile or glance to the side, you could sense jaws set in anger and hearts bursting with hatred. They had only knuckled under because compelled to by starvation.[18]

Right beneath the painting Vincent wrote, "they who bear the burdens." Three women walk and move bent over under the burden of the bags of coal on their backs. A railway bridge and a church tower can be seen in the background. At the side of the road is a tree covered in ivy to which a crucifix has been attached.[19] These miners' wives are to be viewed as modern pilgrims. From a wooden frame on the tree Christ on the cross sees these pilgrims going past.

According to Vincent van Gogh, one of the roots of fundamental truths of the Gospel as well as the whole Bible is: "Light that shines in the darkness" (John 1:5).

> Who has ears for that? Experience has taught us that those who work in darkness, in the heart of the earth, such as the miners in

17. Sund, *True to Temperament*, 96.
18. Quoted by De Leeuw et al., *De Haagse School*, 304. Cf. Zola, *Germinal*.
19. Bailey, *Van Gogh in England*, 122.

the black coal mines are very much affected by the Gospel and also believe it. (November 15, 1878)

Both the Bible and literature offer light in the darkness of the modern era.

Literature as Light in Darkness

Vincent believed that writers like Michelet, Carlyle, and Eliot were in the vanguard of modern society; their books were full of the real world (December 21, 1881). Harriet Beecher Stowe was among them as well. Even though the book had been written years before, Vincent said the following about *Uncle Tom's Cabin*, which discussed slavery (June 1879):[20]

> It is so finely felt; it is so affective, it is so masterful. It is written with so much love, so much seriousness and so faithfully, in line with truth and with a knowledge of the matter at hand. (June 1880)[21]

He saw clear parallels with the situation of the miners with whom he worked.[22] After his mental collapse in March 1889 Vincent read *Uncle Tom's Cabin* again. He did so extremely attentively because it was a book by a woman, written, she claimed, while making soup for her children—so he wrote to his sister Wil (April 30, 1889).

What he meant exactly by the understanding of the reality of his time "in a modern way" becomes clear when he points out that when the painter Puvis de Chavannes paints a portrait of a serene old man, the latter is reading a yellow novel with a rose and brushes for aquarelles in a glass of water beside him. The yellow color indicates, in his view, that the old man is receptive to new ideas. He thought that this portrait was proof that this painter was prepared to abandon the Elysian fields (i.e. the ivory tower) for the "intimacy of our time" (August 4, 1888; December 15, 1889).[23] For Vincent, this portrait remained the perfect figure: "It gives comfort, gives a clear view of modern life, despite the inevitable sadness" (December 15,

---

20. He wrote Gauguin and his brother that he read the book in the Borinage for the first time after his dismissal as evangelist (July 1880). Sund, "Favoured Fictions," 267, note 11.

21. Like Charles Dickens.

22. Soth, "Van Gogh's Images," 158.

23. Druick and Zegers, *Van Gogh en Gauguin*, 90.

1889). In Arles he himself painted *Woman Reading a Novel* with a yellow book in her hand! (November 16, 1888).[24]

One of Vincent's deepest (unfulfilled) desires was to do a painting of a bookshop with a yellow-pink display window, at night, with dark figures passing by. He found that to be a thoroughly modern motif, for books are figurative sources of light (November 21, 1889). Books, reality, and art are all of a piece for him. He borrowed the name of his painting *Still Life with French Novels and a Rose* from the subtitle of a book, *Braves Gens* (Brave People) by Jean Richipin, that examines the life of Parisian artists. In this painting Vincent combines the yellow French novels with a rose that has not yet fully opened. The books represent the despondent modern period and the buds embody the "consoling things."

In Arles he worked this theme out again and was now able to symbolize the comforting idea of a hopeful, burgeoning life more directly through almond blossoms, the earliest herald of spring. The painting was intended to be a birthday present for his sister Wil, with whom he discussed the French naturalist novel.[25] He argued that if one wanted to know life as it is, "then these naturalists paint life as we ourselves feel it and thus satisfy our need that people tell us the truth" (summer, autumn, 1887).

The painting also contains French books whose titles are not legible, but there could have been many, such as Zola's *La joie de vivre (The Joy of Life)*, Michelet's *L'Amour (Love)*, or Hugo's *Les Misérables*. He thought Zola's books were the best of all at that time (October 13, 1883). These men and women, who could be considered to be in the vanguard of modern civilization, call to us, Vincent says:

> Whoever you are with a heart in your body, help us found something real, permanent, and genuine. Limit yourself to one task; love one woman. Let your trade be a modern one.[26] Create a free, modern soul in your wife and redeem her from the terrible prejudices that shackle her. Do not doubt God's help if you do what God wants you to do. God wants the world to be reformed in this age by the reform of morals (cf. Romans 12:2), by renewal of the light and the fire of eternal love. You will succeed by that means and you will have a good influence in smaller and larger circles, depending on your circumstances. (November 19, 1881)

24. A letter to his sister and brother.

25. Druick and Zegers, *Van Gogh en Gauguin*, 90.

26. Like Michelet, Beecher Stowe, Thomas Carlyle, George Eliot and many others. Cf. October 30, 1877; July 2, 1883. Druick and Zegers, *Van Gogh en Gauguin*, 355, note 20.

But Vincent became involved in a heated dispute with his father on the significance of literature for modern society. In that discussion he said that his father and mother had probably read Goethe's *Faust* because Rev. Ten Kate had translated it, "for now that a minister translated it, it shouldn't be too immoral (what is that?)" (December 21, 1881). He thought that his uncle Stricker was more liberal in his thinking than his father but nonetheless held that

> both are standing in front of a wall that writers like Beecher Stowe and Michelet have knocked down at a certain spot. Neither minister knows this spot, for they have not penetrated deeply enough into new ideas. (November 19, 1881)[27]

Their response to Victor Hugo's *Les Misérables*—the story of a man, Jean Valjean, who is persecuted by society because of crimes he had committed earlier—is evident in a letter from his parents to Theo: "[Vincent] sent us," they wrote, "a book by Hugo, but that man chooses the side of the criminals and he calls not bad what is truly bad." In his father's eyes, that is unacceptable even if it is done with the best of intentions.[28] Vincent was very impressed by that book and viewed it as a standard for a long time. As soon as his father saw him with books by Michelet or Hugo in his hands, he thought immediately of arsonists, murderers, and immorality.

> I have often told Dad, "Read a book like this, even if it is only a few pages, and you will be moved by it." But Dad stubbornly refuses. (November 18, 1881)

Vincent thought that

> if his father would understand Hugo's real intention, he could even be of some use in his sermons because he sometimes had a very different view of a text.

His father, however, thought that Vincent's way of seeing things was unacceptable and disregarded it regularly. Nonetheless, Vincent did not as a result view his father as the enemy but as a friend—though he would be even more of a friend if he was less afraid that he would contaminate him with "French fallacies" (November 23, 1881).

---

27. During that summer he read one book by his uncle Stricker about the minor prophets. He hopes that in that time more sympathy will develop between them. "I do not want to 'defeat' but to gain him." Cf. November 23, 1881.

28. Druick and Zegers, *Van Gogh en Gauguin*, 367, note 243.

> The Bible is indeed eternal and imperishable, but Michelet gives
> such surprisingly practical and clear hints, immediately applicable
> in this fast, hectic modern life in which we find ourselves. (No-
> vember 23, 1881)

Starting with the bad and broken marriage relationships and family situations in connection with the impure views concerning the significance and
the position of the woman in the family and society, Michelet wanted to
show how moral liberation can be attained through genuine love.[29]

The degree to which Vincent connected painters and writers and
other artists with the exegesis of the Gospel is also apparent in how he dealt
with Michelet's work (July 1880). In London he advised Theo to stick with
his own ideas and, if he doubted they were good, to test them on the ideas
of him who said: "I am the way, the truth, and the life" (John 14:6), or that
of a humane person like Michelet (August 10, 1874). He read the latter's *Du
prêtre, de la femme, de la famille* (The Priest, the Woman, and the Family),
in which Michelet shows that love contains much more than what we usually look for. To him, this book was both a revelation and a gospel. "Such
books are good precisely because they witness to *life*."[30]

Vincent does not view the Bible and literature as alternatives; he sees
writers like Michelet and Beecher Stowe as a continuation of—and not a
repetition of—the Gospel (July 2, 1889).

> They do not say that the Gospel is no good anymore; rather, they
> show us how applicable it is in our modern time and in our life.
> They say things out loud that the Gospel only whispers to us in
> germinal form. Literature interprets the message of the Bible. (No-
> vember 23, 1881)

Vincent elaborates on the relationship between reading the Bible and
literature in *Still Life with Open Bible*. It is exemplary for his view and understanding of the relationship between the Bible and literature. The starting point for him is Rembrandt's *The Holy Family in the Evening*.[31] When
Vincent was still working in his family's art business in Paris in July 1875,
he had a copy of this work by Rembrandt hanging in his room: a large old
Dutch room at evening time, a candle on the table where a young mother
is reading the Bible while sitting by her child's cradle. An old woman is

---

29. Miedema, *Vincent van Gogh*, 104.
30. He says that he read those books. September 7, 1875.
31. Cf. October 6, 1875.

listening. He sent a copy of it to both of his sisters, Anna and Willemien. He did miss something more personal and intimate in it that he found in modern painters (July 21, 1882).

He painted *Still Life with Open Bible* in Nuenen after his father's death. The painting has two books, the Bible and Zola's *La joie de vivre*. The Bible in the painting belonged to Vincent's father who had died a few months earlier.[32] The extinguished candle next to the Bible alludes to his father's extinguished life. The Bible is open at the fifty-third chapter of the book of Isaiah ("Isaï" in French) and the chapter number is written in Roman numerals: LIII. This chapter is about the "suffering servant of the Lord," the "man of sorrows" who is brought to the slaughter like a lamb and whose wounds bring about healing: the wounded healer. In the Christian view, this text is a foreshadowing of Jesus's suffering (April 21/22, 1883).

Years earlier, Vincent had advised his brother Theo to read this chapter (beginning of September 1876). He told him about his English friend, Harry Gladwell, whom he had lived with in Paris for some time. At that time he talked about Gladwell as a Christian who would become more and more of one. When he sat next to him, he had the same feeling that he often had, as if he was a son in the same family and a brother in the faith because he loved: "the man of sorrows and acquainted with grief"—thus citing Isaiah 53:3 (September 7, 1877).[33]

The main character in Zola's *La joie de vivre*, Pauline Quenu, is orphaned at the age of ten and moves from Paris to her distant relatives, an aunt and uncle in a poor fishing village, where her family exploits her terribly. Nonetheless, Pauline herself remains the embodiment of selflessness and self-denying love. The power of love transcends all sorrows of injustice, pain, and mortality.[34]

By deliberately connecting the Bible with Zola's novel, Vincent wanted to interpret this text for the modern period. In his view, Zola translated the message of the "man of sorrows" in Isaiah for modern people today. The heroine Pauline is an example for him of a contemporary "woman of sorrows."

32. He received this Bible in order to send it to Theo, but used it first as model (beginning of November 1885). On the fly-leaf two names are written: Johannes Duyser, Minister in Helvoirt. Ths (Theodorus) van Gogh, Minister at Nuenen 1885. Later the Bible was in use by the Remonstrant and Mennonite Church of the city of Leyden. Today it is in the Van Gogh Museum Amsterdam.

33. Cf. October 30, 1877.

34. Edwards, *The Shoes of Van Gogh*, 45. Maurer, *The Pursuit of Spiritual Wisdom*, 75.

Light and Dark (Chiaroscuro)

According to Vincent, it is the artist's task to reproduce the effect of light, whether that be sunlight, candlelight, or light from the fire in the hearth.[35] The Bible and literature are sources of light for him. Already early, in 1877 when he was in Dordrecht and twenty-three or twenty-four years old, he expressed his desire to view life by the light of what was written: "Your word is a lamp for my feet, a light on my path" (Psalm 119:105) (March 16, 1877). His upbringing had acquainted him as a child already with Thomas à Kempis's *The Imitation of Christ*, which has been called the most translated and popular religious and edifying book after the Bible. It emphasized practical everyday piety: imitating Christ's humility and self-denial, particularly his way of the cross.[36] According to Vincent, it was

> a splendid book that gives much light because it expresses so nicely how good it is to engage in the holy struggle of the observation of duty and the inner joy that can be found in doing good and doing well what one does. (November 10, 1876)

He called *The Imitation of Christ* a peculiar book that contained such deep and serious things that one could not read it without emotion and almost fear, at least if it was read with a sincere desire for light and truth (September 4, 1877).

Vincent discussed William Holman Hunt's *The Light of the World* a few times.[37] Hunt was one of the founders of the Pre-Raphaelites, the name for a British brotherhood set up in 1848 to achieve the common ideals of its members.[38] According to these artists, art had been degenerating since the creation of ideal types of physical and moral beauty by the Italian painter Raphael. They held that the time had come to renew painting's ties to nature. In their art they strove for creative simplicity, innocence, and seriousness, as well as attention for nature from before the time of the high Renaissance.

35. Quoted from the book of the etcher F. Bracquemond, *Du dessin et de la couleur*, 139–40, which he found very beautiful, September 1885. Uitert, *Van Gogh in Brabant*, 224.

36. Stolwijk et al., *De Keuze van Vincent*, 52, 60. He sends copies of the work to Theo that are easy to carry in one's pocket (March 3, 1878) and to his sisters, Anne and Willemien ("read faithfully in it") October 1875.

37. Cf. December 10, 1889. Landow, *William Holman Hunt*, 1979.

38. The three most important founders were, including Hunt (November 17, 1889): Dante Gabriel Rossetti (cf. November 17, 1889), and John Everett Millais (July 20, 1873; March 1, 1885), all of whom were mentioned in his letters. He once ran into Millais on the street in London, just after having seen several of his paintings (July 15, 1877). Hammacher, *Van Gogh*, 57.

The movement was very literary right from the start. In addition to religious subjects, they also chose literary ones.[39] Hunt expressed his own conversion experience in *The Light of the World*. To attain "symbolic realism," he painted the work mainly at night by the light of a lamp. The risen Christ, who knocks at the door of the soul (Revelation 3:20), is depicted with a crown of light, thorns, and gold on his head and a lantern in his hand. The door he is knocking on is the door of the soul. This door had to have been shut a long time—the weeds on the threshold are high[40]—but the strands of ivy are also symbolic of continuing life and thus of the resurrection.[41]

Asking himself where the peasants and poor women in Brabant found support in their hard lives, Vincent's wondered if it was not precisely that image of Christ, the name's miraculous power and appeal. Is that not what Hunt painted in his *Light of the World*? (March 16, 1877). Later, in Arles, he would find the depiction of Christ by one of the other Pre-Raphaelites considerably more serious than the attempts by Paul Gauguin or Émile Bernard to paint Christ in the Garden of Gethsemane (November 17, 1889).[42] The English Pre-Raphaelites did that "with more seriousness, conscience, knowledge, and logic" (December 10, 1889).

Painters of the Light

Rembrandt, the painter of chiaroscuro, played an important role throughout Vincent's whole life. When he was doing preparatory studies in Amsterdam to become a minister he visited the Rembrandt collection in the Trippenhuis, the predecessor of the later Rijksmuseum (September 18, 1877). He told how he turned left at the railway station, where there were many mills, along a road to a canal with elm trees (May 19, 1877). Everything reminded him of Rembrandt's etchings. Every day he walked through the Jewish quarter to go to Mendes da Costa, his teacher in Latin and Greek, on Jonas Daniël Meijerplein (August 18, 1877). The Dutch Jewish painter Jozef Israëls, whom Vincent so admired, had the same sensation. When he left the Trippenhuis, everything on the street appeared to him to have come out of Rembrandt's work.

39. Stonyk, *Nineteenth-Century English Literature*, 122–23; Buser, *Religious Art*, 90–92.

40. Gibson, *Symbolisme*, 74–75. www.artchive.com/artchive/Hunt/hunt.html.

41. Upstone, *The Pre-Raphaelite Dream*, 21.

42. Namely, Millais.

> From the Trippenhuis to Hoogstraat, then along Sint Anthonie-breestraat and finally Jodenbreestraat, where I lived at that time a few doors away from the famous house where Rembrandt had worked for so many years, I looked at the picturesque crowd, the busy-ness, the warm Jewish mugs with their drab gray beards, the women with their pinkish hair, the carts full of fish and fruit and all kinds of wares, the houses, the people, the sky—it was all Rembrandt, it was Rembrandtesque.[43]

When Vincent took his long walks through outlying districts of Amsterdam and the sand works on the Eastern line, he could not express how beautiful it was there in the twilight, which Rembrandt had painted; the sky illuminated by the glow of the setting sun, the row of houses and towers, with lights in the windows everywhere, the reflections in the water, people and vehicles like small black figures like those one sometimes sees in Rembrandt's painting. In the naval dockyard in Amsterdam, where he lived with his uncle Johannes van Gogh, he spoke of

> a beautiful sight, where everything is dead silent and the lanterns are burning and the starry sky up above. When all sounds cease - God's voice is heard under the stars. (June 4, 1877)

That reminded him of Charles Dickens's words about a "Blessed Twilight," an expression he often cited (September 18, 1877).

The great Dutch painters are known for having "something" with light. That obtains for Rembrandt especially, the "master of light and darkness." Vincent thought that Rembrandt was aptly called a magician (October 10/11, 1885; second half of December 1888):

> a magician who is also essentially a prophet if he does not have to be faithful to the literal, as in a portrait; if he can poeticize, be a poet, he is a creator.[44]

The latter is expressed, in his view, in *The Jewish Bride*:

> What an intimate, infinitely sympathetic painting, painted with a passionate hand. . . . That people have to die several times to be able to paint like this is certainly applicable here. (October 10/11, 1885)

---

43. Dekkers, *Jozef Israëls*, 48.

44. Quote from Carlyle, *On Heroes*, 126. Cf. Druick and Zegers, *Van Gogh en Gauguin*, 373, note 209.

Rembrandt delves so deeply into the mysterious that he says things for which no language exists. Rembrandt achieves a "metaphysical magic" via chiaroscuro (December 28, 1885).

In connection with the Dutch painter Johannes Vermeer from Delft and the Dutch landscape painter Jacob I. van Ruisdael, Vincent spoke of the "mysterious light effect" in both (June 10, 1882). He also admired the effects of light in the work of Jan Hendrik Weissenbruch, one of the painters of The Hague School (July 20, 1873). Weissenbruch, who became the best painter of cityscapes, especially in The Hague, in the second half of the nineteenth century, is striking because of his refined play of light and shadow.[45] Weissenbruch was one of the painters whom Vincent was very fond of (January 1874). Before he went to London for the first time, he became personally acquainted with him in The Hague, already in August 1877—thus before he chose painting as his profession. He visited him in his studio and was clearly impressed by his person and work (August 3, 1877). When Vincent himself was working as a painter in The Hague, in February 1882, Weissenbruch visited him in turn (February 13, 1882).

Weissenbruch was attempting to recreate his experience of nature:

> When you walk outside in nature and see something beautiful, which stops you short, then you cannot keep your hands in control and you have to paint.[46]

His landscapes were primarily bearers of light and cloudy skies. Sky and light are the great magicians. The sky determines the painting. "Painters," Weissenbruch said, "can never look at the sky enough."[47]

Vincent saw two watercolors by Weissenbruch in Paris that he found exceptionally beautiful: one is of a mill beside a canal, a blue sky with a small cloud hiding the sun; the other is of a canal with boats, at evening in the moonlight (May 21, 1889). It was primarily Weissenbruch's handling of nature and light that struck him. In Saint Rémy he wrote about the remarkable vistas of the canals that Weissenbruch made. That is one of the reasons he went to the south, to experience a different light and to get a clearer view of the "Japanese" way of feeling and drawing as soon as he could see nature under a clearer sky and a brighter sun (September 7/8, 1889).

---

45. Van der Mast and Dumas, *Van Gogh*, 98–99.
46. Sillevis and Tabak, *Het Haagse School boek*, 234.
47. Sillevis and Tabak, *Het Haagse School boek*, 234.

Self-Portrait

For one of his self-portraits in Paris Vincent used the just published book, 1887, by Frederik W. van Eeden, *De kleine Johannes* (Little John), as a source of inspiration. In a time that was paralyzed by unbelief and disillusionment about the progress of knowledge, Van Eeden describes a mythical journey from light to darkness and back again.[48]

As soon as the sun goes down, little John and Windekind (Child of the Wind) talk. Windekind was born out of the chalice of the wind, the first rays of the moon, and the last ones of the sun.[49] When little John wonders whom he should pray to, it helps him to look at the splendor of nature. He is witness to a splendid show of light, a sunset on the infinite ocean, and thus catches a glimpse of eternity.[50]

Van Eeden describes little John seeing the appearance of dark Death on the beach.

> . . . a small black shape. It becomes larger and larger—a human being slowly approaches, striding quietly over the tossing, fiery waves. It is a human being; his face is pale and his eye deep and dark. As deep as the eyes of Windekind, but in their look was infinite gentle sadness, such as John had never seen in other eyes.
>
> "Who are you?" John asks, "Are you a man?"
>
> "I am more!" he says.
>
> "Are you Jesus? Are you God?" John asks.
>
> "Do not mention those names," the shape says. . . .
>
> "I recognize you. I want to be with you."
>
> John stretches out his hands. But the man points to the glistening vessel that is slowly drifting forward on the fiery road.
>
> "See!" he says, "That is the way to everything you have been longing for. There is no other. Without both of them you will not find it. Make your choice now. There is the Great Light, there you will be what you desire to know. There!"—and he points to the dark east—"where humanity is and its woe, there is my road. . . ."
>
> Then John slowly turned his eyes away from Windekind's beckoning shape and stretched out his hands to the serious man. And

48. Van Eeden, *De kleine Johannes*, 216. Druick and Zegers, *Van Gogh en Gauguin*, 97.

49. Van Eeden, *De kleine Johannes*, 12.

50. Van Eeden, *De kleine Johannes*, 52–54. Druick and Zegers, *Van Gogh en Gauguin*, 147.

with his escort, he went to meet the cold night wind, the difficult path to the great dark city where humankind was and its woe.[51]

When Vincent described his self-portrait, he wrote:

> A pink-gray face, with green eyes, ash-colored hair, wrinkles on the forehead and around the mouth, stiff, wooden, a very red beard, very unkempt and sad, but the lips are full, a blue smock of rough linen. . . . You will say that this is something like the face of death in Frederik van Eeden's book.

The Language of Nature

When Vincent was drawing and painting in The Hague he found that it was not so much the language of the painters one should be listening to as the language of nature (July 21, 1882). Now he understood better why the painter of the Hague school, Anton Mauve, his uncle and teacher at the time, once said to him about a half year prior:

> But don't talk to me about the French painter Jules Dupré; talk to me rather about the side of the ditch or something like that. . . . Feeling the things themselves, reality, is much more important than feeling paintings, at least it is more fruitful and more inspiring. . . . It is the duty of the painter to completely immerse himself in nature and to use all his intelligence and feeling in his work so that others can understand it. The feeling and love for nature will always find an echo sooner or later with people who are interested in art. (August 1, 1882)

According to Vincent, there was a riddle hidden in nature. Life in the abstract is a riddle as such, and reality turns it into a riddle within a riddle. "Who are we to solve it?" (November 5, 1882). Vincent held that people do not get anywhere if they do not make wrestling with nature a central occupation. If an artist attentively studies other master artists, he will discover that he has penetrated deeply into reality at certain moments.

> Their creations will also be viewed as real to the extent people have the same kind of eyes, the same sentiment as they. . . . Precisely because one has to look long and hard at nature before they are convinced that what the greater masters have painted as the most gripping nevertheless has its ground in life and reality itself. . . . For

---

51. Van Eeden, *De kleine Johannes*, 152–54.

> my part, I see no other way than to wrestle with nature until she
> gives up her secret. (January 24, 1885)

Vincent became involved in a discussion with his painter friend Anthon van Rappard about penetrating into nature and reality. When Van Rappard was working at the academy, Vincent wrote him that academic people were not worth anything (September 30, 1881). He believed that Van Rappard was more of a true realist who wanted to know nature and reality, but the academy stood in the way of the more serious, warmer, more fruitful life awakening in him. He advised him, "Let the mistress go and fall head over heels in love with your own true love: nature or reality." Vincent himself fell in love with this lady, although "she still resisted him and did not want him." He fought for her and sought the key to her heart (January 24, 1885). Vincent drew a comparison with various kinds of mistresses in this context.

> There are mistresses who make you nervous, flatter you, and set you afire; women of marble, sphinxes, cold adders, who want to bind men to themselves without giving themselves completely and without reservation. These mistresses paralyze and petrify men. To these mistresses I say: "Listen, my beauty, wherever you come from, you who say that your true intentions are the beautiful and the sublime. In any case, you do not come from the womb of the living God nor from the womb of a woman. Go away, sphinx. Do you resemble an adder or a snake less than they?"

He warned his friend that he had to free himself from this "woman of marble," "otherwise he would freeze to death."

> Thank God there are other women: Nature or Reality. It costs a great deal of inner struggle to win one. They demand nothing more or less than complete surrender of heart, soul, and mind, all the love that is in us, and then they give themselves. These true ladies, however, although "innocent as doves, are as cunning as serpents" (Matthew 10:16), and can discern all too well who is sincere and who is not. That Lady Nature, that Lady Reality, renews, gives new strength, invigorates. Where does she come from? Not very far from you and me. Her intentions? To love and be lovable, to give life, to renew, heal, and maintain, to work, answer love with love, be good primarily, be useful, be of service for something, to light the fire for example, to give a sandwich to a child or a glass to a sick person (cf. Matthew 10:42). To know her duty, she does not

consult her head but her heart. But she is actually not a mistress at all. As Michelet says, "A lady is a lady." (September 12, 1881)[52]

When Vincent worked on a painting he sometimes changed a motif, but in the end he did not invent it and found it ready made in nature. All he had to do was draw it out of there (October 4, 1888).

> Nature always begins with resisting the artist, but whoever absorbs it seriously does not allow himself to be upset. Nature is certainly "ungraspable," but people have to tackle it with a firm hand. And after we have wrestled and struggled with nature for some time, nature begins to be more accommodating and submissive. The struggle with nature sometimes has what Shakespeare called *The Taming of the Shrew*. (October 12–15, 1881)

Vincent used nature in symbolic ways. He painted ivy, pollard willows, oleanders, sunflowers, olive trees, and cypresses. Oleanders symbolize burgeoning love, but they are also known to be poisonous, for honey made by bees from oleanders can cause mental illness. Vincent knew about this meaning when he painted a spherical cedar or cypress with oleanders in the background in a park across from the "Yellow House" and then spoke of the "insanely rampant growth of oleanders." "Those damn plants bloom in a way as if they could succumb at any moment to their own rampant growth" (September 27, 1888). He planned to put oleanders in barrels at the entrance to his house, the "Yellow House" in Arles (September 22, 1888). The connotation of the oleander is expressed in his work when he places oleanders next to Zola's *La joie de vivre* (*The Joy of Life*) in *Still Life: Vase of Oleanders and Books*.

Ivy

Ivy has a great deal of symbolism attached to it. Dickens saw it as eternal. Because its tendrils fasten on to things so affectionately, ivy is also the symbol of faithful love and friendship. As a plant with leaves that are always green, the ivy immediately evokes the idea of immortality and, with tendrils attaching themselves to dead trees and continuing to live, remaining green, it became the symbol in the Middle Ages of the continued existence of the soul after the death of the body. A Dutch proverb says: "The ivy winds high around an oak, and no fierce wind can tear it loose. If someone

52. He means November 12. Cf. February 15, 1883 (two letters).

has God's support, then he will quickly climb higher, no accident can harm him."[53] The vitality of the plant turns it into a symbol of the joy of life. Ivy already played a role in the Egyptian cult of the resurrecting, popular god Osiris, and it became a symbol of life on graves and early Christian sarcophaguses.[54]

Vincent was particularly fascinated by the way in which ivy overran all other trees and plants. From his room in Dordrecht he could look out on gardens with pine trees and poplars and the backs of old houses covered in ivy. He then referred to the poem "The Ivy Green" from Charles Dickens's *Pickwick Papers*.

Oh, a dainty plant is the Ivy green,
That creepeth o'er ruins old!
Of right choice food are his meals, I ween,
In his cell so lone and cold.
The wall must be crumbled, the stone decayed,
To pleasure his dainty whim:
And the mouldering dust that years have made
Is a merry meal for him.
Creeping where no life is seen,
A rare old plant is the Ivy green.

Fast he stealeth on, though he wears no wings,
And a staunch old heart has he.
How closely he twineth, how tight he clings,
To his friend the huge Oak Tree!
And slily he traileth along the ground,
And his leaves he gently waves,
As he joyously hugs and crawleth round
The rich mould of dead men's graves.
Creeping where grim death has been,
A rare old plant is the Ivy green.

Whole ages have fled and their works decayed,
And nations have scattered been;
But the stout old Ivy shall never fade,
From its hale and hearty green.
The brave old plant, in its lonely days,
Shall fatten upon the past:
For the stateliest building man can raise,

53. From W.H. Frh. von Hoberg (1675).
54. Biedermann, *Prisma*, s.v., klimop; Lurker, s.v., Efeu.

Is the Ivy's food at last.
Creeping on, where time has been,
A rare old plant is the Ivy green.[55]

In Arles Vincent attempted to console himself with the idea that illnesses are to the human being what ivy is to the oak (April 25–28, 1889). During his stay in hospital in Saint Rémy he used the motif of trees covered in ivy as the subject of drawings and paintings.[56] He wrote to his sister Wil concerning a cancer patient she was assisting that he found it very brave of her that she did not recoil from that Gethsemane.

> Ivy has a preference for old willows with no branches. Each spring it searches out the trunk of the old oak. Precisely in the same way, cancer, that mysterious plant, attaches itself to people whose life consisted of nothing more than passionate love and devotion. However awful the mystery of those pains may be, the terrible thing of it is holy, and is there not also something sweet and sad in it, as we see an abundance of moss on old thatch roofs? (April 30, 1889)

Sunflowers

Vincent said sunflowers were characteristic for him, whereas the peony and the hollyhock were characteristic, respectively, for his less well-known artistic brothers, the still life painters Georges Jeannin and Ernest Quost (January 22, 1889).[57] Traditionally, sunflowers symbolize the love of God, as in the Dutch emblem literature, volumes with symbolic plates accompanied by captions (sixteenth to eighteenth century). Rev. Eliza Laurillard, who influenced Van Gogh, gave sunflowers loaded significance.[58]

> That is the why the idea could arise in a poet's soul: "the Lord God is a sun" (Psalm 84:11). But then we should wish for the radiance of this sun to shine on our spirit and heart, just as we wish that the radiance of the sun shining in nature will bring light and joy to our homes, and life and fruitfulness into our garden. Yes! As we

---

55. Dickens, *The Pickwick Papers*, 85–86.
56. Leeuw et al., *De Haagse School*, 163.
57. Cf. January 23, 1889; February 2, 1890; February 10/11, 1890 (letter to Aurier).
58. Werness, "The Symbolism," 52.

wish that our mind be like the sunflower, turning continually to the Great Light, in order to receive the rays it sends down.[59]

On 23 January 1889 Theo wrote in a letter to his wife, Jo Bonger:

For me, there is something like the flowers turning to the sun in the idea of progress. Impossible to keep them from doing so and why? They will wither all the more quickly then. (August 23, 1888)

Vincent first painted sunflowers from July to September 1887 during his time in Paris.[60] Towards the end of his stay in Paris, in February 1888, he painted four works, each of which shows two or four large, even monumental, cut sunflowers on a table.

As soon as he was able, Vincent intended to go to the south of France for a time, where there was even more color and sun (summer, autumn, 1887). When he finally did leave, he literally turned toward the sun, as the French word for sunflower expresses so strikingly: *tourne-sol*. He passionately wanted Theo to see and feel the sun of the south as well:

a sun, a light that I, for lack of better word, can only call yellow, pale sulphur yellow, pale lemon yellow, gold. How beautiful yellow is! (August 13, 1888)

Vincent produced various still lifes with sunflowers for his artists' house in Arles. He wanted to make decorations in the "Yellow House" using nothing other than large sunflowers, twelve panels, "light on light," the whole of "a symphony in blue and yellow" (August 21, 1888; September 9, 1888; August 16, 1888):

bright or dull chrome yellows, standing out sharply against blue backgrounds of the lightest Veronese blue, with a frame of thin slats, painted in red lead . . . comparable to the effect of stained-glass windows in a Gothic church. (August 18, 1888)

He consoled himself with the sight of sunflowers, which, in his view, symbolized gratefulness (February 20, 1890).

59. Laurillard, *Geen dag zonder God.* Kôdera, *Vincent van Gogh,* 111, note 118.

60. Van Kooten and Rijnders, *De schilderijen,* 181; Vellekoop and Van Heugten, *Vincent van Gogh,* 311–12. Cf. Van Tilborgh and Vellekoop, *Vincent van Gogh.*

Trees

To Vincent, the olive tree was just as changeable as the willow or pollard willow in the north. He called the latter picturesque, even though they seem monotonous. The willow is the tree that belongs in the Netherlands. Just as the willow was important for the north, so the olive tree and cypress were important in the south of France (November 21, 1889).

In Etten Vincent drew a pollard willow as a living being and also stated explicitly that one should not rest before something of life entered into the drawing (October 12–15, 1881). In The Hague he described a pollard willow that hung lonely and dejectedly over a pond and that he drew and painted (July 26, 1882). In Nuenen he made a drawing of a parsonage garden in the snow with one figure, under which he wrote a caption in French, *mélancholie* (September 15, 1883).

Just as in all of nature, he saw an expression in trees, a soul, as it were:

> a row of pollard willows sometimes resembles a procession of old men. Young grain can possess something inexpressibly pure and gentle that awakens a similar emotion like the expression of a sleeping child. The grass trampled flat on the side of the road looks tired and dusty like the inhabitants of a slum. . . . When it last snowed, I saw some savoy cabbages that were freezing and that reminded me of a group of women I had seen early one morning standing in a water and fire cellar in their thin skirts and old shawls. (November 5, 1882)

The cypress is a tree that can become very old and always remains green. It functions as an attribute of divinities like Saturn and is identified with Chronos ("Time"), the father of Zeus (Jupiter), the patron god of graybeards. The evergreen and long-lived tree with its long-lasting wood is a symbol of a long life. It is often planted in cemeteries and is thus, primarily in the Mediterranean world, a typical tree in churchyards and is often depicted on sarcophaguses. In Christianity, the cypress appears in the depiction of Paradise, and it is used as a symbol of hope for life after death.[61]

Van Gogh painted cypresses in a park in Arles: "A somber, completely black cypress," *un funèbre cypres* (September 27, 1888). He called the somber cypresses the opposite of sunflowers but nonetheless equal to them. In Saint Rémy, cypresses kept Vincent busy in the final days of June 1889. He compared them to a nice Egyptian obelisk—which is connected with

---

61. Biedermann, *Prisma*, 296; *Prisma van de symbolen*, s.v., cipres.

the worship of the sun—for at creation the first rays of the sun fell on the cypress (June 25, 1889).Japan: The South, Nature, and the Sun

Vincent discovered Japanese printing for the first time in Antwerp. Japan was opened to the West in 1860. Various important French writers showed interest in Japanese art,[62] and Jules and Edmond de Goncourt circulated it.[63] Vincent saw his leaving Paris for the south of France also as a departure for "Japan" and the painting of light. The train journey from Paris to Arles produced a great deal of emotion in him. "I just sat looking to see if it was already Japan! Childish, hey?" (October 17, 1888).

It was still winter (February 1886) when he arrived in Arles. To him, the landscapes in the snow with the white peaks against a sky as clear as the snow were just like the winter landscapes that the Japanese made (February 21, 1888). He envisioned himself now in "Japan" and saw new things (March 14, 1888).

He imagined he was in Japan and therefore he only had to open his eyes and paint whatever made an impression on him (September 9 and 16, 1888). He said of a study of Arles, a city surrounded by a field full of yellow and purple flowers: "You know, this is just like a Japanese dream" (May 12, 1888).

In Arles he began to lead the life of a Japanese painter, living in nature more and more (September 22, 1888). He had gone south and there plunged into work in order to see another light and to get a clear image of the way the Japanese felt and drew, to view nature under a clearer sky and to see it more brightly (September 7/8, 1889). He held that if one studied Japanese art, one was an indisputably wise, philosophical, and intelligent man who

> passes his time ... with what? With studying the distance between the earth and the moon? No! With studying the politics of Bismarck? No. He studies ... one single blade of grass.

This blade of grass leads him to draw all kinds of plants, then the seasons, the grandest sight of landscapes, finally animals, and the human form.

> Look, this is how he passes his time, and life is too short to do everything. Look, is that not almost a true religion that is taught

62. Émile Zola is painted by Edouard Manet in front of a Japanese screen with a Japanese print on the wall.

63. Vincent quotes the proverb of the De Goncourts: "Japonaiserie forever" (November 28, 1885); Hulsker, *Lotgenoten*, 381. For objections to the claim that they were the first, see Sund, *True to Temperament*, 117.

us by the simple Japanese who live in nature as if they themselves were flowers? (September 24, 1888)

Vincent held that the Japanese art could not be studied without making a person more cheerful and happy (September 14, 1888). He believed that for Theo and for him in the south, the most reliable remedy was the sun, the nice weather, and the blue sky (September 29, 1888).

This inspiration by "Japan" led to his self-portrait as a *bonze*, a "simple worshipper of the eternal Buddha," whereby he painted his eyes as somewhat slanted in Japanese fashion. A *bonze* is someone who points the way to enlightenment (October 4, 1888).[64] The book by Pierre Loti, *Madame Chrysanthème*, with illustrations of Buddhist monks, possibly served as a source for that self-portrait.

Vincent was struck in particular by what he had read about the many points of comparison between the life of Buddha and Christ. Buddha's birth, just like Jesus's, was miraculous and occurred on 25 December. When the Buddha withdrew to the desert to purify himself, he was also tempted by an evil spirit. When he was thirty-five, after seven years of meditation and abstinence, Siddhartha became "the Enlightened one" (the Buddha). In 1888 Vincent was thirty-five; his head in his self-portrait is shaved, just like the Buddha's.[65]

The Four Evangelists: The Seasons and their Colors

When Vincent was working in London in May 1876 he became acquainted with the activities of the famous nineteenth-century English minister C.H. Spurgeon, whose work as an evangelist he admired.[66] He later regretted that he never went to hear Spurgeon's two American followers, Dwight Lyman Moody and Ira David Sankey, in London (May 12, 1876). During his months in Dordrecht, Spurgeon was one of his favorite writers.[67] The latter once said that nature, just like the Bible, had four evangelists, namely, the four seasons: spring, summer, autumn, and winter.[68]

64. Maurer, *The Pursuit of Spiritual Wisdom*, 77. Collins, *Van Gogh and Gauguin*, 88–89.

65. Merlhès, *Paul Gauguin*, 114–20. Cf. Collins, *Van Gogh and Gauguin*, 105–6.

66. Bailey, *Van Gogh in England*, 148.

67. He read his "Juweeltjes" (Gems), in any case. Cf. Kôdera, *Vincent van Gogh*, 17.

68. Spurgeon, *Teachings of Nature*, 231. Kôdera, *Vincent van Gogh*, 22–23, 106, notes 61, 62.

Vincent saw the seasons in terms of colors (August-October, 1886). Spring is delicate, green, young grain, and pink apple blossoms. Fall is the contrast between yellow leaves and violet tones. Winter is snow with black silhouettes. A summer effect is, in his view, not easy to express, but

> as . . . in summer the opposition of blue to an element of orange in the auburn of the grain exists, so one could paint a painting in precisely each one of the contrasts of the complementary colors (red and green, blue and orange, blue and orange, yellow and violet, white and black) that can express the mood of the seasons well. (beginning of June 1884)

The fall, for which he had an explicit preference, offers the complete range.

He wanted to express the love of two people by a marriage of two complementary colors, their mingling and their contrasts, the mysterious vibrations of related tones. He expressed the idea by the brilliance of a clear tone on a dark foundation, hope by means of a star and passion by means of the rays of the setting sun (September 3, 1888). For him, there are colors that make a pair, complement each other like man and woman. Vincent thought that the nature of the south could not be painted precisely with the palette of the north. His uncle Anton Mauve was a master in gray. But

> [t]he palette of the present is absolute color: sky blue, pink, orange, vermillion, high yellow, bright green, deep red, and violet. If you bring in all colors, you achieve calm and harmony. (March 30, 1888)

In Arles he had to paint the rich and beautiful aspects of nature. The uglier, older, meaner, sicker, and poorer he became the more he wanted to balance that by making gleaming, well-structured, and brilliant colors.

> Jewelers are old and ugly as well before they know how to set the precious stones properly. And to arrange colors on a painting in order to have them vibrate and come into their own through their contrasts—that is like setting jewels or designing clothes. (September 9, 16, 1888)

In Auvers he said that "these last days" were "like a revelation of colors" for him again (May 11/12, 1890).

Stars in the Night

In Nuenen Vincent painted not only when it was light but also in the evening in the huts by the light of a lamp, when he could scarcely discern something on his palette in order to grasp something, if possible, of the peculiar effects of light at night, such as a large cast shadow on the wall (March 1, 1885).

In Arles as well, years later, he took great pleasure in painting night scenes or night effects on the spot (September 16, 1888). He preferred to paint immediately on the spot and not first, as was usual, only to draw at night and then do the painting during the day.[69] He could indeed mistake blue for green, blue lilac for pink lilac, given that it was impossible to properly discern the character of the tone, but it was the only way to finally move beyond that conventional black night "with that pathetic pale and whitish light, while a simple candle provides the richest hues of yellow and orange" (April 9, 1888). He had the feeling that night was more colorful than the day,

> colored with violet, blue, and the most intense green hues. Some stars are lemon yellow, others have a pink, green, forget-me-not blue glow. To paint the starry sky it is not sufficient at all to place white dots on an indifferent black.

At that time he was busy painting *Café Terrace at Night*, namely, the café on the Place du Forum in Arles, where he usually went with his friend, the Belgian painter, Eugène Boch (October 2, 1888). He reported that the French writer Guy de Maupassant begins his masterwork *Bel-ami* (summer, autumn, 1887) with a description of a starry night in Paris with lighted cafés on the boulevard, almost the same motif that he himself was painting now (September 9 and 16, 1888).[70] He had gas lighting installed in the "Yellow House" so that he could do portraits there by gaslight.[71] He later found that his studio looked nice in the evening in that light (October 28, 1888).

Before he moved into the "Yellow House" he stayed in the Café de la Gare on the Place Lamartine from May to September 1888, a café that was run by Joseph Michel Ginoux and his wife Marie, a stone's throw from the "Yellow House." He painted this café in *The Night Café* (*L'Assommoir*). *Assommoir* is the French word for night café or bar. When he was in The

69. Van Kooten and Rijnders, *De schilderijen*, 239.

70. Actually *Yvette* is meant. Cf. Nemeczek, *Van Gogh in Arles*, 123, note 27.

71. Van Kooten and Rijnders, *De schilderijen*, 241, note 6; 260.

Hague (April 1883) he thought a great deal about Zola's *Assommoir* and five years later he thought of it again when he was in Arles. Although he did not cite Zola's novel as a literary inspiration for this painting, this story of a washerwoman who is ruined by drink could have been a model for it. In The Hague, when his relationship to Sien was ending, he did in any case cite Zola's words with approval:

> But the women are not bad, for their errors and their downfall are caused by the impossibility of living an irreproachable life in the midst of the gossip and slander of the corrupt suburbs. (August 22/23, 1883)

A night café stays open all night. The "night owls" can thus take refuge there if they have no money for a hotel or are too drunk to be admitted to them. It is a "rendezvous house," where every now and then one can see a prostitute sitting at a table with her client (September 18, 1888).

Van Gogh painted the work in three successive evenings by gaslight (August 6, 1888). He attempted to depict the awful human passions using red and green:

> The room is blood-red and dull yellow, a green billiards table in the center, four lemon yellow lamps with orange and green light. Everywhere there is struggle and conflict between the most divergent green and red; in the figures of the three sleeping tramps in the empty and high room, violet and blue. The blood-red and the yellow-green of the billiards table contrast with the small bit of Louis XV green of the bar on which a pink bouquet is standing. The white clothing of the owner, who is watching in a corner of the hothouse, becomes lemon yellow, pale green, and luminous.

Vincent tried to express the sense that "the café is a place where you can destroy yourself, go insane, or commit crimes." With the contrasts of soft pink, blood-red, and burgundy, soft green, he wanted to express an atmosphere of a hellish oven in a pale sulphur color, "as the true dark forces of a bar and yet with the appearance of Japanese cheerfulness" (September 8, 1888).

The painting of his own bedroom (September 5/6, 1889) was intended to be the counterpart of this night café. The walls are pale violet, and on the floor are red tiles and pine furniture (October 17, 1888). The wood of the bed and of the chairs is yellow like fresh butter, the sheet and the pillows in very bright lime green, the blanket scarlet, the window green, the washbasin blue, and the doors lilac. The shadows and cast shadows are omitted; it is colored in flat and bright hues, like Japanese prints. Hanging on the walls are portraits, a mirror, a towel, and some clothes (October 16, 1888). The sturdiness of the furniture is intended to express imperturbable rest and thus forms a contrast with the unrest of *The Night Café* (January 23, 1889). Vincent wanted to achieve absolute rest by the three pairs of complementary colors:

> red and green, yellow and purple, blue and orange, supplemented by black and white, with the mirror with a black frame as the only white note in order to bring in the fourth pair of complementary colors. (October 17, 1888)

He often did not know what he was doing because he worked like a sleepwalker. He thought that the colors should suggest rest or sleep. This painting was intended to give rest to the mind, or rather, the imagination. He wanted to attain a simple effect.[72] Making something simple with loud colors, however, is not easy, and he would have liked to show that one can be simple with colors other than gray, white, black, and brown. He definitely wanted other artists to have the same yearning and need for simplicity that he had.

> In today's society, however, an ideal of simplicity makes life more complicated, and whoever who cherishes that ideal only gets, just like me, to the point that he cannot do what he wants. (October 2022, 1889)

Doctor Gachet

Vincent returned to the north in the last weeks of his life. He would, Theo assured him, find it as interesting as a new country. On Theo's initiative he left Saint Rémy for Auvers to be treated by Doctor Paul-Ferdinand Gachet (October 5, 1889). When he arrived in Auvers, he learned that Daubigny's widow still lived there (May 21, 1890). In a sketch and a painting of the Daubigny garden he made, the figure in black walking towards a group is Daubigny's widow.[73]

Theo had heard of Doctor Gachet from the painter Camille Pissaro. He was a homeopathic doctor who painted in his spare time and maintained

---

72. As can be found in Eliot's *Felix Holt*.
73. Maurer, *The Pursuit of Spiritual Wisdom*, 112.

contact with all the impressionists (October 4, 1889).[74] Theo thought he looked a bit like Vincent (March 29, 1890), and he himself thought so later as well (June 5, 1890). Gachet had lost his wife some years before, an event that dealt him a severe blow. He had a nineteen-year-old daughter, Marguérite,[75] and a sixteen-year-old son, Paul. Gachet was up to date on what the concerns of painters were at the time, was a great friend of the painters of the "new school," and helped them as much as he was able. He graduated from the University of Montpellier as a doctor of medicine in 1858 with a dissertation on the subject of melancholy among painters![76] According to Vincent, Gachet was very nervous and eccentric, a condition that was probably not helped by the death of his wife. He gave Vincent the impression of being just as sick and washed out as Theo and Vincent themselves were but called him a "top doctor and his profession and his faith [kept] him going." Gachet showed him a great deal of sympathy and said that he was welcome in his home as often as he wanted to come. Gachet told him that work was still the best medicine for getting better. Vincent found a true friend in him, something like another brother, so alike physically and with respect to character (June 5, 1890).[77] Gachet showed that he was impressed by Vincent's painting of Madame Ginoux, *The Arlésienne* (June 3, 1890). Vincent was planning to do a portrait of Gachet, and when the latter asked, he did so (May 20, 1890). The painting shows two books in front of Gachet on his red garden table with legible titles, *Germinie Lacerteux* and *Manette Salomon*, by Edmond Huot de Goncourt and his brother Jules Huot, French writers who even made paintings, etchings, and drawings for a time (November 8–12, 1885). They were the pacesetters of the so-called naturalist school.

The De Goncourt brothers wrote documentary novels and chose their subjects from the world of prostitution and the environs of a hospital (half of February 1886). These "great thinkers of today," as Vincent called them, were devoted to the study of the history of eighteenth-century French culture[78] and the French Revolution. Vincent learned much from their work

---

74. Maurer, *The Pursuit of Spiritual Wisdom*, 106. Cf. November 16, 1889.

75. Cf. Alyson Richman, *De muze van Vincent* (Amsterdam: Sijthof, 2007).

76. *Étude sur la mélancholie* (1858). Zemel, *Van Gogh's Progress*, 220.

77. Cf. June 4, 1890; May 25, 1890; June 3, 1890.

78. De Goncourt, *L'Art du dix-huitième siècle*, November 18–20, 1885, January 12–16, 1886.

"about the 'end of the century (*fin du siècle*)' in which we now live." (beginning of January 1886).

Manette Salomon evokes the conception of the art of the 1840s. The main character, a painter who was married to Manette, is described as nervous and sensitive. Modern art is discussed in the novel: "What will remain are the landscape painters" (September 5/6, 1889.[79]The other novel is their magnus opus, *Germinie Lacerteux,*[80] a moral tragedy based on the sad life of their own maid, in which they portray her progressive physical and mental decline under the influence of alcohol and hysteria. Only after her death did the brothers come to the realization that the girl had lived a double life, full of alcohol abuse and slovenly eroticism. Jules de Goncourt described this discovery as the greatest shock of his life.[81]

If people want to know the truth about life, they can, in Vincent's view, turn to such a book (summer, autumn, 1887).[82] To him, the French naturalist novels symbolize the gloomy modern period that the doctor's melancholic attitude expresses. A small dark-red branch with foxglove represents the healing effect (for the treatment of heart disease) of hope and comfort (June 5, 1890).[83] The bowed posture and the balled fist that supports the head is a traditional sign of melancholy, as Albrecht Dürer depicts it in his *Melencolia I* (1514),[84] to which Vincent refers (September 24, 1880). He related how Millet, thinking back on his first wife, "takes his head between his two hands with a gesture as the great darkness and inexpressible melancholy of that period inundated him anew" (beginning of April 1884).[85]

That traditional pose of melancholy can also be seen in Vincent's bowed female figures in *Sitting Woman*, possibly Sien, *Mourning Woman Seated on a Basket*, with her face in her hands, and Madame Ginoux, *The*

79. Dorn et al., *Van Gogh*, 224.

80. Cf. July 6–8, 1883; January 22, 1889.

81. Arnold Heumakers, "God and Sex," *NRC* (date unknown), on Edmond and Jules de Goncourt's *God, Geld en Sex*, translated into Dutch by Edu Borger (Utrecht: De Arbeiderspers, 1996).

82. Werness, "The Symbolism," 53. Books were important to Vincent but not to Dr. Gachet, according to Gachet's son (Sund, "Favoured Fictions," 264). Vincent is all right with the fact that his sister is not that enthusiastic about this masterpiece by De Goncourt. She prefers Tolstoy to find energy for the work she is doing. "But would it be wrong for me to love French novelists so much?" (September 15, 1889).

83. June 3, 1890, draft letter to Gauguin. Uitert et al., *Schilderijen*, 268–71.

84. Dürer, *Albrecht Dürer*, 1953. Dorn et al., *Van Gogh*, 221.

85. Referring to Millet's biographer Sensier.

Arlesiénne. When Gachet talked about Belgium and the time of the painters from yesteryear, "a smile would appear on his grief-lined face" (May 20, 1890).

For Vincent, painting a portrait was not a matter of producing a photographic likeness, but he used color to express the character of the person (June 12, 1890). Gachet's face has

> the color of an overheated brick and is tanned by the sun with a blue background of hills: his clothes—a blue jacket—are ultramarine blue, which sets off his face better and makes it paler, despite the fact that it is brick-red in color. The hands of the doctor who delivers babies are whiter than his face.

He has a melancholic expression, "with passion, as well as an expression of desire like a cry." He bears the "sad expression of our time," even though that was not, perhaps, intended (June 17, 1890).

CHAPTER FOUR

The Art of Living

Living and the Task of Living

WHILE HE WAS IN Amsterdam Vincent reflected on the purpose of his life, something he had discussed earlier with Theo. He believed that they were agreed that the end should be kept in view and that victory after a whole life of work and struggle was better than victory before that struggle! (April 3, 1878).

When he was working as a painter in Etten in 1881, Vincent argued that the life force of "love" should receive the most attention.

> There is no genuine independence, no true freedom, no unshakable independence other than through love. Without love we fall, sooner or later; with love we win in the end. It is first through love that our sense of duty becomes evident and our work clear to us. Through loving and fulfilling the duties of love we do God's will and find peace with God that stills our conscience. (November 23, 1881)

At the beginning of his life as a painter, when he was still in Belgium, the question of his purpose in life and the why of his life continued to preoccupy him. He saw himself as a caged bird.[1]

> A bird in a cage in the spring knows very well that there is a purpose he could serve; he feels very well that there is something to do, but he can't do it. What is it? He doesn't recall it very well but

1. Last winter he studied *Le dernier jour d'un condamné* by Victor Hugo (September 24, 1880). Perhaps this led him to the description of a bird in a cage. Sund, *True to Temperament*, 40.

does have a vague idea of it and says to himself: The other birds build nests and have young and raise them. And then he hits his head against the bars of the cage. But the cage does not yield and the bird goes crazy with the pain. "He's good-for-nothing," says another bird passing by, that is, a kind of rentier. Nonetheless, the prisoner lives and does not die; nothing of what takes place on the inside can be seen on the outside, he does well, he is reasonably happy in the sunshine. Then the season of the great migration comes: an attack of melancholy . . .

"But," say the children who look after him in his cage, "He has everything he needs, doesn't he?" He looks outside, at the rough, stormy skies, and deep down he feels resistance to his lot. "I sit in a cage, I sit in a cage, and thus I lack nothing, you stupid children! I have everything I need. O, give me, please, the freedom to be a bird like other birds." A good-for-nothing human being resembles a good-for-nothing bird like this. . . .

But you can't always point to what locks you in, what walls you in, what you seem to bury, but nevertheless I feel the intangible bars, gates, walls—is all that my imagination, an illusion? I don't think so. And then you ask yourself: "My God, will this last for a long time, is it forever, for eternity?" Being friends, being brothers, loving—that opens the prison with its sovereign power, by a very powerful enchantment. Whoever does not have that stays dead. But where affection blossoms, there life blossoms as well. (July, 1880)

In the beginning period of his life as a painter Vincent found inspiration primarily in illustrators in English magazines. And so, similarly, when—ten years later in January/February 1890—he again felt trapped he found inspiration then in an exhibition by the French artist and lithographer Gustave Doré.[2] He made a painting of Doré's *Newgate Exercise Yard* (February 10, 1878), where the prisoner in the middle of the circle of prisoners taking their exercise in the walled-in prison yard points to Vincent's own imprisonment in the psychiatric institution in Saint Paul de Mausole in Saint Rémy, aside from the question of whether this figure displays Vincent's own traits or not.[3]

2. He knew Doré's works about London, and he found them splendid and full of feeling, such as his *Shelter for beggars* (September 18/19, 1878).

3. Hulsker doubts this (*Lotgenoten*, 436). Walther and Metzger, *Alle schilderijen*, 587, 612.

Born to Faith

In 1881 in Etten, where his father had been called as a minister, he fell in love in the parsonage with his cousin Cornelia Adriana (Kee) Vos-Stricker, the daughter of his uncle and aunt. She had been a widow for three years after the death of her husband, Christoffel M. Vos. Vincent had visited them often when he was in Amsterdam (September 18, 1877).

Kee was several years older than he and had a child. He was very determined to marry her (November 10/11, 1881), but she firmly rejected his marriage proposal: "No, never ever," Kee stated explicitly (November 10/11, 1881). Precisely at that time he was rereading Jules Michelet's *l'Amour* (Love) and *La femme* (Woman), which, as he himself said, clarified so many things that would otherwise have remained mysteries. Michelet said, "If you want to become a man, a woman has to breathe on you." Vincent wondered if the opposite was true, that a man had to breathe on a woman to make a woman of her. He himself was convinced of this. He wanted to place other words over against her "never": "My dear, I love you and you will love me," and: "You must have loved, must have stopped loving, and must love again!" (November 9/10, 1881).

His own mother refused to put in a good word for him with Kee. When Kee spoke to his mother in confidence and poured out her heart he would have liked to have seen her embrace his cause with some more sympathy instead of agreeing with her "No, never ever." He supposed that his mother had prayed a very nice prayer for him to have the strength to resign himself to Kee's rejection of him (November 9/10, 1881). This prayer was never heard and instead gave him strength for action. Kee's mother thought it ill-becoming that he did not resign himself to her daughter's refusal. When he said that he thought resignation to be very un-Christian and that neither Jesus nor Paul were examples of that, he was no longer welcome (November 23, 1881).

According to him, Kee was in a kind of prison without knowing it. The hypocrisy of ministers and pious women made more of an impression on her than on him. It did not occur to her that God actually begins only when we say what Multatuli (a Dutch author known for his subversive and critical writings during the colonial period) concludes his "Gebed van een onwetende" ("Prayer of an Ignorant Man"): "(O God, there is no God)":

> See, that God of the ministers, I found him to be as dead as a doornail, but does that make me an atheist? The ministers think I am—whatever—but, look, I love, and how could I feel love if I

> myself did not live or others did not live, and if we do live, there is
> something wondrous about that. Call it God or human nature or
> whatever you want, but it is certainly something that I can't define
> in a system, although it is very alive and real, and, look, for me,
> that's God for me or just as good as God. (December 21, 1881)

The cold, appalling reception he was given by Kee's parents in Amsterdam shocked him. A friend in need is a friend indeed. He wondered if the ministers, J.P. Stricker and Theodorus van Gogh, looking so "reverend-like" in their togas and gray hair, would dare to preach about love in the way people talked about it in private. In contrast to their sermons he gave his own in the form of a painting: *Painting of a Horse* by Anton Mauve, an interpretation of the attitude of acceptance, of resignation (November 21, 1881).

> I have never heard a good sermon on resignation, nor can I
> imagine a good one, except for this painting by Anton Mauve of
> a yearling being dragged up the dunes. (December 29, 1881)[4]
> It is resignation, but of the real sort; not the kind ministers talk
> about. Those nags, those poor, battered nags, black, white, brown;
> they stand there patiently, subdued, resigned, and still. They still
> have to drag the heavy barge along the lowest end later. The job
> is done. They stand still for a moment, panting. They are covered
> in sweat—but they don't grumble, they don't protest—they don't
> complain. They got past that years ago. They have resigned them-
> selves to only living and working. Nevertheless, they have to go to
> the skinner [who skins dead livestock] tomorrow; they are ready
> for that. (March 11, 1882)[5]

Vincent found a high, practical, silent philosophy in that painting, which seems to say that being able to suffer without complaint is the only thing that is practical, that is the knowledge, the lesson we must learn, the solution to the problem of life (March 11, 1882).

When he was later admitted to hospital in Saint Rémy, he believed that one could be healed by great resignation to suffering and death by distancing oneself from one's own will and love for oneself. But that did not appeal to him. He loved to paint, to see people and things, and everything that is part of—perhaps artificial—life. True life was elsewhere, but he did not believe he belonged to that category of people who are prepared to live and also to die at any moment (September 7/8, 1889).

4. I would rather look at a horse by Mauve, July 11, 1883.
5. Cf. December 29, 1881.

Religions Disappear, but God Remains

Vincent was irritated by his parents' attitude to his relationship with Sien. They objected strenuously on financial grounds to his marrying her, and that is why he saw ministers as the most godless people and dullest materialists in society—not so much on the pulpit but certainly in private life. He thought that his father and mother should be content with the simple side of life, and he would be proud of his father if he was a genuinely poor village pastor in the pure sense of the Gospel. He thought he could expect him to collaborate in helping save a poor woman and that he would take her part because she was poor and alone. He thought what his father did was inhuman—and twice as much so since he was a servant of the Gospel (June 3, 1883).

He did temper his words shortly afterwards, however. He felt that his father's error lay more in his words than in his heart and disposition, and he was again moved by the help his father offered Sien by giving her an overcoat against the cold! (June 5/6, 1883).

Distancing himself from the institution of the church and ministers, Vincent, like Thomas Carlyle in the latter's "philosophy of old clothes," put the dogmas of the church behind him. In his 1836 novel, *Sartor Resartus: The Life and Opinions of Herr Teufelsdröck* (i.e. The Tailor Retailored), Carlyle asks for a Creator who pours the old truths into a new mythical form that fits the present.[6] Vincent compared this to an exhibit of impressionistic painters that was taking place in Paris at the time (August–October, 1886). When a crowd of visitors returned bitterly disappointed and even indignant from the exhibit, they were acting just like good Dutch people who had just left a church service and a moment later were listening to the speech by the socialist leader Domela Nieuwenhuis.

> Indeed . . . in ten or fifteen years' time, that whole edifice of a national religion collapsed, whereas the socialists are still there and will be there for a long time, even though neither you [his sister Wil] nor I belong very much to either persuasion. (June 22, 1888)

Vincent read Carlyle's "philosophy of old clothes," as he called *Sartor Resartus*, in The Hague. Thomas Carlyle's *Sartor Resartus* is a combination of novel, autobiography, and essay, in which a hero tells of his misfortune in love and the difficulties he has with religion. In his philosophy of clothes

---

6. Carlyle, *Sartor Resartus*, 147. Druick and Zegers, *Van Gogh en Gauguin*, 380, note 129.

he attempts to indicate the difference between the appearance of things and their reality. The appearance of an individual depends on the clothes he or she is wearing; the reality of that individual is the body under the clothes. Carlyle sees an analogy here to institutions like churches. They may be useful emblems of the spiritual powers they clothe, but they wear out eventually and must be replaced by new ones. The underlying spirit must be kept alive at all costs. Clothes hide the body, just as the world of nature clothes the reality of God. The discovery of these realities behind the appearance is the first step to a solution for the dilemmas of life.[7]

As far as religion is concerned, Vincent saw all dogmas as old clothes. He said that Carlyle's book was much disparaged and its author viewed as a monster. But Vincent defended him. In his view, Carlyle had learned much from Goethe, or even more from a certain man who wrote no books but whose words, although he did not write them down himself, were still around, namely, Jesus Christ. Long before Carlyle, Jesus had also relegated many forms to "old clothes" (March 5, 1883).

When Vincent was in the Catholic psychiatric institution Saint Paul de Mausole in Saint Rémy for treatment, he was preoccupied with the same relationship with certain forms of institutional religion. This hospital was housed in a former monastery that had been built in the Middle Ages by an order and had been used to treat mentally ill people since 1605. In the first half of the nineteenth century it became a full-fledged psychiatric hospital for mentally disturbed people, with separate male and female wards.[8] The priests there made a sad impression on Vincent. He did meet interesting nuns (April 30, 1889), but it annoyed him that they believed in the Holy Virgin of Lourdes.

Vincent sensed he was a prisoner in an institution where unhealthy religious deviations were fostered rather than healed (September 7/8, 1889). He knew that these nuns had their own faith and their own way of doing good. He had attacks of religious mania like a superstitious person and had confused and horrible thoughts in those old cloisters that he had never had when he lived in the "North," i.e. the Netherlands and Belgium. He thought that his already long stay in hospital in Arles and his stay in this

7. In this first book by Thomas Carlyle his Calvinistic youth as well as the German Romantic influence are noticeable. Goethe held a great attraction for him. Cf. Abrams, *The Norton Anthology*, 932–33.

8. Van Kooten and Rijnders, *De schilderijen*, 279.

institution were sufficient to explain those attacks. He would rather have left immediately (September 19, 1889).

Nevertheless, he confessed that, during his stay, religious thoughts sometimes also brought him comfort (September 7/8, 1889). For him, the criticism of institutions did not entail a break with faith! Quoting Victor Hugo, he said: "Religions disappear, but God remains" (cf. Matthew 24:35) (beginning of June 1885).[9] In a letter of condolence to Theo after Vincent's death, Gauguin cited one of Vincent's favorite expressions, "La pierre périra, la parole restera" (the stone erodes, the word remains).[10] Vincent's painting *Starry Night*,[11] with the mountains rolling like waves and the flame-shaped cypresses in the foreground, shows strikingly enough a church with a prominent steeple—a symbol of a deeply rooted faith in the midst of an uncertain, limitless universe (June 17/18, 1889).[12]

Vincent's critical statements about the church and about ministers were closely connected to differences of opinion with his parents on the relationship with his cousin Kee Vos and later with Sien Hoornik.

> Oh, I am no friend of present-day Christianity, even though its founder was sublime—present-day Christianity, I have seen through it too well. It even fascinated me, its ice-coldness in my youth—but I've had my revenge since then. Through what? Through worshipping love, which they, the theologians, call sin, by respecting a whore, etc. and not "would-be" respectable, religious ladies. The woman is always heresy and demonic for the one side. For me, it is the opposite. (October, 1884) . . . There are (as a rule with exceptions) no more unbelieving, hardened, and more worldly people than ministers and, above all, ministers' wives. (November 19, 1881)

Although relations between him and his parents were strained a few years later in Nuenen, they improved when he took care of his mother after she broke her thigh (January, 17 1884). The differences of opinion between him and his father and mother receded to the background. For his mother he painted "the little church with the hedge and the trees" (January 24, 1884),

9. He says that Victor Hugo had just died and been buried in Paris in June (May 22, 1885).

10. Druick and Zegers, *Van Gogh en Gauguin*, 265, 376, note 6.

11. Possibly in connection with Daudet's *Les Étoiles*. Sund, *True to Temperament*, 304, note 64.

12. Druick and Zegers, *Van Gogh en Gauguin*, 285–86. Cf. Pabst, *Van Gogh Album*, 2, 22–23.

which became known as *Congregation Leaving the Reformed Church in Nuenen*. A plaque above the church door reads (in Dutch): "My house will be called a house of prayer" (Matthew 21:13).[13] Even though it was intended for his mother, he wanted to seal the new relationship with both parents.[14]

He did some more work on the painting later, putting some members of the congregation in the foreground who are, strikingly enough, wearing Catholic mourning clothes. Obviously, he wanted to include the reference to mourning in front of the church where his father worked and who had succumbed to a stroke on the threshold of his parsonage on 26 March 1885. He thus brought the painting up to date for the sake of his mother.[15]

When Vincent painted his *Starry Night over the Rhone* at night outside under gaslight (September, 29, 1888), where the city, illuminated by gaslight, is reflected in the blue river (October 2, 1885), he speaks of his immense need for "should I say the word—religion" (September 29, 1888). He quoted the American poet Walt Whitman who spoke of the starry night as "a manifestation of eternity." In the future and even in the present this poet saw a world full of health, full of a generous and upright physical love, of friendship, of work in connection with the great starry firmament, something that cannot be called anything else than God and eternity, both of which have again gained their place above this world. "You have to laugh at first, it's so innocent and pure, and for the same reasons it makes you think" (August 28, 1888).[16] Whitman and Vincent use (according to Werness) the image of the star to embody their most visionary and spiritual experiences:

> Human life and death are inseparably connected with the immensely mutual reaching into one another of cosmic rhythms, which offer comfort and reassurance, even in the face of the distant and spectacular beauty of the universe.[17]

In Nuenen Vincent did a painting of the ruins of the old church tower of a Roman Catholic church, *The Old Church Tower at Nuenen (The Peasant's Churchyard)*. The tower was demolished a week later; the steeple was

13. De Brouwer, *Van Gogh en Nuenen*, 28. Matthew 21:25 is mistakenly mentioned; see also Van Tilborgh, *Vincent van Gogh*, 60, note 60.

14. Van Tilborgh, *Vincent van Gogh*, 60.

15. Van Tilborgh, *Vincent van Gogh*, 63–65. See also pages 110–13.

16. Francis Viélé-Griffin translates "From Noon to Starry Night" ("Du midi a la nuit étoilée"). Sund, *True to Temperament*, 288, note 40.

17. Werness, "Whitman and Van Gogh," 38–40.

already gone (May 11, 1885), and for him this ruin represented the passing of religion. It showed him how faith and religion decayed, even though it was solidly established, and how the life and death of peasants was and remains the same: "constantly growing and wilting like the grass and the flowers that grow in the churchyard" (beginning of June 1885).

On 30 March 1885 his father was buried in the accompanying cemetery, in the north section, which was reserved for Protestants. Instead of a wooden cross, he was given a gravestone on which was written (in Dutch): "Here lies Theodorus van Gogh, born 8 February 1822, died 26 March 1885 Pastor and teacher in Nuenen from 1882 to 1885."[18]

Vincent was attracted by the theme of churchyards. That was the case in Drenthe, after he arrived in Hoogeveen (Drenthe), and the theme also came up, after Nuenen, in Paris, in the form of *Churchyard in the Rain*, and during his short stay on the Mediterranean coast, in *Saintes-Maries with Cemetery*.[19]

Our Life is a Pilgrimage

The theme of life as a pilgrimage appears throughout in his life and work. In Dordrecht he quoted (without giving the poet's name) the poem "De Pelgrimstogt" (The Pilgrimage), which is about a pilgrim who already by virtue of wandering is searching for the heavenly city.

HOMESICKNESS FLOWS THROUGH

the heart of a pilgrim.
Wandering, he searches
for the heavenly city,
city of pleasures, of
eternal joys That
God's Angel had once
promised him . . . .
Holy melancholy
mollifies my soul.
Burning sighs
rise up from my heart.
Dully, he sinks down

18. De Brouwer, *Van Gogh en Nuenen*, 70. Van Tilborgh, *Vincent van Gogh*, 158, note 1.
19. Cf. Dijk and Van der Sluis, *De Drentste tijd*, 315.

on the flowery bed.
Languishing, his eyes
pierce the distance.

. . .

Sweet as the scents
of flowers, he disappears.
The pilgrim springs up
strengthened by his word.
Difficult paths
he trod bravely.
Finally, there the
Heavenly gate shines.

She opens her wings
like the arms of the Mother
who has expected
her son in yearning.
Jubilant songs
greet the weary one,
who has so bravely
completed his journey. (February 28, 1877)

As an artist, he retained the sense of being a traveler on the way to a destination (August 6, 1888). He compared it to the march of soldiers in retreat: "How much we feel their tiredness! We also march in life, don't we, though we aren't soldiers?" (October 17, 1888). During his life, he sought support in the examples from the life and work of other artists. He says about the painting of a woman in the snow, *Way of Flowers, Way of Tears*:[20]

> Now, my wife (Sien) no longer walks the way of flowers like she did when she was younger, and did what she wanted and what she felt like doing, but life has become thornier for her and a way of tears. (May 9/10, 1883)

He was strongly aware of how difficult the road of an artist is. He wrote to Anthon van Rappard that they both were viewed as "good-for-nothings by others, as bores or boring, both in their work and as people." Vincent emphasized that they had to be tough for their own sakes and not be discouraged or upset by others who thought they knew a better direction than what they themselves were attempting to follow. He thought that they

20. James J.J. Tissot, *Voie des fleurs, voie des pleurs*.

should not have any illusions but should be prepared to be misunderstood, despised, and deplored (November 1, 1882).

He did believe, however, that it was the duty of every artist to "Let your light shine before people" (Matthew 5:16). Vincent sought more and better opportunities than exhibitions to bring art to the people. He did not want to hide the candle under a bushel but to put it on a candlestick (Matthew 5:15) (second half of March 1884).

Early Puritans of New England Going to Church (London, July 20, 1873) and *Pilgrim Fathers* are two paintings he liked very much (October 6/7, 1883).[21] They had been painted by the popular illustrator George H. Boughton, who cherished a preference for New England. Vincent's ideas have an affinity with motifs in Boughton's work. The bare landscape motifs (gnarls, thistles, branches) display a close connection with his work in Drenthe. Boughton's "*'God Speed' Pilgrims Setting Out For Canterbury*" fascinated him.[22] In his view, it was not actually a painting but an inspiration.

> A dusty dirt path leads over the hills to a mountain where the holy city can be seen, illuminated by the sun setting behind the gray evening clouds. In the distance on the right is a mountain ridge that looks blue in the evening mist. Above the hills one can see the beauty of the sunset, the gray clouds set off with an edge of silver, gold, and purple. The landscape is a plain or a stretch of wilderness covered by grass and heather with here and there the white stem of a birch tree with its yellow leaves, for it is autumn. A road leads through the landscape to a higher mountain very, very far away, on the top of which is a city wrapped in a halo by the setting sun. . . . A pilgrim is walking on that road, staff in hand. He has been traveling for quite some time now and is very tired. And then he meets a woman, a shape in black that reminds one of the words of Paul: "sorrowful, yet always rejoicing" (2 Corinthians 6:10). The angel is placed there to encourage the pilgrims and to answer their questions. The pilgrim asks: "Does this road go all the way up the mountain?" The answer is "Yes, right to the end." He asks again: "And does the trip last the whole day?" And the answer is: "From morning until evening, my friend."[23] And the pilgrim goes on,

21. Hammacher, *Van Gogh*, 10, 56, 108.

22. According to Sund, *True to Temperament*, 259, note 76, it is probable that Vincent had *The Bearers of the Burden* in mind, which shows four people on a winding road towards hills in the distance.

23. Poem by Christina G. Rossetti, "Up-hill," the sister of the painter and poet Dante Rossetti.

sorrowful yet always rejoicing, sad because it is so far and the road is so long. She is filled with hope when she looks up at the eternal city far away shining in the evening glow. (August 26, 1876)

Exile and Strangers on the Earth

On 29 October 1876 Vincent preached in the Methodist church in Richmond on the text: "I am a stranger on the earth, hide not Thy commandments from me" (Psalm 119:19) (September 1, 1876).[24]

The following story about Vincent was found in an album that was not discovered until the 1990s. He did allude to this story in letters (June 29, 1875) that we did have before the album was found. A Frenchman went to England because of family difficulties and there became a teacher, married, and had a child. When he became mortally ill he wanted to return to France to die. When he was back in the Granville harbor, he asked to be brought to the beach to see the sunset. One day, when he felt the end approaching, he asked for a priest and then, after confession, asked to be left alone with his wife. He told her, "I love you" and collapsed and died. Vincent added: "He loved France, Brittany in particular,[25] and nature and there he saw God. That is why I am telling you the story of this stranger on earth, who was one of its true citizens." The man in question was Jean Baptiste Loyer, the husband of Vincent's landlady in London.[26]

Vincent's sermon was on the theme of "being a stranger," which is characteristic for human pilgrimage (October 31, 1876).

> It is an old faith and it is a good faith that our life is a pilgrim's progress—that we are strangers in the earth, but that though this be so, yet we are not alone for our Father is with us. We are pilgrims, our life is a long walk, a journey from earth to heaven.
>
> The beginning of this life is this. There is one who remembereth no more Her sorrow and Her anguish for joy that a man is born into the world. She is our Mother. The end of our pilgrimage is the entering in Our Fathers house, where are many mansions, where He had gone before us to prepare a place for us. The end of this life is what we call death—it is an hour in which words are spoken, things are seen and felt that are kept in the secret chambers of the

24. Silverman, *Vincent van Gogh*, 66, 69, 116–17.

25. Normandy is actually meant here.

26. Bailey, "Vincent van Gogh," 16–17.

hearts of those who stand by, it is so that all of us have such things in our hearts or forebodings of such things. There is sorrow in the hour when a man is born into the world, but also joy—deep and unspeakable—thankfulness so great that it reacheth the highest Heavens. Yes the Angels of God they smile and they rejoice when a man is born in the world. There is sorrow in the hour of death—but there too is joy unspeakable when it is the hour of death of one who has fought a good fight. There is One who has said, I am the resurrection and the life, if any man believe in Me, though he were dead, yet shall he live. There was an Apostle who heard a voice from heaven, saying: Blessed are they that die in the Lord for they rest from their labour and their works follow them. . . .

We are pilgrims in the earth and strangers—we come from afar and we are going far. The journey of our life goes from the loving breast of our Mother on earth to the arms of our Father in heaven. Everything on earth changes—we have no abiding city here—it is the experience of everybody: That it is Gods will that we should part with what we dearest have on earth—we ourselves, we change in many respects, we are not what we once were, we shall not remain what we are now. From infant we grow up to boys and girls—young men and young women—and if God spares us and helps us—to husbands and wives, Fathers and Mothers in our turn, and then, slowly but surely the face that once had the 'early dew of morning' gets its wrinkles, the eyes that once beamed with youth and gladness speak of a sincere deep and earnest sadness—though they may keep the fire of Faith, Hope and Charity—though they may beam with Gods spirit. . . .

And when everyone of us goes back to daily things and daily duties, let us not forget—that things are not what they seem, that God by the things of daily life teacheth us higher things, that our life is a pilgrim's progress and that we are strangers in the earth—but that we have a God and Father who preserveth strangers, and that we are all brethren. Amen. (October 29, 1876)

Vincent was familiar with John Bunyan's *Pilgrim's Progress*,[27] of which he had made an excerpt in Amsterdam (October 30, 1877). John Bunyan, the son of a coppersmith or tinker, a trade that he himself also practiced, was a soldier in the Parliamentary Army in England and also a lay preacher. He became a Baptist minister in Bedford. Because he was not authorized to preach, he was put in prison and remained there for several years. While in

27. *Pilgrim's Progress from this World to that Which is to Come: Delivered under the Similitude of a Dream.*

prison he wrote *Pilgrim's Progress*, an allegorical description of the journey of "Christian" from the city of destruction to the Heavenly City. "Christian" is guided by an "Evangelist" to the light that shines from the city in the distance. He travels with fellow pilgrims, like "Faithful," and "Hopeful," through many dangers and temptations, ultimately reaches his destination, and is admitted to the Heavenly City. The pilgrims' goal is a visual liberation: seeing Christ in the kingdom of heaven. There they see their Redeemer face to face, now they live only by sight.[28]

This book was widely read in the nineteenth century in England and was one of the foundations of Methodism (living according to the methods of the Bible), a pietistically tinged revival movement in the eighteenth century that had great influence on evangelical movements elsewhere, including the Netherlands. Bunyan's work is permeated by a piety directed against the institutional church. The book rejects reason and celebrates the religion of feeling.[29]

Vincent could find his own personal religious experiences reflected in the pilgrim "Christian" in *Pilgrim's Progress* who is always moving forward.[30] In 1876 he considered himself a pilgrim, like "Christian" and "Mr Great-heart." He was certain he would be led on the right path, like the pilgrims in Bunyan's story through all temptations.[31] Years later (August 6, 1888) he referred to John Bunyan. Works like *The Bearers of the Burden* and *At Eternity's Gate* evoke Bunyan's world, the heavy labor of the laden pilgrim.[32]

Walkers on a Pilgrimage

While he was in Saint Rémy Vincent took long walks (October 25, 1889). During the great difficulties he underwent in his treatment, he nevertheless saw the way forward. He thought constantly of the "preface" of the book *Le conscrit* (The Conscript) in which Henry Conscience, a Flemish novelist, relates that he felt his affection for people ebbing away during a period of serious illness despite all his efforts to the contrary. His feeling of love returned, however, through long walks in an open field (September 5/6,

28. Cf. Bailey, *Van Gogh in England*, 96–98.
29. Bailey, *Van Gogh in England*, 98.
30. Stolwijk et al., *De Keuze van Vincent*, 53.
31. Bailey, *Van Gogh in England*, 100.
32. Bailey, *Van Gogh in England*, 103.

1889). Vincent depicted walkers as if they were on a pilgrimage, people on their way somewhere. When he made a large painting of a ravine—two large rock masses close to Saint Rémy, with a small brook flowing between them and a third mountain that closed off the ravine (October 8, 1889)— two very small travelers in the mountainous landscape between seem to be searching for the unknown, with red notes as points of light (March 20, 1890).

In *Cypress in Starry Night* as well, we can see walkers or pilgrims who point to Vincent himself. *Country Road in Provence by Night* is one of the last paintings from Saint Rémy when he was getting ready to leave for Auvers.[33] He painted

> a cypress with a star, a night sky with a moon with no glow, no more than a thin crescent rising from the dark shadow of the earth, a star with an exaggerated shine, a soft pink and green shine in the ultramarine light in which clouds are floating. The road is below, with high yellow reeds beside it and behind it the low blue Alpine mountains: an old inn with windows lit up by orange light, and a very tall, straight, and very dark cypress. On the road is a yellow carriage to which a white horse is hitched and two late walkers, workmen who are going home with spades slung over their shoulders. (June 17, 1890)

It is not improbable that he put himself in the painting in one of the figures in the foreground with red hair and beard.

There are more examples from this period in which he was ill in which he painted a corresponding pair of figures such as *Several Figures on a Road with Trees*,[34] also with a man who appears to lead the way with an upraised arm. Just as in his *Lane with Poplars* from Nuenen, the walkers here lend the painting their own meaning and purpose. That religiously tinged association seems to be strengthened by a busy night sky, the cypress as the symbol of death (*Un funèbre cyprès*) (September 27, 1888), and the insignificance of the walkers in the foreground. Because the figures are prominently present, the image of the human being as pilgrim is evoked.[35]

33. Painted between May 12 and 15 1890. Van Kooten and Rijnders, *De schilderijen*, 355.

34. Hulsker, *Lotgenoten*, 452.

35. Uitert et al., *Schilderijen*, 260, 265. Van Kooten and Rijnders, *De schilderijen*, 355–59.

Pilgrims Together on the Road

In all the places in the Netherlands, England, Belgium, and France where Vincent lived and worked he was a passionate walker. His letters teem with the descriptions of how he experienced nature during his walks and what he felt inside. These "wanderings and pilgrimages" reveal a passionate emotional life.[36] Vincent also took long walks through Amsterdam, and small lanes and roads appear already in his early sketches in Etten. When the leaves were falling he made a sketch of *Road with Pollard Willows* and speaks about a ploughman in connection with pilgrimage (October 12, 1881). Passing a certain spot in Brussels made him think of Hippolyte Boulenger's *Avenue of Poplars* (March 1, 1884)[37] and the poem "Tristement" ("Sorrowful") by François J.E. Coppée made him think of that painting. In his time, Coppée was viewed as a "poet of ordinary people." A grieving woman who wanders in a lane in the fall becomes the metaphor of deep sorrow. The final verse reads:

> And I have a heart so full of fall and widowhood
> That I always dream, under a bright clear sky
> Of a figure in mourning—against a cold landscape
> And, at the first wind of winter, the leaves that fly.
> (March 1, 1884)[38]

Avenue of Poplars near Nuenen is the last painting that Van Gogh made in November 1885 in Nuenen. In the autumn or sunset he saw an infinite poetry and a mysterious striving in nature (first half of February 1886). For him, there was a gentle melancholy in the falling leaves (February 7, 1883).[39] This avenue of poplars facing Nuenen and the Roman Catholic Clemens Church is

> a study in color of the effect of autumn in the twilight, whereby a strip of color above the horizon constitutes the strongest light effect. The foreground is covered entirely with fallen yellow autumn leaves. Here and there the sun makes glittering spots on the

---

36. Hammacher, "Van Gogh-Michelet-Zola," 17.

37. Cf. May 7, 1888.

38. Van Uitert, *Van Gogh in Brabant*, 220. *Ouvres Completes Poésis (1864–1887)* (Paris: Alphonse Lemerre, n.d.). Cf. Coppée, cited in Van Uitert, *Van Gogh in Brabant*, 433.

39. With reference to Gustave Doré.

fallen leaves that are alternated by the long cast shadows above in between the autumn leaves. (November 15–20, 1885)[40]

The walker gives the painting her own meaning. She is clearly going somewhere and thus perhaps symbolizes human existence as a pilgrimage.[41]

At the beginning of November 1888, Van Gogh did four studies of Les Alyscamps in Arles (November 2, 1888). Arles was once one of the last centers of power of the Roman Empire and was also called the second Rome.[42] It developed into the Rome of Gaul under the Roman emperor Augustus, and Les Alyscamps (Champs Elysées or Elysian Fields), a long lane of poplars with tombs from the Roman and early Christian period on both sides, dates from that time. It was one of the oldest roads leading into the city. It was a tourist attraction already in Vincent's time and an ideal place for the residents of Arles to walk intimately arm in arm.[43]

Vincent painted lilac poplar trunks that stand like pillars along a lane with a row of old Roman tombs left and right in blue lilac. The ground is covered with a thick carpet of orange and yellow fallen leaves. They are still falling like snowflakes. And in the lane black figures of couples in love are walking. A second canvas shows the same lane with an old man and a fat, rotund woman. Couples in love appear in two of the works. The image of life as a pilgrimage toward death, borrowed from John Bunyan's *Pilgrim's Progress*, also played a role in this road that led along the sarcophaguses.[44]

Plunging into the Open Sea of Reality

In his correspondence with his painter friend Anthon van Rappard, Vincent makes clear how one must become involved in the true reality around one and plunge into it. However difficult it was, this act would yield results. Here Vincent used the image of the raging sea on which one must become a fisherman and leave the wharf for the open sea.

From his youth onward, he understood that the ship of life could be driven about by all kinds of winds. He used such images until the last

40. Cf. end of October 1884; second half of August 1885. Van Uitert, *Van Gogh in Brabant*, 224–25.

41. Uitert et al., *Schilderijen*, 56–57.

42. Nemeczek, *Van Gogh in Arles*, 7–10.

43. Van Kooten and Rijnders, *De schilderijen*, 253–57, Druick and Zegers, *Van Gogh en Gauguin*, 171–72; Van Uitert et al., *Schilderijen*, 177.

44. Van Uitert et al., *Schilderijen*, 177.

months of his life, and his sketchbook contains a drawing of a sailboat (between October 29 and November 15, 1883).

In November 1881 he wrote from Etten that he held that love, fully developed, would make people better than the opposite passion, "Ambition and Co.," would.

> But precisely because love is so strong, we are usually not strong enough when we are young to keep our rudder straight. The passions are the sails of the ship, and someone who surrenders himself completely to his feelings gets too much wind: his boat takes on water and he dies—or resurfaces. Someone who, in contrast, raises the sail Ambition and Co. and no other on his mast sails through life, straight through the sea, without incident, without any capers, until—until ultimately circumstances arise in which he notices: I do not have enough sail. Then he says, everything, everything I have I would give for one more square sail, and I don't have it. He becomes desperate. But now he thinks he can still raise a different sail. He remembers that sail he despised until now, that he stored up until this point as ballast. And that sail saves him. The sail Love must save him. If he does not add that sail, he will not make it. (November 12, 1881)

He found it difficult to define what kind of love he had then. He saw his physical passions as quite weak, perhaps because of a year of serious poverty and hard work, but he viewed his intellectual passions as strong. In the sermon we cited earlier from October 1876 in England he says:

> Our earlier life might be compared to sailing on a river, but very soon the waves become higher, the wind more violent, we are at sea almost before we are aware of it—and the prayer from the heart ariseth to God: protect me o God, for my bark is so small and thy sea is so great. (October 31, 1876)

Vincent saw the human heart as very much like the sea: it has its storms and its tides, and there are pearls in its depths. This image of the sea returned to him constantly, literally and figuratively. He urged Van Rappard to throw himself completely into reality, into the open sea as his proper element. He himself could not master the sea and could not maneuver like he wanted.

> If we do not drown or are not crushed against the rocks in the surf, we will become true seamen. Everyone who shoves off to the depths must go through a time of toil and rummaging about. In the beginning you catch few fish, but you learn to know the

waters and to steer the boat and that is something essential at any rate. And after a while we catch many fish—and big ones too! (November 2, 1881)

Where did Vincent want others to float to?

To the open sea! . . . But a person can hold out for long on the open sea—he has to have a hut on the beach with a fire in the hearth, with a wife and children around that hearth.[45]

He wanted to stimulate others

to become fishermen on the sea we call the Ocean of reality, but for myself and for my fellow human beings whom I sometimes turn to, I want specifically that hut. (November 23, 1881)

In Amsterdam, in April 1878, he wrote that great artists always

shove off to the depths, that is what we have to do as well if we want to catch fish, and if it sometimes happens that we work the whole night and do not catch anything, then it is good not to give up but to "cast the nets once more at dawn" (Luke 5:1–11). (April 3, 1878)

Collaboration with Other Artists

As of 1880, the beginning of his life as a painter, Vincent always imagined himself as living and working with another artist.[46] He had a great need to live in a community and he deeply wanted to work with other artists. He always thought it foolish for painters to live alone (May 28, 1888).

Before he was transferred to London Vincent worked from 1867 to 1873 in The Hague as the youngest staff member in the shop owned by the art dealer Goupil, where H.G. Tersteeg was in charge. Writing to Vincent's parents, he called Vincent an "industrious, diligent boy." The relationship between Vincent and his chief, who was eight years his senior, must have been good at that time. Vincent was initially also the protégé of Anton Mauve, a well-known painter in The Hague. Mauve had married Vincent's cousin and, like Vincent, was the son of a minister. He was Vincent's elder by fifteen years and coached him in the beginning of his life as a painter.

45. Cf. Dickens, *The Cricket on the Hearth*. McChesney Alhadeff, "Van Gogh's 'Worship of Sorrow,'" 63.

46. Jo Bonger, "Introduction," in Van Gogh, *De Brieven*, 28.

The relationship between Vincent and Tersteeg and Mauve changed very quickly during his second stay in The Hague, at the beginning of 1882. Tersteeg possibly influenced Mauve here. The former began to lose confidence in Vincent and reproached him for all kinds of things. He insisted that he paint "marketable things" (small drawings in watercolor). Mauve was not very sure of Vincent's talent and his disposition toward him changed. Vincent reported: "Mauve's sympathy that, to me, was like water to a half-withered plant, dried up." Attempts to reconcile with Mauve failed. When Vincent encountered him once by chance in The Hague, he refused to come look at Vincent's work.

> "I will certainly not come to you, it is completely over. . . . You have a vicious character." Then I [Vincent] turned around, I was in the dunes, and I went home alone.

Vincent thought about forming a kind of society of painters where warmth and cordiality and a certain harmony held sway. He saw more good in a society of painters than in the association of their works with one another via expositions. He considered the spirit of concord and respect for one another to be of great importance (March 21, 1883). Already in The Hague he spoke of his love for his studio "like [the love] a skipper would have for his barge" (March 3, 1883). He dreamt in The Hague of a "studio with a cradle, as a protection against storms" (July 6, 1882).

But his relations with other painters in The Hague were disappointing for him. When he arrived there, he went to all the studios he could to seek contact and make friends. But the artists did not come to see him because of Sien and because of his views about painting. With a variation on the saying by the preacher-poet, Petrus de Genestet ("I did not find it in books and from 'the learned' I learned, oh, so little") he said, "I did not find it in the studio, and from painters/experts I learned, oh, so little" (second half of March 1884).

Vincent recognized that he had little success with dealing with people who were very fond of external forms. That the contact with artists in The Hague ceased completely for him did make him feel abandoned sometimes. On the other hand, however, it directed him to what was eternally beautiful in nature. He thought of Robinson Crusoe who did not lose courage in his loneliness but set about in such a way that he created a working environment around himself through his own searching and toil. As a result, he had a very active and stimulating life (September 18/19, 1882).

For him, painting the peasant life was something serious. He would have reproached himself if he had not attempted to produce "paintings in such a way that they could give serious things to think about to those who thought seriously about art and life" (April 30, 1885). In the summer of 1887 he wrote from Paris that it would be better to enjoy life than to do away with oneself. The following summer in Arles he said that his work during the harvest period was no easier than that of the peasants who were bringing in the harvest. Precisely at that time he felt almost as happy in the artist's life, although that was not real life, as he could have been in the ideal life, true life (June 29, 1888).

In August, a few months before Gauguin arrived, he sometimes felt he was no match for the situation as it was and thought he needed to be wiser, richer, and younger to win—but he did not value winning at all. For him, painting was only a means for coping with life (August 29, 1888).

On Board my Little Yellow House

Vincent found it difficult to work alone because solitude could lead to all kinds of storms and dangers. He spoke about this in terms of the sea, borrowed from religion (Mary as star of the sea) and from literature, in particular Pierre Loti, a French writer who was also a naval officer. Through Loti, he gained a great deal of sympathy for the life of fishermen in storms and dangers. That Gauguin had also been a sailor played a role here as well. Together they discussed Loti's *Pêcheur d'Islande* (An Iceland Fisherman) (October 28, 1888).[47]

After he was disappointed with his contacts with artists in The Hague, he did not seem to be able to realize his ideal of collaboration until Arles in 1888, where he wanted to board "the ark of his little yellow house" (January 22, 1889). He hoped that "that enterprise would not be shipwrecked."[48] He wanted to create a home there, not one with a wife and children but one with a family of artists. Vincent even abandoned the idea of fathering any children, though he could produce ideas and paintings. He wanted to have a kind of monastery there for struggling artists, where they could live together as simple monks with Gauguin as their abbot (October 3, 1888).

47. When at the end of the novel the central character dies he married with the sea. Sund, *True to Temperament*, 309, note 128.

48. Druick and Zegers, *Van Gogh en Gauguin*, 270.

Gauguin obviously agreed with the idea that artists living together was more advantageous. He used the image of sailors who, when they had to move heavy cargo or raise anchor, sing together to keep up one another's spirits and courage, and so that they could endure until the task was complete. That was, in Vincent's view, exactly what artists were missing (June 12, 1888). In his final year, he complained that sufficient friendship was not always found among artists or someone's qualities were exaggerated or too neglected (February 1890).

In May 1888, Vincent hoped, however, that Gauguin would come to Arles and join him as a friend, along with Émile Bernard, and that his own brother Theo would lead a society of impressionists in France. Vincent saw a society of artists in front of him, "the studio of the South" (June 7, 1888), and wanted to found that artists' colony in the house he was going to occupy: the "Yellow House" (January 22, 1889). He also used the image of a ship, the "little ark." He bought twelve (!) chairs with wicker seats for his "Yellow House" (September 9, 1888), a number that recalls Jesus's twelve disciples (September 29, 1888).[49] He called Theo one of the first or *the* first apostle (art) dealer (October 3, 1888). He felt that painters should join together, like the "brothers of the common life" did on the Dutch heaths in their time. Here he had in mind the "modern devotion" with which the name of Thomas à Kempis is connected (August 14, 1888).

He also referred to the collaboration of the modern French writers, the De Goncourt brothers, and their luminous idea of working and thinking in a community (February 14, 1886).[50] The brothers were gloomy, it is true, at the end of their lives, but they were sure of their ground. "Man, they were something! If we get along better than now, why not?" (December 28, 1885 and first half of February 1886). It was his intention that he and his brother set up such a studio and leave a studio that could be continued by others to the next generation (September 17, 1888).

On 1 May 1888 already he spoke about Gauguin perhaps coming south (May 1, 1888), and on 23 October his dream came true when Gauguin arrived in Arles. He hoped for the success of their enterprise and that Gauguin would feel at home. As soon as Gauguin arrived, their conversations revolved around the "fantastic plan for a society of painters" (October 3, 1888). But Gauguin would be the only painter to come, and their living and working together would last no longer than nine weeks

49. Cf. September 9 and 16, 1888.
50. He refers to the Introduction of their book *Chérie*.

(63 days). Vincent saw Gauguin's sudden and swift departure from Arles around Christmas 1888 as a betrayal. Left behind alone in his small yellow house, Vincent was deeply shaken and called Gauguin "the Bonaparte of impressionism." He compared the latter's departure from Arles with the little corporal's return from Egypt: he too had returned to Paris. Because Gauguin had been a sailor, Vincent remarked: "The captain shouldn't be the first to abandon ship, should he?" (January 17, 1889).[51]

That brought him to the book, the *Pêcheur d'Islande* (An Iceland Fisherman) by the French writer Loti (October 28, 1888). Sea voyages play an important role in the stories by this French naval officer who wrote about Brittany (where Gauguin lived before he came to Arles) with its harbors, where women wept for their husbands and sons who never returned from the sea, who grew up to die at sea.[52] *Pecheur d'Islande* is about a fisherman and his young wife whom he married just before his final fatal voyage, and Loti describes the torments of the woman, who waited in vain for the return of her husband. In December 1888 Vincent still hoped the shipwreck of his sailing venture, the "Yellow House" (ark), could be prevented. In his imagination Gauguin and he could prevent such a destructive shipwreck as that described by Loti at the end of his novel.[53] In February 1890, he compared "painting" with the "raft" that "nevertheless comes safely to shore after the shipwreck." He was aware that he had not yet set foot on the shore of a new continent at all, just as Moses himself did not enter the promised land (Deuteronomy 4:21–22) (November 3, 1883).

A Comforting Beacon on Dangerous Seas

In the period before Gauguin's departure from Arles, Vincent made various paintings of Augustine Roulin, the wife of the civil servant Joseph Roulin. The latter, with whom Vincent became close friends, was a civil servant in the post office at the Arles station. Vincent was deeply affected by the prospect of Roulin's transfer to Marseille, where he had been given a new position starting 21 January 1889 (January 22, 1889). Roulin was good for him during his crisis. Although he was not old enough by far to be a father to him, Roulin did have a quiet seriousness and responded with tenderness toward him, like the tenderness an old soldier might feel for a younger one.

51. Cf. Collins, *Van Gogh and Gauguin*, 98.
52. Stolwijk et al., *De Keuze van Vincent*, 57–59.
53. Soth, "Gauguin, Van Gogh," 297.

Roulin continued to correspond with Vincent when he was admitted to Saint Rémy (May 22, August, October 24, 1889).

Between December 1888 and March 1889 Vincent painted Roulin's wife, Augustine, several times as *La Berceuse* (The Rocker). He worked on it in the Christmas season, at the time of his first nervous breakdown, working then on what would become a series of five similar portraits (January 22, 23, 28, 1889). These paintings were intended as an illustration of an old Breton legend. When Breton fishermen were in a storm at sea one night, they suddenly saw a vision: an old woman was sitting in the prow of the boat in front of them singing a cradle song. They were not afraid of her, for they knew that she was "the rocker," the old nanny who rocked them to sleep when they were small and now reappeared to rock them to rest on the tossing boat (January 23, 1889).

In order to have the rocker function as a Madonna in a ship's galley, Vincent wanted to place her in the middle with the two canvasses with sunflowers on the right and left, thus forming a triptych. The yellow and orange tones of the head have more of a sheen because of the yellow panels (May 22, 1889). The sunflowers on both sides serve as floor lamps or candlesticks (January 28, 1889).

Loti's book aroused Vincent's sympathy for fishermen who have to face the dangers of the sea to feed their families. The novel opens with a description of a shrine of the Virgin Mary, the patron saint of fishermen, hanging on the wall of the ship's cabin. An image of the Holy Virgin was fixed in a place of honor, where the midship was divided: she must have listened in fatal hours to many a passionate prayer: at her feet two small bouquets of artificial flowers and a rosary were nailed.[54] Conversations with Gauguin about the Icelanders and their dismal isolation on the dreary seas, exposed to all dangers, led Vincent to the idea of producing a painting that would have the sailors, when they saw it in the ship's cabin, feel a rocking motion reminding them of their own cradle song. The sea is described in that book as a nanny who rocks the sailor in the cradle-like hull of the ship.[55] Vincent saw *La Berceuse* both as a rocking mother with a cradle cord in her hand and as someone who sings a cradle song next to the cradle. By hanging the image on a ship, the ship becomes the cradle that is rocked by the modern Madonna and the fishermen become the children who are rocked, comforted, and protected by her. Vincent tried to paint her in such

54. Edwards, *The Shoes of Van Gogh*, 85–86.
55. Sund, "Van Gogh's *Berceuse*," 215. Akikawa, "La Berceuse," 57–58.

a way that a sailor would feel as if he was thinking of a woman on land while he himself was at sea, just as Mary is a source of comfort for the Icelandic fishermen in Loti's story. Vincent associates his painting of Augustine Roulin, surrounded by colored wallpaper[56] and holding a cradle cord, with the image of the Holy Virgin with flowers and a rosary (January 28, 1889).

Vincent was again inspired, as in Paris, by Frederik van Eeden's *De Kleine Johannes* (Little John), saying that he borrowed the title *De Wiegster* (The Rocker) from Van Eeden (January 23, 1889). He brought Little John's nursery, a room decorated with a pattern of large, gaudily colored flowers, to life again. Vincent's view was that his painting was "very parallel" to Van Eeden and his way of writing, although he himself did it with color.[57]

The decorative background also refers to the decorative tapestry that early Flemish painters painted behind Mary.[58] Vincent said he sang a cradle song while painting, thinking of the woman who rocked the sailors, and hoped that in *La Berceuse* people could hear a melody "in the colors here" (February 3, 1899). He himself, however, called the work badly painted; he found the color prints in the bazaars infinitely better—an allusion to Épinal, a city in Vosges where popular prints were published in the eighteenth century (May 22, 1889).

Savior from the Fear of Death

The dramatic break that occurred between Vincent and Paul Gauguin at the end of 1888 led Vincent to reflect on the "madness" that afflicts many artists. Even though he felt artists like Gauguin and he were somewhat mad, Vincent did feel that he was enough of an artist to stand up to the fear of that. "Everyone has a neurosis at some time, a *horla*, the St. Vitus dance, or something else" (January 28, 1889). In Norman dialect *horla* means "stranger,"[59] a "ghost figure" that appears in Guy de Maupassant's story *The Horla* and falls into a state of paranoia and madness.[60]

---

56. Druick and Zegers, *Van Gogh en Gauguin*, 271, note 22. With references to the Dutch book by Frederik van Eeden, *De kleine Johannes* (*Little John*).

57. Druick and Zegers, *Van Gogh en Gauguin*, 271, and note 22. Van Eeden, *De kleine Johannes*, 7, 140.

58. Jan van Eyck. Cf. Druick and Zegers, *Van Gogh en Gauguin*, 270.

59. Collins, *Van Gogh and Gauguin*, 168.

60. Cf. Guy de Maupassant, *De Horla*, published in 1887. Vincent read it in Paris. Druick and Zegers, *Van Gogh en Gauguin*, note 217.

Looking back at the conflict with Gauguin and his mutilation of his own ear in December 1888, Vincent wrote to Gauguin:

> In my foolishness or nervous illness or madness—I do not have a very good idea of what I should call it or name it—my thoughts have sailed many seas and I have dreamed of the Dutch ghost ship, *The Flying Dutchman*. (January 22, 1889)

The Flying Dutchman (January 22, 1889) is the name of the ship and the captain who sold his soul to the devil and now has to sail a ship manned with the dead with full sail into the wind. Anyone who encounters him is doomed. Vincent later saw his own work as a kind of antidote for the madness that afflicts artists (January 28, 1889). Are artists like Delacroix, Hector Berlioz, and Wagner not all affected by that artists' madness? Nevertheless, Vincent claimed to persevere because, according to him, the antidote and the comfort that they offer were more decisive. "Does not art, after all, just like music, bring comfort to dejected hearts?" January 23, 1889).

It is striking that precisely in that same letter about the ghost ship and the *horla* Vincent included a drawing with symbolic meaning: a fish with *ichtus,* the Greek word for fish, written in it. The early Christians in Rome used this symbol of the fish in the catacombs: each letter has a particular meaning: *Iesous Christos Theou Uios Soter*: Jesus Christ, Son of God, Savior (January 22, 1889).

Empty Chairs

The painting of an empty chair is very suggestive: it represents the owner who has left. In a letter from Isleworth (1876), Vincent quoted the poem *The Three Little Chairs*, which describes two aged parents sitting at their hearth gazing at the empty chairs of their three children who had died (November 25, 1876).[61]

> The Three Little Chairs
> They sat by the bright wood fire,
> The grey-haired dame and the aged sire,
> Dreaming of days gone by;
> The tear-drops fell on each wrinkled cheek,
> They both had thoughts they could not speak,
> And each heart uttered a sigh—

61. Bailey, *Van Gogh in England*, 126.

For their sad and tearful eyes descried
Three little chairs placed side by side

. . .

Then the sire shook his silvery head,
And with trembling voice he gently said:
"Mother, these empty chairs!
They bring us sad, sad thoughts tonight,
We'll put them for ever out of sight,
In the small dark room upstairs."

But she answered: "Father, no not yet,
For I look at them, and I forget
That the children are away;

. . .

"So let them stand there, though empty now,
And every time when alone we bow
At the Father's throne to pray,
We'll ask to meet the children above,
In our Saviour's home of rest and love,
Where no child goes away." (November 25, 1876)

When Vincent's father visited him once in Amsterdam in August 1878, they spent the time in his room looking at his work and discussing all kinds of things. After he brought his father to the station and watched the train until he could no longer see its smoke, he returned to his room and was overcome by emotion, like a small child, as soon as he saw his father's empty chair at the table on which the books and writings of the previous day were still lying (February 1878).

Vincent had already used the image of the empty chair when he was seventeen. Charles Dickens's final, uncompleted novel, *The Mystery of Edwin Drood*,[62] was said to be illustrated by Luke Fildes. Fildes came to Dickens's room on the day he died and the next day (June 10, 1870) drew the study and writing desk with an empty chair. Fildes's *The Empty Chair* appeared in the Christmas issue of *The Graphic* (1870) and Vincent was very much impressed by this memorable image of Dickens (December 11, 1882).

Empty chairs—there are many, and there will be more and sooner or later, instead of Von Herkomer, Fildes, Frank Holl, William Small, etc., only "empty chairs" will be left. Empty chairs are symbols of the mortality of an artist. What they can leave behind is

62. Vincent knew the book. June 10, 1882. Bailey, *Van Gogh in England*, 138.

their work. The illustrators have created the images that accompany modern literature.

Vincent would depict "empty chairs" himself at various times. He painted the empty chairs of Gauguin and himself and thus saluted the English illustrators who inspired him with their work. Vincent said that a few days before Vincent and Gauguin parted in December 1888, when his sickness forced him to enter an institution, he attempted to paint Gauguin's empty chair. In fact, however, he painted this canvas already in November, when there was still nothing that indicated an (official) break between the two—although Vincent did suspect Gauguin's imminent departure (February 10/11, 1890). He also painted his own chair. This chair, of pinewood and completely yellow with a wicker seat, was on a red tile floor in the studio. He gave this chair an everyday appearance. He painted both their empty chairs and called them "quite funny" (November 23, 1888).

In both studies he attempted to attain a light effect through using bright colors. Each chair is intended to be the counterpart of each other. His is much simpler than Gauguin's. He gave the former a "day effect,"[63] using yellow, red, and blue, and Gauguin's a "night effect," red and green, with which both chairs are given their own specific meaning (January 17, 1889).[64]

> The luxury chair has armrests in dark red-brown and the seat is green straw. The carpet has a rich pattern. Against the wall is a burning gas lamp. A burning candle takes the place of the one who is absent. (November 23, 1888)[65]

Yellow and pink books, two modern French novels, are on the chair. The meaning that Vincent gives to the painting of his own chair is clear if it is brought into connection with the two self-portraits from January 1889, where he can be seen with a bandage around his head: *Self-Portrait with Bandaged Ear* and *Self-Portrait with Bandaged Ear and Pipe*. We see here the same elements as in the two paintings of the chairs.

His *Still Life around a Plate of Onions*, done shortly after he left the hospital in Arles, can also be seen as a kind of self-portrait: a candlestick

---

63. Van Uitert et al., *Schilderijen*, 184–85. For a survey of the empty chairs see Kôdera, *Vincent van Gogh*, 154.

64. Werness, "Some Observations," 133.

65. January 17, 1889; February 10/11, 1890. Kooten and Rijnders, *De schilderijen*, 261–62.

(represents light and life), (sprouting) onions, and a pipe with a paper bag of tobacco.[66] The *Almanach de la Santé* (Almanac of Health) on the table is a symbol of his own struggles with his illness and healing through ordinary means (February 3, 1889).[67]

The Struggle to Live

It is striking that Vincent painted a pipe and tobacco. That has to do with a kind of exorcism of his inclination toward suicide. After the departure of his friend Gauguin he painted *Plate with Onions* the following month, which brought elements from both paintings of the chairs together: the burning candle, the earthly onions, a pipe and tobacco, a bottle of wine, and a letter—objects of physical and mental comfort! (April 30, 1889). He put his own name under the onions; that had to have been, for him, an excellent symbol of "his own humble, unpretentious desire for growth and productivity." [68]

To understand the significance of the pipe in this painting, one must keep in mind how often Van Gogh referred to smoking. When he worked in the art shop in The Hague in March 1873, he recommended that Theo smoke a pipe. "It's good whenever you get annoyed, as happens to me quite often now." In 1876, at the boarding school in Isleworth, he often, for example, smoked a pipe late in the evening. "The tobacco is quite dreary here" (March 17, 1873).

Vincent often referred to his inclination toward suicide. After he had brought someone to the station in Amsterdam in August 1879 and put him on the train, he breakfasted on a piece of dry bread and a glass of beer:

> That is a means Dickens recommends to those who are the point
> of committing suicide as very suited to making them abandon that
> resolution at least for some time. (August 17, 1877)

After he fell passionately in love for some time with Kee Vos and had recovered from his infatuation in the winter of 1882 in The Hague, he was overcome by an inexpressible melancholy. He then reflected a great deal

66. Kooten and Rijnders, *De schilderijen*, 261–62.

67. *Manuel Annuaire de la Santé* by F.H. Raspail. Maurer, *The Pursuit of Spiritual Wisdom*, 82.

68. Druick and Zegers, *Van Gogh en Gauguin*, 268.

about something "Father" Millet said: "I have always thought that suicide was an act of a dishonest man." Vincent himself thought that

> the emptiness, the inexpressible misery inside me allows me to think and understand that there are people who jump into the water—but he far from approves of such and finds something to hold on to in that word mentioned and by seeking a remedy through work. (July 6, 1882)

In the fall of 1883, during his lonely stay in Drenthe, Vincent spoke of times of great melancholy and the notion of suicide, but he did not view it as appropriate for Theo and himself. "May our conscience keep us from that" (July 6, 1882).

Back in Nuenen in November 1883, he drew *Young Man with a Pipe*.[69] In the summer of 1887 in Paris, when he was afraid that he would not be able to live off his painting and lacked the desire to marry and have children, he was so completely disheartened that he was ready to commit suicide when he was thirty-five. He sometimes blamed the miserable profession of painting for this, and he referred to the French poet and writer Jean Richepin: "Love for art makes true love disappear." But he also wrote: "It's better to enjoy life than to do away with yourself" (summer, 1887).

In August 1888, in Arles, he proposed that one should be able to live on a piece of bread, despite working the whole day, and one should still have the strength to smoke and drink a glass "for you need that in those circumstances. Then life is almost a delight." He also advised his painter friend Bernard to smoke a pipe in peace and quiet and to drink coffee. The next year, when he was in the institution in Saint Rémy, he wrote how religion had brought him much fear for many years and that the feeling of emptiness and tiredness had made him depressed. He suggested that remorse and guilt were possibly bacteria, just like love.

> I take the remedy that the incomparable Dickens prescribed for suicide every day. That remedy consists of a glass of wine, a piece of bread and cheese, and a pipe of tobacco. (April 30, 1889)[70]

The doctor treating him added the following to a letter Vincent wrote to Theo

---

69. Van Heugten, *Vincent van Gogh*, 99.
70. Dickens actually talks about beer.

to tell you that he has recovered from his crisis completely, that he has returned to complete presence of mind, and that he has begun to paint again as before. His suicidal tendencies have disappeared; only upsetting dreams still remain, and they are already showing signs of disappearing and decreasing in intensity. (September 3/4, 1889)[71]

In September 1889 Vincent wrote that he was attempting to become better, "just as everyone who wants to commit suicide but attempts to reach the bank because he finds the water too cold" (September 7/8, 1889).

In addition to tobacco and alcohol, writers also constituted a remedy for melancholy. When Vincent felt the need to have a good laugh, he read Guy de Maupassant and Voltaire (summer, autumn, 1887).[72] Vincent cited Voltaire various times, both in Saint Rémy and earlier, in Arles and Paris. A statement by the philosopher ("Father Pangloss") from Voltaire's *Candide* became his motto: "Everything is going as good as it conceivably can, in the best of all possible worlds" (August 1886). Vincent calls Pangloss "an excellent optimist" (May 3, 1888). Nevertheless, the advice of Dickens, "Father Pangloss," and others would not ultimately avail and he would die "smoking his pipe."[73]

Working to Distraction

Before and after the crisis around Christmas 1888 in Arles, when he cut off his ear, Vincent cited various other painters who had worked to the point of distraction, such as Henri de Braekeleer, Jules Dupré, Adolphe J.T. Monticelli, Torquato Tasso, and, in particular, Hugo van der Goes. In Antwerp, Vincent had seen the work of the Belgian painter Henri de Braekeleer (November 25-27, 1885), who was considered to be a herald of the advent of impressionism. He called him a famous colorist and someone who engaged in rigorous analysis (December 8-15, 1885). His serious mental illness between 1880 and 1884 had an enormous influence on his style: the colors receive livelier accents and light effects.[74] He also read that Jules Dupré,

71. Hammacher, *Van Gogh*, 197.

72. Sund, *True to Temperament*, 140.

73. Du Quesne-Van Gogh, *Vincent van Gogh*, 69.

74. Cf. *Grote Winkler Prins Encyclopedie, s.v.* July 20, 1873. He is one of the painters that Vincent loves, January 1874.

a French painter and engraver of the Barbizon school, seemed to be mad (end of October 1885).

He also thought a great deal about Adolphe Joseph Thomas Monticelli:

> A great man—somewhat crazy and not just a little bit either—dreaming of the sun, love, and joy, but always tormented by poverty, with an extremely refined feeling for coloration, a rare type of man. Very sadly, he died in Marseille, probably after having gone through a true Gethsemane.

Vincent was certain that he was continuing Monticelli's work in Arles, as if he was his son or brother (August 27, 1888). He disputed the idea that Monticelli died of alcohol consumption and quoted a doctor who told him that he had found Monticelli "always eccentric," but that he was only "a bit insane" at the end (July 6, 1889). Van Gogh also reflected on Alfred Bruyas, an art collector and patron with a striking influence on the impressionists who worked in the south. He left his collection to the Musée Fabre in Montpellier (January 7, 1889), to which Gauguin took Vincent about the middle of December 1888 (second half of December 1888).[75] Certain portraits by Bruyas moved him, and he saw how sad and tormented his face was. Vincent told Gauguin he owed Bruyas a great deal and, while he saw himself following in Monticelli's footsteps, he was following even more in Bruyas's (January 7 and 9, 1889).[76]

He also mentioned the Italian painter Torquato Tasso and referred to the portrait *Tasso in Prison* by Delacroix. Tasso was kept in an institution for seven years because he displayed symptoms of paranoia. Delacroix portrayed him in the psychiatric asylum as a man with a red beard and hair, the very picture of the oppressed, ridiculed, and misunderstood artist.[77]

Vincent also cited the example of the Flemish painter Hugo van der Goes in connection with "artist's madness" in Arles. In the summer of 1888 he discovered that he looked as wild as Van der Goes, as painted by the Belgian Émile Charles Wauters. Van der Goes entered holy orders at the height of his career and had a mental collapse five years later. The prior attempted to heal him through musical performances. Wauters's painting *The Madness of Hugo van der Goes* depicts one of those therapy sessions: Van der Goes in the foreground is painted in dramatic fashion, unshaven,

75. The visit did cause a change in his thoughts. September 5/6, 1889. Hammacher, *Van Gogh*, 169.

76. Cf. Stolwijk et al., *De Keuze van Vincent*, 252–54.

77. Jobert et al., *Delacroix*, 62, 118.

wide-eyed, and wringing his hands, while a self-satisfied calm priest directs a choir.[78] Vincent thinks that he is more like the calm abbot in the painting than like the insane painter (July 25, 1888).

That theme of "artist's madness" kept coming up in his correspondence in the last half year of his life. After his admittance to the hospital in Arles at Christmas he hoped that he would have nothing more than "an ordinary artist's eccentricity," with a high fever afterwards as a result of a loss of a great deal of blood because an artery had been cut (January, 7, 1889). When he was kept in quarantine in Arles at a certain point, he wrote that he would rather die than cause and experience so many problems (February 3, 1889). He held that "suffering without complaining" was the only lesson one had to learn in this life (April 10, 1889)[79] and referred to a very old tomb not far away, predating Christ, on which was written: "Blessed be Thebe, daughter of Telhui, priestess of Osiris, who never complained about anyone" (January 7, 1889). The "true South"—is that not more or less where one finds sufficient wisdom, patience, and peace of mind to be like that good Thebe? (March 29, 1889).[80]

At the end of April 1889, he wanted to be admitted to the psychiatric institution, Saint Paul de Mausole in Saint Rémy. The Protestant minister Frédéric Salles spoke to him about that (April 21, 1889): he hoped that the nature in Saint Rémy would do him more good than the medicine (April 24, 1889). His fear of insanity decreased considerably when he saw those who were insane close up (May 22, 1889).

In June 1889 the final paintings made Theo think about the state of mind in which they were made. He spoke of the rare rich coloring, which Vincent had never before attained and was of a quality he had not previously attained.

> But how that head of yours must have worked and how you ventured to the utmost, where dizzy spells are unavoidable.

At the same time Theo was worried:

---

78. Rudolf Wittkoper and Margot Wittkoper, *Born under Saturn : The Character and Conduct of Artists* (New York: W W Norton & Company Incorporated, 1969), 108–13. Cf. Collins, *Van Gogh and Gauguin*, 110.

79. He wrote to his painter friend Paul Signac, who had visited him.

80. Cf. April 30, July 2, 1889.

> For you should not venture into those mysterious regions you can approach but cannot enter with impunity before you are completely healed. (June 16, 1889)

Vincent toiled like one possessed; he had an insane rage to work like never before (September 5/6, 1889). He saw work as a remedy, the best lightning rod to divert the illness. He did believe that healing could come by a great resignation to suffering and death through distancing oneself from one's own will and self-love. But that was not for him, however. He liked to paint, liked to see people and everything that was part of their lives. True life was perhaps something else, but he did not believe that he belonged to the category of those who were prepared to suffer at any time (September 7/8, 1889).

Over time, the environment of Saint Rémy began to close in on him in an inexpressible way. After more than a year of having patience, he wrote:

> I have to get out of here, I am dying of boredom and grief here. Dear brother, my patience is at an end, I can't do it any more, I have to go somewhere else, even if it is only an emergency measure. I have not done anything to anybody; is it right then to supervise me like a dangerous animal? No, thank you. I object to that. It makes me so sad to leave in this way that the sadness will be greater than the madness; I also think I have the necessary self-confidence. (May 4, 1889)

The emotions that overtook him when looking at nature took him to the edge of oblivion, with the result that he was not able to work for fourteen days (February 10/11, 1890).[81] He saw himself as "battered in the struggle for life" (February 20, 1890). In May 1890 he wanted to return north, thinking he would recover quickly there (May 2, 1890). Nevertheless, as soon as he arrived in Auvers, he felt he was a failure. He thought it was his lot to accept that fact (May 23, 1890). He wrote at the beginning of the final month of his life:

> I still love art and life very much, even though I don't know absolutely but also do know absolutely that I am on the mend. (July 2, 1890)

Already much earlier, in February 1883 in The Hague, he declared that life was merely "a kind of fertilization time . . . and the harvest [was] not here" (February 8, 1883). He was worried and felt dejected because his

---

81. In a letter to Aurier.

brother, who provided for him, thought about leaving his position in the art business. He saw his daily bread in danger, understood the vulnerability of both their lives, and was afraid of being a burden to his brother Theo and his wife. A reassuring letter from his sister-in-law Jo after his visit to Paris was, to him, "a true Gospel, a liberation from the fear he had experienced." It was living proof for him that Theo and Jo understood that he worked and toiled away as hard as they did.

When he had returned to Auvers from visiting Theo and his wife in Paris on 10 July 1890, he went back to work, although the brush almost fell out of his hands. He painted vast grainfields under wild skies and deliberately attempted to bring sadness and extreme loneliness to expression (July 10, 1890).

Christ the Greatest Artist

Vincent spoke about Christ in various ways and at different times. He drew a comparison between Jesus and Socrates and cited Michelet approvingly:

> Socrates arrived in the world as a true sensualist, but he changed so completely through devotion to duty, work, and abandoning insignificant matters that, in the end, face to face with his judges and death, there was something of a god in him, a ray from on high that sheds light on the Parthenon. (January 19, 1889)

He also saw the same phenomenon in Jesus, who started out as just a working man and worked his way up to something else:

> A personality so full of pity, love, goodness, and seriousness that people were attracted by it. In many cases, a carpenter's son becomes a carpenters' boss: narrow-minded, dry, miserly, vain, and, whatever Jesus may be, he looked at things differently from my friend the carpenter on the wharf at Scheveningen, who worked his way up to rack-renter and is quite a bit more pedantic and frets about himself more than Jesus did. (July 27, 1883)

Vincent thinks that the Christian idea of being prepared for death was not shared by Jesus (May 28, 1888). Few literary works would, in his view, find grace in Christ's eyes, except for the gospel of Luke, "so simple in its austere and militant form" (June 23, 1888).

Luke, the writer of the third gospel and the author of the book of Acts, was one of the apostle Paul's co-workers. In addition to being an evangelist, he was also a doctor and above all a painter. The symbol for Luke is the ox. Vincent cites Gustave Doré here: "I have the patience of an ox." He saw something positive here, a resolute honesty.

> Would you not have patience, not learn patience from nature, learn patience from watching the grain slowly grow? . . . If you want to grow, you must fall into the ground. (October 28, 1883)

Since the fifth century, the four evangelists—Matthew, Mark, Luke, and John—have been presented as a tetramorph. That was influenced by the Eastern presentation of the guardians of the four corners of the earth or those supporting the heavens at the four sides of the firmament, a notion going back to the star symbols of the zodiac. The last book of the Bible, Revelation, speaks of four creatures around the throne of God.

> The first creature looked like a lion and the second like an ox; the third had a face like a man, and the fourth resembled a flying eagle. (Revelation 4:7)

The church father Jerome provided the following reasons for the image as follows:

> Matthew has the winged man as symbol because his message begins with Christ becoming man. Mark has the lion because his gospel begins with "the voice of one calling in the desert": John the Baptist. Luke is connected with the sacrificial animal, the ox, because he talks about the priest Zechariah at the beginning of his gospel; John, finally, has the eagle as his symbol, for "the flight of the spirit up to the highest regions" stands out in his gospel.[82]

Vincent knew and admired *Luke Painting the Virgin* by the northern Dutch painter Maarten van Heemskerck.[83] Since the sixth century, the writer of the third gospel, Luke, has also been called a painter. According to tradition, he painted not only the Madonna but also Christ.[84]

Vincent reminded his painter friend Bernard of the fact that the patron saint of painters, Luke—doctor, painter, and evangelist—with nothing more than an ox as his symbol, gives us hope (June 23, 1888).

> The life of our painters pines away under the exhausting yoke of the problems of a profession that almost cannot be practiced on

82. *Prisma van de symbolen, s.v.*, evangelistensymbolen.

83. Vincent knew his work and admired it together with Frans Hals. Druick and Zegers, *Van Gogh en Gauguin*, 228, 373, note 207.

84. Kirshbaum, *Lexikon*, 119–22.

this ungrateful planet and where love for art forces out true love.
If you want to cultivate the land of art, you have to be as patient as
an ox. (June 18, 1888)

Oxen are lucky in that they do not have to work in the miserable profession
of painting. That is why it does Vincent good as a painter to be an ox, and
he admires the ox, the eagle (symbol for John), and the man (symbol for
Matthew) (June 24, 1888).[85]

The problem of the painter's life with regard to material goods made
it, according to Vincent, desirable for painters to work together and form
a society as in the time of the Guild of St. Luke (July 17, 1888), the guild
of artists and craftsmen who placed themselves under the protection of St.
Luke. Such a guild also existed in Amsterdam, co-founded by the painter
Jan Toorop. The artists' guild celebrated the poem by Joost van de Vondel,
which Vincent also knew:

> Like the sunflower that turns its eyes
> to heaven's arch out of love and
> follows with its face
> the all-quickening light,
> the sun, that gives it all its color
>
> and lives there with tree and plant,
> so the art of painting follows
> of its own innate goodwill,
> ignited by a holy fire,
> the beauty of nature.[86]

God as Light, Christ as Sun

On 23 June Vincent wrote a long letter to his painter friend Émile Bernard,
in which he asserts that, in his view, Christ is the heart of the Bible:

> Only Christ, of all the philosophers, has affirmed eternal life, the
> infinity of time, the insignificance of death, the necessity and
> meaning of serenity and devotion, as the most important certainty.
> . . . That is why he, as an artist, is greater than all other artists. He
> scorns marble, clay, and paint, working only with living flesh. The
> peerless Christ does not make any statues, paintings, or books but

85. Cf. Druick and Zegers, *Van Gogh en Gauguin*, 122.
86. Quoted by Druick and Zegers, *Van Gogh en Gauguin*, 77.

living people, immortals. This great artist did not write any books either. Christian literature as a whole would undoubtedly provoke his ire. Few literary works, apart from the gospel of Luke and the letters of Paul, would have found favor in his eyes. . . . This artist did not concern himself with writing books about ideas (feelings), had a great deal less contempt for the spoken word, especially the parable (what a sower, what a harvest, what a fig tree!)[87] . . . . "Heaven and earth may pass away, but my words will never pass away" (Mark 13:1, 2, 31). These spoken words, which he did not even deign to write down, form one of the high points reached by art. Pure creative power . . . . These thoughts, my dear friend Bernard, raise us above art itself. They give us a glance at creating the art of life, at the art of being immortally alive. (June 23, 1888)

Only in the south of France, in Arles, did what he talked about for so many years come to fruition, i.e. the portrayal of light. The amateur painter Anton Kerssemakers remembered Vincent from his Nuenen period:

He stops, suddenly, for a beautiful sunset and, using both hands to shut it out somewhat and with his eyes half closed, exclaims: "How does someone or God, or whatever you want to call Him, do that? How is He is doing it now? We should be able to do that too. God, God, is that ever beautiful, what a shame that we do not have a palette ready, for it will be gone immediately."[88]

"Those who do not believe in the sun from here must be very godless," Vincent thought (August 11, 1888). He remembered that light, space, and color were the essential things in the work of "the unsurpassed painter of the light, Johannes Vermeer," who knew, already two centuries before impressionism, how to paint light through color. In August 1889, he worked in Arles like an insane man to paint light, with yellow as the basic color.[89]

The heavenly dome is of wondrously beautiful blue, the rays of the sun are of pale sulphur yellow, and it is soft and friendly like the combination of sky blue and yellow as in Vermeer. (September 17, 1888)

A month later he wrote to Bernard that he had been looking at the sun becoming brighter for months. That this put him on a special path was confirmed in January 1890 by the art critic Albert Aurier in *Mercure de*

87. Cf. December 26, 1878 in the Borinage.
88. Kôdera, *Vincent van Gogh*, 106, note 65.
89. La fondametale du jaune.

France. The latter was the only important critic of Vincent's work during his life. He called Vincent's directing the viewer's gaze straight to the sun a bold move.[90]

> It remains a fact that I had to work a bit beyond my powers to reach the high yellow note that I reached this summer. If a prison or institution is my lot, why not? (March 24, 1889)

In one of his last letters, possibly the last one, Vincent wrote:

> Well, my work, I risked my life for that, and it has cost me half my mind. Fine, but as far as I know and as far as I can judge, you are not one of those who deals in people. I think you deal in art in a truly human way. (July 24, 1890)

He testifies "to the point of distraction" how the darkness would be overcome by the light of the sun, the symbol of Christ and of God. After all, God is an artist whose work does indeed appear to have failed, or at any rate did not succeed very well. Nonetheless, precisely because one loved the artist and because of his great artistry, God could certainly be expected to fix it!

> I believe more and more that we should not judge God according to this world, for that is a study he did that did not succeed very well. What do you want? If you like the artist, then you can't find any fault with his failed works. Then keep quiet. But you do have the right to demand better. We should, however, see other works by the same hand. This world is of course a rush job, made in one of the unfortunate moments in which the maker no longer knew what he was doing, whose mind was elsewhere. What the legend of our dear Lord tells us is that he did his very best in his study of the world. I am inclined to believe that the legend is based on truth, but the study has been botched in many ways. Only great masters can make such mistakes; that is perhaps the greatest comfort, for then you have reason to hope that the same creative hand will return in the end with an even greater intensity to set things right. (May 26, 1888)[91]

90. Aurier, "Les Isolé." Hammacher and Hammacher, *Van Gogh*.

91. Cf. Edwards, "Van Gogh's Spiritual Quest," 252. Vincent's original sentence (in French) reads: "Il n'y a que les maîtres pour se tromper ainsi, voila peutêtre la meilleure consolation vu que dès lors on est en droit d'espérer voir prendre sa revanche par la même main creatrice."

BIBLIOGRAPHY

Abrams, M.H., general editor. *The Norton Anthology of English Literature*. 6th ed. Volume 2. New York/London: Norton & Company, 1993.

Akikawa, Haruo. "La Berceuse. An Interpretation of Vincent van Gogh's Portraits." *Annual Bulletin of the National Museum of Western Art* (1981) 31–69.

Amiel, Alain. *Vincent Van Gogh aux Saintes-Maries-de-la-Mer*. No pages. Online: http://www.vangoghaventure.com. 2005.

Aurier, G. Albert. "Les Isolés: Vincent van Gogh." *Mercure de France* I/1 (January 1890) 24–29.

Avert, Frans van der, and Heleen van Ketwick Verschuur. *Stad & land. 19de-eeuwse meesterwerken uit het Stedelijk Museum*. Amsterdam: De Nieuwe Kerk, 2003.

Ayala, Roselyne de, and Jean-Pierre Guéno. *Belles Lettres: Manuscripts by the Masters of French Literature*. New York: Abrams, 2001.

Bailey, Martin. "Vincent van Gogh, the Writer." *The Art Newspaper* 35 (February 1994) 16–17.

———. *Van Gogh in England: Portrait of the Artist as a Young Man*. London: Barbican Art Gallery, 1992.

Bank, Jan. "Afscheid van domineesland." *De negentiende Eeuw* XX/4 (1996) 229–46.

Beecher Stowe, Harriet E. *Uncle Tom's Cabin; or, Life Among the Lowly*. First edition 1852.

Berlage, H.P. "Levensbericht van Dr. J.P. Stricker." *Levensberichten der Afgestorvene Medeleden van de Maatschappij der Nederlandse Letterkunde. Bijlage tot de handeling van 1887*, 27–55. Leiden: Brill, 1887.

Bernard, Marc. *Émile Zola in Selbstzeugnissen und Bilddokumenten*. Hamburg: Rowohlt, 1982.

Biedermann, Hans. *Prisma van de symbolen. Historisch-culturele symbolen van A tot Z verklaard*. 4th print. Utrecht: Spectrum, 1993.

Boime, Albert. "Van Gogh, Thomas Nast and the Social Role of the Artist." In *Van Gogh 100*, edited by Joseph D. Mascheck, 71–111. Westport, Connecticut: Greenwood Press, 1996.

———. "Van Gogh's Starry Night: A History of Matter and a Matter of History." *Arts Magazine* (December 1984) 86–103.

Bonger, Jo. "Introduction." In Vincent van Gogh. *De Brieven van Vincent van Gogh*. Edited by Han van Crimpen and Monique Berends-Albert, 1–42. The Hague: SDU, 1990.

Bowman, Frank Paul. *Le Christ des Barricades, 1789–1848*. Paris: Cerf, 1987.

Bracquemond, F. *Du dessin et de la couleur*. Paris: Charpentier, 1885.

Breton, Jules. *Les Champs et la Mer*. Paris: Charpentier, 1875.

Brink, G. van den, and W.T.M. Frijhoff. *De wevers en Vincent van Gogh*. Zwolle: Waanders, 1990.

Bibliography

Brom, Gerard. *De Dominee in onze cultuur*. Nijmegen/Utrecht: Dekker, Van de Vecht & Van Leeuwen, 1924.

———. *Schilderkunst in de 19e eeuw*. Utrecht/Antwerp: Spectrum, 1959.

Brontë, Charlotte. *Shirley*. London: Penguin Books, 1994.

Brouwer, Ton de. *Van Gogh en Nuenen*. Venlo: Van Spijk, 1984.

Bullen, J.B., editor. *The Sun is God: Painting, Literature, and Mythology in the Nineteenth Century*. Oxford: Clarendon Press/New York: Oxford University Press, 1989.

Bungener, Louis. *Het Kerstfeest aan de Pool of God overal. Een nieuw Kerstverhaal*. Utrecht: J.H. van Peursen, 1873.

Bunyan, John. *The Pilgrim's Progress From this World to that which is to Come* (1678). World Classics edition. Oxford: Oxford University Press, 1984.

Buser, Thomas. *Religious Art in the Nineteenth Century in Europe and America*. Book 1. Studies in Art and Religious Interpretation. Volume 28a. Lewiston, New York: The Edwin Mellen Press. 2002.

———. "Van Gogh as a Religious Artist." *Gazette des Beaux Arts* 131 (July–August 1989) 41–50.

Cachin, Françoise, and Bogomila Welsh-Ovcharov. *Van Gogh à Paris*. Edition de la Union. Paris: Musée d'Orsay, 1988.

Callow, Philip. *Vincent van Gogh. Een leven*. Amsterdam: Bert Bakker, 2003.

Carlyle, Thomas. *Heroes, Hero-Worship and the Heroic in History*. London: Chapman and Hall, 1913.

———. *Sartor Resartus. On Heroes and Hero Worship*. London/New York: Dent & Sons, 1959.

———. *Zes lezingen over helden, helderverering en heldengeest in de geschiedenis*. Translated by J. Wesselink-van Rossum. Wereldbibliotheek. Amsterdam: mij. voor goede en goedkoope lectuur, n.d.

Carpenter, Mary Wilson. *George Eliot and the Landscape of Time: Narrative Form and Protestants Apocalyptic History*. Chapel Hill/London: University of North Carolina, 1986.

Cochin, Henry. "Boccace d'après ses oeuvres et les témoignages contemporains." *La Revue des deuxmondes* (15 July 1888) 373–413.

Cocquiot, Gustave. *Vincent van Gogh*. Paris: Ollendorff, 1923.

Collins, Bradley. *Van Gogh and Gauguin. Electric Arguments and Utopian Dreams*. Boulder, Colorado/Oxford: Westview, 2004.

Conradi, Henk. *Vincent van Gogh. Verborgen aspecten van zijn levensverhaal*. Groningen: Boomker Haren, 2002.

Cossée, E.H. "De gehele godsdienst behoort het gevoel. Romantische elementen in kerk en theologie." *De Negentiende Eeuw* 8 (October 1984) 91–107.

———. "Vincent van Gogh en kerkelijk Dordrecht." *Kwartaal en teken van Dordrecht* VI/1 (1980) 1–5.

Davis, Paul. *Charles Dickens A to Z. The Essential Reference to his Life and Work*. New York: Checkmark Books, 1999.

Dekkers, Diewertje. *Jozef Israëls 1824–1911*. Zwolle: Waanders, 2000.

Dewilde, Jan, and Jean-Marie Duvosquel. *Charles Degroux en het realisme*. Gent: Snoeck-Ducaju & Zoon, 1995.

Dickens, Charles. *The Christmas Books*. Volume 1. *A Christmas Carol;The Chimes*. New York, etc.: Penguin, 1971.

——. *The Christmas Books.* Volume 2. *The Cricket on the Hearth; The Battle of Life; The Haunted Man.* Middlesex: Penguin, 1971.

——. *The Christmas Books.* Volume 3. *The Cricket on the Hearth.* New York, etc.: Penguin, 1971.

——. *Hard Times.* London: Penguin, 2003.

——. *Little Dorrit.* London, etc.: Penguin Classics, 2003.

——. *The Mystery of Edwin Drood.* New York, etc.: Penguin, 1974.

——. *Oliver Twist.* London: Penguin, 1966.

——. *The Pickwick Papers.* New York: Heritage, 1938.

——. *A Tale of Two Cities.* London: Penguin, 1970.

Dijk, Wout J., and Meent W. van der Sluis. *De Drentste tijd van Vincent van Gogh. Een onderbelichte periode nader onderzocht.* Groningen: Boon, 2001.

Dirven, Ron, and Kees Wouters, editors. *Vincent van Gogh: Verloren Vondsten. Het mysterie van de Bredase kisten.* Breda: Breda's Museum, 2003.

Dorn, Roland, et al. *Van Gogh. Die Porträts.* Cologne: Dumont, 2000.

——. *Vincent van Gogh en de moderne kunst.* Zwolle: Waanders/Essen: Museum Folkwang/Amsterdam: Van Gogh Museum, 1991.

Druick, Douglas W., and Peter Kort Zegers. Together with Brit Salvesen. *Van Gogh en Gauguin.* Amsterdam: Van Gogh Museum, 2002.

Dürer, Albrecht. *Albrecht Dürer.* 1471- 1528. *Das gesamte graphische Werk. Handzeichnungen.* Introduction by Wolfgang Hüt. Munich: Rogner & Bernard, 1971.

Edwards, Clifford Walter. *The Shoes of Van Gogh. (With Reflections on the Artist by Henri Nouwen).* New York: Crossroad, 2004.

——. *Van Gogh and God. A Creative Spiritual Quest.* Chicago, Illinois: Loyola University Press, 1989.

——. "Van Gogh's Spiritual Quest: Toward a Theology of Vulnerability." In *Van Gogh 100.* Edited by Joseph D. Masheck, 251–8. Westport, Connecticut: Greenwood, 1996.

Eeden, Frederik van. *De kleine Johannes.* Amsterdam: Querido, 1986.

Eliot, George. *Felix Holt. The Radical.* Middlesex: Penguin Books, 1972.

——. *Middlemarch.* New York: Penguin, 1965.

——. *Scenes of Clerical Life.* Edited with an Introduction by Jennifer Gribble. London: Penguin Classics, 1998.

——. *Silas Marner, the Weaver of Raveloe.* First published in 1861. London: Penguin Classics, 1996.

Erftemeijer, Antoon F.W. "Ware werkelijkeid." In *De Godsbeelden van Van Gogh en Mondriaan vergeleken,* edited by Erik L.H.M. van de Loo, et al., 96–130. *Kunst van geloven.* Baarn: Ambo, 1996.

Erickson, Kathleen Powers. *At Eternity's Gate: the Spiritual Vision of Vincent van Gogh.* Grand Rapids: Eerdmans, 1998.

——. "Images After Delacroix." *Christianity and the Arts* (Summer 2000) 14–17.

——. "*Imitation of Christ.* The Book that Influenced Van Gogh." *Christianity and the Arts* (Summer 2009) 9–12.

——. "Testimony to Theo: Van Gogh's Witness of Faith." *Church History* 61/2 (June 1992) 206–20.

——. "Van Gogh's Evangelical Faith." *Christianity and the Arts* (Summer 2000) 6–8.

Ewals, Leo J.I. *Ary Scheffer, 1795–1858: Gevierd Romanticus.* Zwolle: Waanders, 1996.

——. *Ary Scheffer bewonderd door Vincent van Gogh.* Dordrecht: Dordrechts Museum, 1990.

Bibliography

Gachet, Paul-Ferdinand. Étude sur la mélancholie. Paris: unknown, 1864.

Gasten, Andrea. "De poëzie van het Weversbestaan: Enkele literaire invloeden bij Vincent van Gogh." In *De wevers en Vincent van Gogh*, edited by G. van den Brink and W. Frijhoff, 97–103. Zwolle: Waanders, 1990.

Gauguin, Paul. *Avant en Après*. First edition 1903. Paris: G. Crès, 1923.

Gayford, Martin. *The Yellow House. Van Gogh, Gauguin and Nine Turbulent Weeks in Arles*. London: Fig Tree/Penguin, 2006.

Génestet, P.A. de. *De Dichtwerken van P.A. de Génestet*. Collected and published under supervision of C.P. Tiele. 8th reprint. Amsterdam: Elsevier, 1888.

Gibson, Michael. *Symbolisme*. Cologne, et al.: Taschen, 2006.

Gogh, Vincent van. *De Brieven van Vincent van Gogh*. Introduction by Jo Bonger. Edited by Han van Crimpen and Monique Berends-Albert, 1–42. The Hague: SDU, 1990.

Gogh, Vincent van and J. van Gogh-Bonger. *Verzamelde brieven van Vincent van Gogh*. Amsterdam, etc.: Wereldbibliotheek, 1973.

Goncourt, Edmond de, and Jules H. de Goncourt. *L'Art du dix-huitième siècle*. 2 volumes. Paris: Quantin, 1873–1874.

——. *Germinie Lacerteux*. Paris: Carpentier, 1864.

——. *Manette Salomon*. 2 volumes. Paris: Librairie Internationale, 1867.

Graetz, H.R. *The Symbolic Language of Vincent van Gogh*. New York/Toronto/London: Mc Graw Hill, 1963.

Greer, Joan Eileen. *The Artist as Christ; The Image of the Artist in the Netherlands, 1885–1902, with a Focus on the Christological Imagery of Vincent van Gogh and Johan Thorn Prikker*. Dissertation, Free University Amsterdam, 2000.

——. "'Een man van smerten en de versocht in krankheyt.' Het christologische beeld van de kunstenaar in Van Goghs *Stilleven met open bijbel*." *Jong Holland* 3 (1997) 30–42.

Groot, Reindert, and Sjoerd de Vries. *Vincent van Gogh in Amsterdam*. Amsterdam: Stadsuitgeverij, 1990.

Grote Winkler Prins Encyclopedie in 25 delen. 8th reprint. Amsterdam/Brussels: Elsevier, 1979 on.

Hammacher, A.M. "Van Gogh-Michelet-Zola." *Vincent Bulletin* 4/3 (1975) 2–21.

——, and R. Hammacher. *Van Gogh. A Documentary Biography*. New York: Macmillan, 1976.

Hecht, Peter. *Vincent van Gogh en Rembrandt*. Amsterdam: Van Gogh Museum/Brussels: Mercatorfonds, 2006.

Hendriks, Ella, and Louis van Tilborgh. *New Views on Van Gogh's Development in Antwerp and Paris. An Integrated Art Historical and Technical Study of his Paintings in the Van Gogh Museum*. Academic thesis, University of Amsterdam, 2006.

Hermans, Theu, et al. *Ik voel mij thuis daar. Opstellen over het leven en werk van Vincent van Gogh in Nuenen*. Nuenen: Heemkundekring De Drijerhornick, 2003.

Herzogenrath, Wulf, and Dorothee Hansen. *Van Gogh: Fields. The Field with Poppies and the Artist's Dispute*. Bremen: Hatje Cantz, 2002.

Heteren, Marjan van, et al. *The Poetry of Reality. Dutch Painters of the Nineteenth Century*. Zwolle: Waanders/Amsterdam: Rijksmusem, 2000.

Heugten, Sjraar van. *Van Gogh tekenaar. De meesterwerken*. Amsterdam: Van Gogh Museum/Brussels: Mercatorfonds, 2005.

——. *Vincent van Gogh. Tekeningen. Nuenen 1883–1885*. Volume 2. Amsterdam: Van Gogh Museum, 1997.

Hoekstra, Hidde. *Het Oude Testament.* Part 1. *De Aartstvaders.* Utrecht/Antwerp: Spectrum, 1975.

———. *Rembrandt en de Bijbel; Het Nieuwe Testament.* Volume 1: *Het Kerstevangelie.* Volume 2: *Jezus van Nazareth.* Volume 3: *Kruis en opstanding.* Utrecht/Antwerp: Spectrum, 1975.

Hoffmann, K. "Zu van Goghs Sonneblumenbildern." *Zeitschrift für Kunstgeschichte* 31/1 (1968) 27–58.

Hooft, F.L. van 't. "Johannes Paulus Stricker." *Biografisch Lexicon voor de geschiedenis van het Nederlandse protestantisme.* Volume 3. Kampen: Kok, 1988.

Hugo, Victor. *L'Homme qui Rit.* First edition 1869.

———. *Quatrevingt-treize.* First edition 1874. Paris: Classiques Garnier, 1957.

———. *William Shakespeare.* First edition 1864.

Huizinga, J. "De Groninger Richting." *Verzamelde Werken.* Volume VIII, 139–63. Haarlem: Tjeenk Willink, 1951.

Hulsker, Jan. *Lotgenoten. Het leven van Vincent en Theo van Gogh.* Weesp: Agathon, 1985.

———. *Van Gogh en zijn weg. Het complete werk.* 3rd print. Amsterdam: Meulenhoff, 1985.

———. *Van Gogh in Close-up.* Amsterdam: Meulenhoff, 1993.

Hütt, Wolfgang. *Albrecht Dürer. 1471 bis 1528. Das gesamte graphische Werk - Band 2: Druckgraphik.* Volume 2. Munich: Rogner & Bernhard, 1971.

Jansen, Leo. "Literatuur als leidraad: Vincent van Gogh als lezer." *Literatuur* 20 (2003) 20–26.

———. "Van Gogh en de letterkunde." *Literatuur* 20 (2003) 19.

———, and Jan Robert. *Kort geluk. De briefwisseling tussen Theo van Gogh en Jo Bonger.* Amsterdam: Van Gogh Museum/Zwolle: Waanders, 1999.

Jobert, Barthelemy, et al. *Delacroix, Eugène: Staatliche Kunsthalle Karlsruhe.* Karlsruhe: Kherer, 2003.

Kate, J.J.L. ten. *Christus Remunerator, een harptoon.* Amsterdam: unknown, 1858.

———. *Eerste liefde.* Edited by Gerrit Komrij. De Sandwich-reeks 12. Amsterdam: Uitgeverij 521, 2006.

———. *De jaargetijden.* Groningen: Wolters, 1871.

———. *Keurgedichten. Met portret en handschrift.* Terneuzen: "De Schelde", 1920.

———. *Kunst en leven, naar origineele cartons.* Amsterdam: unknown, ca. 1870.

———. *De nieuwe kerk van Amsterdam.* Amsterdam: Centen, 1885.

———. *Nieuwe photographiën met dichterlijke bijschriften.* Amsterdam: Jager, 1870.

———. *Planeeten.* The Hague: Nijhoff/Leiden: Sijthoff/Arnhem: Thieme, 1869.

———. *De schepping, een gedicht.* Utrecht: Kemink en Zoon, 1886.

Kemperdick, Stephan. *Rogier van der Weyden (1399/1400–1464.)* Cologne: Könemann, 1999.

Keulen, Jan van. *Met Van Gogh in de Provence.* The Hague: Staatsuitgeverij, 1987.

Kirshbaum, Engelbert, editor. *Lexikon der christlichen Ikonographie.* Volume III. Rome, et al.: Herder, 1990.

Kôdera, Tsukasa. "Van Gogh and the Dutch Theological Culture of the Nineteenth Century." *Vincent van Gogh International Symposium,* 115–32. Tokyo: Tokyo Shimbon, 1988.

———. "Van Gogh's Utopian Japonisme." In *Catalogue of the Van Gogh Museum's Collection of Japanese Prints,* edited by Charlotte van Rappard-Boon, et al., 11–45. Amsterdam: Van Gogh Museum/Zwolle: Waanders, 1991.

Bibliography

——. *Vincent van Gogh: Christianity versus Nature.* Revised dissertation, University of Amsterdam. Amsterdam: John Benjamins, 1990.

——. "In het zweet uws aanschijns." In *Van Gogh in Brabant,* edited by E. van Uitert, 59–71. Zwolle: Waanders, 1987.

——, and Yvette Rosenberg, editors. *The Mythology of Vincent van Gogh.* Amsterdam: Benjamins, 1993.

Kooten, Toos van, and Mieke Rijnders, editors. *De schilderijen van Vincent van Gogh in de collectie van het Kröller-Müller Museum.* Otterlo: Kröller-Müller Museum, 2003.

Landow, George P. *William Homan Hunt and Typological Symbolism.* New Haven/London: Yale University Press, 1979.

Larence, George E. "The Methodism of Vincent van Gogh." 1979. Unpublished thesis. In Van Gogh Museum Library. 1979.

Laurillard, E. *Figuren en Tonen, platen met bijschriften.* Collected by Dr. E. Laurillard. Amsterdam: Centen, 1882.

——. *Geen dag zonder God, stichtelijke overdenkingen voor iederen dag des jaars.* Amsterdam: Centen, 1869, 1870, 1876.

——. *Met Jezus in de natuur.* Amsterdam: unknown, 1881.

——. *Kunst-juweeltjes voor de salon-tafel met bijschriften van E. Laurillard.* Haarlem: Van Binger & Chits, 1871.

——. *Vlechtwerk uit verscheiden kleuren: twintig voordrachten.* Amsterdam: Centen, 1880.

Leeman, Fred, and John Sillevis. *De Haagse school en de jonge Van Gogh.* Zwolle: Waanders/Haags Gemeentemuseum, 2004.

Leeuw, Ronald de, editor. *De brieven van Vincent van Gogh.* Amsterdam: Bert Bakker, 2003.

——, et al., editors. *De Haagse School. Hollandse meesters van de 19de eeuw.* Paris: Grand Palais/London: Royal Academy of Arts/The Hague: Haags Gemeentemuseum, 1983.

——. *Van Gogh Museum.* Zwolle: Waanders, 1997.

Leistra, Josefine. *George Henry Boughton; God speed! Pelgrims op weg naar Canterbury.* Zwolle: Waanders, 1987.

Liagre, Guy. "De jonge Vincent van Gogh, en zijn komst naar België." *Eigen Schoon & De Brabander* LXXXVIII (2005) 209–22.

——. "Een veelkleurig bestaan: De religieuze leefwereld van de jonge Vincent van Gogh en zijn komst naar België (1854–1880)." *Analecta Bruxellensia. Revue annuelle de la Faculté universitaire de Théologie protestante de Bruxelles Jaarboek van de Universitaire Faculteit voor Protestantse Godgeleerdheid te Brussel* 7 (2000) 210–41.

Lodwick, Marcus. *De kunstgids. Symboliek en thematiek van klassieke, Bijbelse en religieuze schilderkunst.* Kerkdriel: Librero, 2006.

Loo, Erik L.H.M. van de, et al., editors. *Kunst van geloven.* Baarn: Ambo, 1996.

Loti, Pierre. *Madame Chrysanthème.* Paris: unknown, 1887, 1888.

——. *Pêcheur d'Islande* (with notes by F. Doucet). 3rd edition. Zwolle: Tjeenk Willink, 1917.

Lövgren, Sven. *The Genesis of Modernism; Seurat, Gauguin and French Symbolism in the 1880's.* Stockholm: Almquist & Wiskell, 1959.

Lubin, Albert J. *Stranger on the Earth. A Psychological Biography of Vincent van Gogh.* New York/San Francisco/Chicago: Henry Holt, 1972.

Luker, Manfred. *Wörterbuch der Symbolik.* 5th print. Stuttgart: Kröner, 1991.

Lutjeharms, L.H. "Abraham Van der Wayen Pieterszen." *Société du Protestantisme Belge; Vereniging voor de Geschiedenis van Belgisch Protestantisme* V (1969) 131–44.

———. *De Vlaamse opleidingsschool van Nicolaas de Jonge en zijn opvolgers (1875-1926).* Brussels: Vereniging voor de Geschiedenis van het Belgisch Protestantisme, 1978.

Masheck, Joseph D., editor. *Van Gogh* 100. Westport, Connecticut: Greenwood, 1996.

Mast, Michel van der, and Charles Dumas. *Van Gogh en The Hague.* Zwolle: Waanders, 1990.

Maupassant, Guy de. *De Horla. Verhalen.* 119–50. Amsterdam: Zephyr, Coppens & Grenks, 1999.

Maurer, Naomi Margolis. *The Pursuit of Spiritual Wisdom. The Thought and Art of Vincent van Gogh and Paul Gauguin.* 2nd print. London: Associated University Presses, etc., 1999.

McChesney Alhadeff, Kitty. "Van Gogh's 'Worship of Sorrow' and Charles Dickens' Religion of Hearth and Home." In *Van Gogh* 100, edited by Joseph D. Masheck, 57–69. Westport, Connecticut: Greenwood, 1996.

Meedendorp, Teio. "Dat zwarte gevaarte van goor geworden eikenhout: De rol van de wevers in de ontwikkeling van Vincent van Gogh." In *De wevers en Vincent van Gogh.* 67–77. Zwolle: Van den Brink & Frijhoff, 1990.

Meekeren, Erwin van. *Leven en ziektegeschiedenis van Vincent van Gogh. "Een rollende steen gadert geen mos."* Amsterdam: Benecke, 2003.

Meier-Graefe, Julius. *Vincent van Gogh. Der Roman eines Gottsuchers.* Munich: Piper, 1932.

———. *Vincent van Gogh.* Utrecht/Antwerp: Spectrum, n.d.

Meissner, W.W. *Vincent's Religion. The Search for Meaning.* New York, etc.: Peter Lang, 1997.

Merlhès, Victor. *Paul Gauguin et Vincent van Gogh, 1887-1888: Lettres retrouvées, sources ignores.* Taravao, Tahiti: Fondation Singer-Polignac, 1989.

Meyers, Jan. *De jonge Vincent.* Amsterdam: De Arbeiderspers, 1989.

Miedema, R. *Vincent van Gogh en het Evangelie.* Amsterdam: Van Munster, 1948.

Moffet, Charles S. "Vincent van Gogh en de Haagse School." In *De Haagse School. Hollandse meesters van de 19de eeuw,* 137–46. Edited by Ronald de Leeuw, et al. Paris: Grand Palais/London: Royal Academy/The Hague: Haags Gemeentemuseum, 1983.

Mooij, Charles de. "Devotionalia en volkskunst." In *Rijke oogst van schrale grond. Een overzicht van de Zuidnederlandse materiële volkscultuur ca. 1700-1900,* edited by C. de Mooij and R. van de Weijer, 144–163. Zwolle: Waanders, 1991.

Murray, A.H. "The Religious Background of Vincent van Gogh and its Relation to his Views on Nature and Art." *Journal of the American Academy of Religion* XLIV (March 1978) supplement, 68–96.

Nemeczek, Alfred. *Van Gogh in Arles.* Munich/New York: Prestel, 1995.

Nordenfalk, Carl. "Van Gogh and Literature." *Journal of the Warburg and Courtlaud Institutes* X (1947) 132–47.

Ommen, Johan van, and Lizet Penson. *Prisma Uittrekselboek Nederlandse literatuur 1880-1945.* Utrecht: Spectrum, 1992.

Pabst, Fieke (ed.). *Vincent van Gogh's Poetry Albums.* Cahier Vincent N°1. Zwolle: Waanders/Amsterdam: Rijksmuseum Vincent van Gogh, 1988.

Bibliography

Pabst, F., and E. van Uitert. "A Literary Life, with a List of Books and Periodicals Read by Van Gogh." In *The Rijksmuseum Vincent van Gogh*, edited by E. van Uitert and M. Hoyle, 68–84. Amsterdam: Meulenhoff/Landshoff, 1987.

Perruchot, Henri. *Het leven van Vincent van Gogh*. Utrecht: Spectrum, 2011.

Pickvance, Ronald. "English Influences on Vincent van Gogh." *Vincent Bulletin* IV 4/1 (1975) 18.

———. Exhibition catalogue. *English Influences on Vincent van Gogh*. Nottingham: University of Nottingham & Art Council of Great Britain, 1974–1975.

———. *Van Gogh in Arles*. New York: The Metropolitan Museum of Art/Abrams, 1984.

Piérard, Louis. "Van Gogh au pays noir." *Van Gogh raconté par lui-même et par ses amis*. Preface by Pierre Courthion. Geneva: Pierre Gailler, 1947.

Pollock, Griselda. "Stark Encounters: Modern Life and Urban Work in Van Gogh's Drawings of The Hague 1881–1883." *Art History* VI/3 (September 1983) 330–58.

———. "Van Gogh and the Poor Slaves: Images of Rural Labour as Modern Art." *Art History* II/3 (September 1988) 406–32.

———. *Vincent van Gogh in zijn Hollandse jaren. Kijk op stad en land door Van Gogh en zijn tijdgenoten* 1870/1890. Amsterdam: Rijksmuseum Vincent van Gogh, 1981.

Prideaux, Tom. *De wereld van Delacroix* 1789–1863. Barcelona: Time-Life, 1979.

Quesne-Van Gogh, E.H. du. *Vincent van Gogh, Herinneringen aan haar broeder*. Baarn: van de Ven, 1923.

Renan, Ernest. *La vie de Jésus*. First edition 1863. *The Life of Jesus*. New York: Carlton, 1927.

Roessingh, K.H. *De moderne theologie in Nederland, hare voorbereiding en eerste periode. Verzamelde werken*. Volume 4. Groningen: Van der Kamp, 1914. Arnhem: Van Loghum Slaterus, 1928.

Romein-Verschoor, Annie. "Meester der menselijkheid." In *Erflaters van onze beschaving. Nederlandse gestalten uit zes eeuwen*, edited by Jan and Annie Romein, 817–40. The Hague/Antwerp: Nederlandse Boekenclub, 1971.

Rooden, Peter van. "De sociale positie van de predikant in de tijd van Haverschmidt." *De Negentiende Eeuw* 18/1 (January 1994) 39–52.

Rosenblum, R. *Modern Painting and the Northern Romantic Tradition*. London: Thames and Hudson, 1975.

———, and H.W. Janson. *Art of the Nineteenth Century. Painting and Sculpture*. London: Thames and Hudson, 1984.

Roskill, Marc. *Van Gogh, Gauguin, and the Impressionist Circle*. Greenwich, Connecticut/ New York: New York Graphic Society, 1970.

Ruiter, Frans, and Wilbert Smulders. *Literatuur en moderniteit in Nederland*. 1840–1990. Amsterdam/Antwerp: Arbeiderspers, 1996.

Schapiro, Meyer. *Vincent van Gogh*. New York: Abrams, 1950.

Scheffer, Ary. *Tekeningen, aquarellen en olieverfschetsen*. Dordrecht: Dordrechtsmuseum, 1979–1980.

Scherer, Susanne. *Religiöse Motive im Bildwerk Vincent van Goghs*. Scientific examination paper, Landau University, 1986.

Schouten, Matthijs, et al. *Veen, turf en Vincent van Gogh*. Assen: Staatsbosbeheer, 2003.

Sensier, Alfred. *Jean-Francois Millet. Paysan et Peintre*. Paris: Paul Mantz, 1881.

Seznec, J. "Literary Inspiration in Van Gogh." *Magazine of Art* 43 (December 1950) 282–88, 306–07.

Sillevis, John, and Anne Tabak. *Het Haagse School boek*. 3rd print. Zwolle: Waanders/The Hague: Haags Gemeentemuseum, 2001, 2004.

Sillevis, John, and Hans Kraan. *The Barbizon School*. The Hague: Haags Gemeentemuseum, 1985.

Silverman, Debora. *Vincent van Gogh in England. Portrait of the Artist as a Young Man*. London: Barbican Art Gallery, 1992.

———. "Weaving Paintings: Religious and Social Origins of Vincent van Gogh's Pictorial Labor." In *Rediscovering History: Culture, Politics and the Psyche*, edited by M. Roth, 137–68, 468–73. Stanford: Stanford University Press, 1994.

Smiley, Jane. *Charles Dickens: A Penguin Life*. New York/London: Viking Adult, 2002.

Soth, Lauren. "Gauguin, Van Gogh and the Fishermen of Iceland." *Burlington Magazine* (April 1989) 296–97.

———. "Van Gogh's Agony." *The Art Bulletin* LXVIII/2 (June 1986) 301–13.

———. "Van Gogh's Images of Women Sewing." *Zeitschrift für Kunstgeschichte* LVII/1 (1994) 105–08.

———. "Van Gogh's *Sorrow* and Millet's *The Shepherdess*." *World and Image* XIV/3 (1995) 9–12.

———. "Vincent van Gogh Reads Harriet Beecher Stowe." *World and Image* X/2 (1994) 156–62.

Spurgeon, C.H. *Spurgeon's Juweeltjes*. Leiden: Hazenberg, 1864. Later editions in Amsterdam, 1872, 1874, 1882.

———. *Teachings of Nature in the Kingdom of Grace*. London: Passmore and Alabaster, 1896.

Steen, J. "Christianity versus Nature." *Jong Holland* 7/1 (1991) 52–57.

Steiner, George. *Real Presences. Is There Anything in What We Say?* London/Boston: Faber & Faber, 1889.

Stellingwerff, J. *Mensen en boeken*. Goes: Oosterbaan & Le Cointre, 1963.

Stolwijk, Chris, and Richard Thomson. *Theo van Gogh 1857–1891 Art Dealer, Collector and Brother of Vincent*. Amsterdam: Van Gogh Museum/Zwolle: Waanders, 1999.

Stolwijk, Chris, et al., editors. *De Keuze van Vincent. Van Goghs Musée imaginaire*. Amsterdam: Van Gogh Museum/Antwerp: Mercatorfonds, 2003.

Stonyk, Margaret. *Nineteenth-Century English Literature*. London: MacMillan, 1983.

Strauss, D.F. *Das Leben Jesu, kritisch bearbeitet*. Tübingen: Osiander, 1835.

Stricker, J.P. *Jesus van Nazareth. Volgens de historie geschetst*. Amsterdam: Kraay, 1868.

———. *Een laatste woord bij het neerleggen van mijn Evangeliebediening in zonderheid gericht tot de vrijzinnige leden der Ned. Herv. Kerk*. Amsterdam: unknown, 1884.

———. *De oorsprong der moderne richting*. Amsterdam: unknown, 1874.

———. *De Schriftelijke nalatenschap der Oud-Israelitische profeten, Wijzen en Dichters*. Amsterdam: Loman, 1880.

Sund, Judy. "Favoured Fictions: Women and Books in the Art of Van Gogh." *Art History* II/2 (June 1988) 255–67.

———. "The Sower and the Sheaf: Biblical Metaphor in the Art of Vincent van Gogh." *Art Bulletin* LXX/4 (December 1988) 660–76.

———. *True to Temperament: Van Gogh and French Naturalist Literature*. New York: Cambridge University Press, 1992.

———. "Van Gogh's *Berceuse* and the Sanctity of the Secular." In *Van Gogh 100*, edited by Joseph D. Masheck, 205–25. Westport, Connecticut: Greenwood, 1996.

Taillandier, Yvon. *Corot*. Milan: The Uffici Press, 1974.

Bibliography

Takashina, Sjuhi. "Vincent van Gogh and French Literature." In *Vincent van Gogh. International Symposium*, 405–17. Tokyo: Tokyo Shimbun, 1988.

Tasso, Torquato. *Gerusalemme liberata Jerusalem Delivered*. Translated by Edward Fairfax. 2nd print. New York: Capricorn Books, 1963.

Tibbe, Lieske. *R.N. Roland Holst, 1868–1938. Arbeid en schoonheid vereend. Opvattingen over gemeenschapskunst*. Amsterdam: Architectura & Natura, 1994.

Tilborgh, Louis van. "De bijbel van Vincents vader." *Van Gogh Bulletin* 3/2 (1988) 13–14.

———. "A Kind of Bible: The Collection of Prints and Illustrations." In *The Rijksmuseum Vincent van Gogh*, edited by E. van Uitert and M. Hoyle, 38–44. Amsterdam: Meulenhoff/Landshoff, 1987.

———. "Het liefstelijke dat ik ooit gemaakt heb." *Kunstschrift* 34/3 (1990) 50–51.

———. "De Parijse zelfportretten van Van Gogh." *Van Gogh Bulletin* 2 (1994) 2–7.

———. *The Potato Eaters; De aardappeleters*. Cahier Vincent 5. Zwolle: Waanders, 1993.

———. "Starry, Starry Night. Van Goghs Sterrennacht." *Kunstschrift* 38/6 (November/December 1994) 36–39.

———. *Van Gogh en Japan*. Amsterdam: Van Gogh Museum/Brussels: Mercatorfonds, 2006.

———. "Van Goghs Stilleven met Bijbel." *Van Gogh Bulletin* 1 (1994) 13–14.

———. *Van Gogh en de zonnebloemen*. Amsterdam: Van Gogh Museum, 2008.

———. "Vincent van Gogh and English social realism." In *Hard Times; Social Realism in Victorian Art* (exhibition catalogue), edited by Julian Treuherz, 119–25. Manchester, etc.: Manchester City Art Gallery, etc., 1987–88.

———, and Marije Vellekoop. *Vincent van Gogh. Schilderijen. Nederlandse periode. 1881–1885*. Amsterdam: Van Gogh Museum, 1999.

———, Sjaar van Heugten, and Philip Conisbee. *Van Gogh & Millet*. Zwolle: Waanders/Amsterdam: Rijksmuseum, 1988.

Tralbaut, Mark Edo. *Over godsdienstige richtingen in Vincents tijd*. Van Goghiana VI, 103–8. Antwerp: Pierre Peré, 1970.

———. *Over godsdienstige richtingen in Vincents tijd*. Van Goghiana VII, 103–8. Antwerp: Pierre Peré, 1970.

———. *Over een predikthema van Vincent van Gogh*. Van Goghiana VI, 111–17. Antwerp: Pierre Peré, 1968.

———. *Vincent van Gogh*. New York: Viking, 1969.

———. *Vincent van Gogh in zijn Antwerpse Periode*. Amsterdam: Strengholt, 1948.

Treuherz, Julian, et al. *Dante Gabriel Rossetti*. Zwolle: Waanders/Amsterdam:Van Gogh Museum/Liverpool: Walker, 2004.

Uitert, E. van, editor. *Van Gogh in Brabant. Schilderijen en tekeningen uit Etten en Nuenen*. Zwolle: Waanders, 1987.

———. *Vincent van Gogh in Creative Competition: Four Essays from Simiolus*. Zutphen: Nauta, 1983.

———. *Vincent van Gogh. Leven en werk*. Amsterdam: Landshoff, 1976.

———, and M. Hoyle, editors. *Het Rijksmuseum Vincent van Gogh*. Amsterdam: Meulenhoff/Landshoff, 1987.

———, et al. *Schilderijen*. Amsterdam/Otterlo: De Luca Edizione d'Arte, 1990.

Upstone, Robert. *The Pre-Raphaelite Dream. Paintings and Drawings from the Tate Collection*. London: Tate, 2003.

Vanbeselaere, Walther. *De Hollandsche periode in het werk van Vincent van Gogh*. Antwerp/Amsterdam: Sikkel, 1937.

Vellekoop, Marije, and Sjraar van Heugten. *Vincent van Gogh. Tekeningen. Antwerpen & Paris 1885–1888*. Amsterdam: Van Gogh Museum, 2001.

Verkade-Bruining, A. *De God van Vincent. Beschouwingen over de mens Van Gogh*. Amsterdam: Wereldbibliotheek, 1990.

———. "More About Michelet." *Vincent Bulletin* IV/4 3 (1975) 22–23.

———. "Vincent's Plans to Become a Clergyman." *Vincent Bulletin* III/4 (1974) 14–23; IV/4 1 (1974) 9–12.

Visser 't Hooft, W.A. *Rembrandts weg tot het Evangelie*. Amsterdam: Ten Have, 1956.

Voolen, Edward van. "Israëls: zoon van het oude volk." In *Jozef Israëls 1824–1911*, edited by Diewertje Dekkers, 55–70. Zwolle: Waanders, 2000.

Walther, Ingo F. *Schilderkunst van het Impressionisme. Deel I. Het impressionisme in Frankrijk*. Cologne: Taschen, 2006.

———, and Rainer Metzger. *Alle schilderijen*. Cologne, et al.: Taschen, 2003.

Welsh-Ovcharov, Bogomila Maria. *Van Gogh à Paris*. Musée d'Orsay, 2 February–15 May 1988. Paris: Ministère de la Culture et de la Communication, Editions de la Réunion des musées nationaux, 1988.

———. *Van Gogh in Perspective*. New Jersey: Englewood/Prentice, 1974.

———. *Vincent van Gogh and the Birth of Cloisonism*. Toronto: Art Gallery of Ontario/ Rijksmuseum Vincent van Gogh, 1981.

Werness, Hope B. "Some Observations on Van Gogh and the Vanitas Tradition." *Studies in Iconography* 6 (1980) 123–36.

———. "The Symbolism of van Gogh's Flowers." In *Van Gogh* 100, edited by Joseph D. Masheck, 43–55. Westport, Connecticut: Greenwood Press, 1990.

———. "Whitman and Van Gogh: Starry Nights and Other Similarities." *Walt Whitman Quarterly Review* II (Spring 1985) 35–41.

Wesseling, H.L. "Ary Scheffer en het Frankrijk van zijn tijd." In *Franser dan Frans*, 86–106. Amsterdam: Bert Bakker, 2004.

Wessels, Anton. *"A Kind of Bible." Vincent van Gogh as Evangelist*. London: SCM Press, 2000.

———. *Een soort Bijbel. Vincent van Gogh als Evangelist*. Baarn: Ten Have, 1990.

Whitman, Walt. *Leaves of Grass. Grasbladen*. Translated by 22 poets. Amsterdam: Querido, 2005.

Wilkie, Kenneth. *Het Dossier Van Gogh*. Baarn: Wereldvenster, 1978.

———. *The Van Gogh File. The Myth and the Man*. London: The Van Gogh Assignment, 1978. Souvenir Press, 2004.

Wilson, A.N. *De begrafenis van God. De ondergang van het geloof in de westerse beschaving*. Amsterdam: Prometheus, 2000.

Wyllie, Anne Stiles. "Vincent's Childhood and Adolescence." *Vincent Bulletin* IV/4 2 (1975) 4–27.

Zemel, Carol. "Sorrowing Women, Rescuing Men: Van Gogh's Images of Women and Family." *Art History* 10/3 (1987) 351–68.

———. *Van Gogh's Progress. Utopia, Modernity, and Late-Nineteenth-Century Art*. Berkeley/Los Angeles/London: University of California Press, 1997.

Zola, Émile. *L'Assomoir*. 1877. Translated into English by L.W. Tancock. Harmondsworth: Penguin Classics, 1970.

———. *Edouard Manet: étude biografique et critique*. 1867.

———. *La Faute de l'Abbe Mouret. Abbe Mouret's Transgression*. 1875. No pages. Online: http://www.gutenberg.org/files/14200/14200-h/14200-h.htm.

Bibliography

———. *Germinal.* 1885. Translated into English by L.W. Tancock. Harmondsworth: Penguin Classics, 1954.

———. *Mes Haines.* 1866.

———. *L'Ouvre.* 1886.

———. *Oeuvres complètes.* Edited by Henri Mitterand. 15 volumes. Paris: Cercle du Livre Précieux, 1966–1970.

———. *Une Page d'amour.* 1878.

———. *Le Rêve.* 1888.

———. *La Terre.* 1887.

———. *Le Vente de Paris.* 1874.

SUBJECT/NAME INDEX

Aeschylus, 25
Abel, 48. *See* Cain.
abandon(ment), 18, 22, 41, 43, 67, 76,
    79, 124, 125, 127, 133, 139
abbey, 56
academy, 90
Achilles, 36
adversity, 18, 23, 41, 74
Agamemnon, 36
agony, 59
alcohol, 18, 103, 135, 136
almond trees, blossoms, 60, 61, 62, 80
Almond Blossom, 62
Alsace, 71
Alone in the World, 16. *See* Jozef Israels.
Along Mother's Grave, 16. *See* Jozef
    Israels.
Alpine mountains, 119
altar(piece), 54, 66
Amsterdam, 2, 5, 8, 9, 10, 16, 27, 31, 37,
    40, 46, 52, 64, 86, 105, 107, 117,
    120, 123, 131, 133, 141
angel, angelic, 55, 58, 59, 60, 113, 115,
    117
anguish, 37, 116
antidote, 130
apostelate, religious, 15
apple, 98
Arabia, 11
ark, 125, 126
Arles, 13, 22, 25, 27, 28, 45, 55, 56, 58,
    60, 62, 65, 66, 73, 80, 85, 91, 93–
    96, 98, 99, 100, 10, 121, 125–27,
    132, 134–37, 142
Arléssienne, 63, 73, 74, 102, 104. *See*
    Madame Ginoux.

art of life, 142, *passim*
art business, 82, 139
art dealer, XVII, 2, 16, 40, 51, 61, 123,
    126
art trade, 2, 3, 19
art of the word, 27
art of lines and colors, 27
artistry, 143
ash trees, 56
Asnières, 62
L'Assomoir, (French for night café) 99,
    100. *See* Café de la Gare, Night
    Café, Émile Zola.
At Eternity's Gate, 19, 28, nt. 59, 37, 118
atheist, 107
Au "Charbonnage" Café, 77. *See* the
    Borinage.
autumn, 27, 97, 115, 120, 121,. *See* fall.
Auvers, 63, 67, 98, 101, 138, 139
avarice, 48
Avenue of Poplars near Nuenen, 120
Avignon, 55

Baptist minister, 117
Barbizon, 19, 20, 136
bark, 4, 122
batter, 108, 138
beacon, XI, 54, 127
beam, 57, 66, 117
Bearers of the Burden, The, 19
Beethoven, Ludwig von, 30
Bedford, 117. *See* C.H. Spurgeon
bedroom, 61, 100
Belgium, Belgian, IX, XVI, 10, 104, 105,
    110, 120
Berlioz, Hector, 130

Bethlehem, 12, 46, 70
birch tree, 115
blazing, 66, 67
"Blessed Twilight," 86. *See* Charles
    Dickens.
blood, 137
blood-red, XIII, 58, 100
blossom, 14, 17, 56, 60, 61, 80, 98, 106
Blossoming Almond Branch in a Glass, 60
boat, 23, 24, 87, 123, 128
Boccaccio, Giovanni, 56
Bonger, Jo, wife of Theo van Gogh, 73,
    94
book of books, 26
book of nature, XVII, 68
books, XIV, XVI, 4, 7, 8, 9, 14, 15, 24, 25,
    27, 31, 35, 43, 47, 49, 51, 55, 59,
    70, 71, 73–75, 77–84, 88, 89, 97,
    102, 103, 110, 118, 124, 127, 128,
    131, 132, 139–42
bookshop, 4, 39, 80
Bonte, Madame, wife of Rev. Bonte, 12
bonze, 97. *See* Buddhist monks
Borinage, the, XVI, XVII, 10–13, 23, 29,
    31, 45, 50, 67, 70, 75, 76, 78
box trees, 60
Braat, Frans, 5
Brabant, 1, 2, 39, 40, 51, 85
Bretagne, 71
Brittany, 116, 127
brother(ly), XVI, 1, 11, 14, 21, 23, 24, 33,
    40, 49, 63, 83, 93, 102, 103, 106,
    136, 138, 139
Brothers of the Common Life, 126. *See*
    Thomas à Kempis.
Brussels, 2, 10, 20, 44, 75, 76, 120
Buddha, 97
Buddhist monks, 97

Café de la Gare, 63, 73, 99. *See* Arles,
    Madame Ginoux.
Café Terrace at Night, 99. *See*
    L'Assommoir, Émile Zola, Place
    de Forum.
Cain, 48
Calvin, John, 5, 6
canal, 85, 87

candle, 72, 82, 83, 99, 115, 132, 133
candlelight, 84
candlesticks, 115,128, 132
Canterbury, 115
Carbentus, Anna Cornelia 1. *See* mother
    Vincent,
carpenter, 139
Carton, Sidney, 47. *See A Tale of Two
    Cities* (Charles Dickens).
cathedrals, 54
cedar, 91
Celestian City, 37. *See* John Bunyan.
cemetery, 77, 95, 113
Chagall Bible, XV
chair, (empty), 36, 37, 73, 100, 126,
    130–33
chalice, 54, 88
charity, 11, 42, 44, 117
Chavannes, Pierre Puvis de, 79
chiaroscuro, VII, 63, 70, 72, 73, 84, 85,
    87. *See* Hamens Rembrandt.
child(dren), XVI, 1, 3, 6, 8, 14, 18, 28, 34,
    36, 38, 41, 43, 52, 57, 61, 62, 71,
    72, 73, 75, 76, 79, 82, 84, 88, 90,
    95, 106, 107, 116, 123, 125, 128,
    130, 134
chimney, 26, 76, 77
Christ, XVII, 7, 12, 26, 28, 39, 43, 46, 54,
    55, 58–62, 64, 78, 84, 85, 97, 110,
    118, 137, 139–41, 143. *See* Jesus.
Christian, 5, 7, 12, 24, 35, 59, 64, 118,
    121, 139
Christian faith, 47
Christian laborer, 5
Christian literature, 142
Christian religion, 47
Christian sarcophaguses, 92
Christian values, 51
Christian view, 83
Christianity, 6, 7, 24, 25, 31, 95, 111
Christus Consolator, 3. *See* Ary Scheffer.
Christus Remunerator, 3 *See* Ary
    Scheffer.
Christmas, 3, 4, 11, 30, 71, 73, 74, 127,
    128, 131, 135
Christmas Carol, 74
Christmas feeling, 72

Christmas fire, 72

Christmas night, 70, 72, 73

Christmas story, 36. *See* Charles Dickens.

Chronos, 95

church, 1, 3, 7–9, 12, 18, 25, 26, 28, 30,
    51, 53, 57, 64, 70, 71, 78, 109–12,
    115

Church, Dutch Reformed, 2

church father, 140

church, Gothic, 94

church history, 25

church, institutional, 7, 28, 118

churchyard, 40, 95, 113

Churchyard in the Rain, 113

City, Celestial, 37

city, eternal, 116

city, heavenly, 113, 118

cityscapes, 87

civilization, 41, 48, 80

civilized people (circles), 37, 53

class, 70

class (working), 17

class, poor, 39

Clemens Church, Roman Catholic, 120.
    See Nuenen.

cloud, 55, 58, 69, 115, 119, 187,

coal, coal-burners, coal-mine(r), 12, 19,
    75, 76, 78, 79

colorist, coloration, coloring, XIV, 30,
    135–37

comfort(ing), 7, 25, 29, 30, 47, 52, 67, 79,
    80, 103, 111, 112, 127, 128, 129,
    30, 133

communion with nature, 19

compassion, 19, 44, 50, 54

complain, complaint, XVII, 51, 65, 108,
    126, 137

composer, 30. *See* Ludwig von
    Beethoven.

comrades, 74

confidence, XIII, 107, 124

*Congregation Leaving the Reformed
    Church in Nuenen,* 112

conscience, 16, 17, 38, 49, 73, 85, 105,
    134,

Conscience, Henri, 118

consolation, 143 nt. 91

constitution, 46

continent, new, 127

cornfields, 64

Costa, Mendes da, 30, 64, 85

country life, 20

Country Road in Provence by Night, 119

courage, courageous, 9, 28, 67, 76, 124,
    126

cradle, 82

cradle song, 129

craftsmen, 50, 141

creator, 86, 109

crescent, 119

Cricket on the Heart, 36. *See* Charles
    Dickens.

crimes, 81, 100

cross, 12, 59, 66, 78, 84, 113

crucifixion, 45, 78

Crusoe, Robinson, 37, 124

cultivate, 141

culture, Dutch, XVI

culture, French, 102

culture, minister, 8

cynicism, 47

cypress, 55, 56, 91, 95, 96, 111, 119

Cypress in Starry Night, 119

dark(ness), XVII, XV, 8, 11, 36, 41, 43,
    45–47, 51, 54, 55, 60, 63, 67, 69,
    70, 72, 75–80, 84, 86, 88, 89, 100,
    103, 119, 132

David, king, 31

death, XVII, 6, 8, 21, 24, 33, 37, 57–63,
    67, 68, 83, 88, 89, 90, 91, 92, 95,
    98, 102 103, 107, 108, 111–13,
    116, 117, 119, 121, 129, 131, 138,
    139, 141, 143

Denis, Esther, 12,

Denis, Jean-Baptiste, 12

depressed, depression, depressing, 51, 71

de profundis, 52

desert, 97, 140

Deserted—The Foundling, 18. *See* Frank
    Holl.

despair, desperation, XVII, 9, 29, 43,
    49, 74

despondent, despondency, 43, 59, 80

destination, 24, 56, 118

devotion, 57, 93, 126, 139, 141

diaconate men, 50

digger, 18, 20, 57, 58

disciples (of Jesus), 54, 126

dissenters, 51

dogma(tics), 2, 26, 28, 31, 109, 110

Dordrecht, 3, 4, 5, 35, 39, 40, 84, 92, 97, 113

dove, 90

drawing, XIII, 13, 14, 16, 19, 32, 36, 38, 41–45, 50, 56, 57, 58, 66, 72, 73, 77, 78, 87, 89, 93, 95, 102, 122, 124, 130

dream(ing), 3, 5, 28, 30, 38, 39, 51, 52, 62, 77, 96, 120, 124,126, 130, 135, 136

Drenthe, 19, 30, 43, 51, 113, 115, 134

Du prêtre, de la femme, de la famille (The Priest, the Woman, and the Family), 82. *See* Jules Michelet.

eagle, 140, 141 (symbol for John)

Early Puritans of New England Going to Church, 115

earth(ly), 4, 6, 7, 9, 16, 28, 37, 42, 43, 58, 62–65, 67, 70, 75, 78, 96, 116, 117, 119, 133, 140, 142

eccentric, eccentricity, 102, 136, 137

eclipse(d), 70

Eilandskerk, 6,

Eindhoven, 54

elm tree, 85

Elysian fields, 79, 121

emblem books, literature, XVI, 93

empty chair(s), 130, 131, 132

Empty Chair, The, 131. *See* Luke Fildes.

England, XV, XVI, 2, 3, 4, 5, 10, 29, 39, 44, 52, 71, 75, 115–18, 120, 122

enlighten(ment), 70, 97,

Épinal, 129

epitaph, 65

etcher, etchings, 14, 42, 59, 63, 64, 72, 76, 84 nt. 35, 85, 102

eternal(ly), 21, 47, 62, 64–66, 82, 91, 113, 124, 141

eternal Buddha, 97

eternal city, 116

eternal love, 80

eternal moral laws, 42

eternal poetry of Christmas night, 70, 72

eternity, manifestation of, 112

Etten, 2, 3, 5, 36, 71, 95, 105, 107, 120, 122

eyes, 14, 21, 36, 42 nt. 16, 43, 46, 54, 60, 72, 75, 76, 81, 88, 89, 96, 97, 114, 117, 131, 137, 139, 141, 142

Evangelism Committee, 10, 12. *See* Belgium.

evangelist, XV, XVI, XVII, 3, 10, 12, 13, 28, 29, 31, 45, 63, 67, 70, 75, 79, nt. 20, 97, 118, 139, 140

Evangelist, the four (seasons), 97, 140. *See* C.H. Spurgeon

Evans, Mary Ann, 25. *See* George Eliot.

Evening, 73. *See* Hamens Rembrandt.

Evening: The Watch (after Millet), 73

exorcism, 133

exploitation, 51

face, facial, XIV, 18, 35, 37, 44, 45, 50, 54, 55, 63, 65, 72, 88, 89, 104, 112, 117, 118, 136, 139–41

factory (workers), 51, 52, 53, 76

faith (ful), XI, XIV, XV, XVI, XVII, 4, 6, 7, 11, 13–15, 20, 26, 28, 38, 39, 79, 42, 47, 48, 72, 84 nt. 36, 83, 86, 91, 102, 110, 111, 113, 116–18

faith, catholic, 54

faith, christian, 47

faith, confession of, 2

faith, convential, 15

faith, natural, 10

faithfulness, 50

fall, (season), 32, 60, 66, 98, 120, 134. *See* leaves (fallen)autumn.

farmers, 13, 20, 30, 36, 45, 51, 65

Father in heaven, 117

Father House, our, 116

father of Vincent, XVI, 1, 2–5, 8, 10, 18, 23, 28, 40, 42, 61, 64, 69, 71, 81, 83, 107, 109, 111–13, 131

Father Pangloss, 135. *See* Pangloss

Faust, 81. *See* Goethe, ten Kate

La Faute de l'abbé Mouret, 56. *See* Zola

fear, XVII, 3, 22, 33, 42 nt. 16, 55, 59, 60, 65, 84, 129, 134, 137, 139

Felix Holt the Radical, 51, 101 nt. 72. *See* George Eliot.

fertility, 61

Feuerbach, Ludwig, 7. *See* Johannes Paulus Stricker.

fever, 137

fig (tree), 31, 56, 142

fields, XIII, 19, 20, 31, 43, 45, 53, 54, 60, 65–67, 96, 118

Field under a Stormy Sky, 65

Figures on a Road with trees, 119

fire, 19, 36, 37, 73, 84, 90, 95, 123, 130, 141

fire, Christmas, 72

fire, evangelical, 26

fire of eternal love, 80

fire of faith, 117

firmament, 63, 112, 140

fish, 24, 83, 86, 122, 123, 130

fishermen, 121, 123, 125, 127, 128, 129. *See* Paul Gauguin, Pierre Loti.

Fishing Boats on the Beach at Les Saintes-de-la-Maries, 24

flowers, 56, 94, 96, 113, 114, 128, 129

"Flying Dutchman," The, 130

Fontaine, Jean de la, 6

France, 22, 27, 50, 55, 56, 63, 64, 77, 94, 95, 96, 97, 116, 120, 126, 142

French Legion, 33

freedom, 6, 105, 106

friend, friendship, 4, 10, 13, 20–, 31, 32, 33 nt. 67, 37, 38, 45, 55–57, 60, 62, 74, 75 nt. 12, 76, 81, 83, 90, 91, 92, 99, 102, 106, 108, 111, 112, 115, 121, 124, 126, 127, 133, 134, 137 nt. 79, 139, 140–42

funeral, 18, 26, 47, 64, 77

Gachet, Marguérite, 102

garden, 8, 26, 55–57, 60, 85, 92, 93, 95, 101, 102

Garden of Eden, XVII

Garden of Gethsemane, 85

Garden of olives, 59, 60

Garden of Paradise, 58

Garden of the Poet, 55, 56. *See* Giovanni Boccaccio, Petrarch.

Garden of the Poet, The, 55,

gaslamp, 54

gaslight, 99, 100, 112

Gaul, 121

Germinal, 27, 77, 78. *See* Émile Zola.

germinate, germination, 31, 64, 65, 66

Germinie Lacerteux, 55, 102, 103. *See* Edmond and Jules Huot de Goncourt.

Gethsemane, XVII, 58, 59, 60, 85, 93, 136

Ginoux, Joseph Michel, 99

Ginoux, Madame, 63, 73, 74, 102, 104. *See Arléssienne.*

Gladwell, Harry, 31, 83

glow, 36, 73, 86, 99, 116, 119

God, 1, 4, 9, 11, 12, 14, 15, 19, 27, 28, 37–39, 42, 44, 52, 64, 67, 70, 72, 75, 80, 86, 88, 90, 92, 93, 105–17, 122, 130, 140–43,

godless, 109, 142

godson, 62. *See* Vincent Willem van Gogh.

God Speed "Pilgrims Setting Out For Canterbury, 115

Goethe, first name or initials, 81, 110

Goncourt, Edmond and Jules Huot de, 25, 55, 96, 102, 103, 126

Gogh, Anna van (sister), 83

Gogh, Cor van (uncle), 40

Gogh, Johannes van (uncle), 2, 5, 86

Gogh, Theo van (brother), XVI, 1, 2, 3, 14, 16, 19, 21–24, 32, 41, 42, 43, 46, 48, 49, 50, 56, 57, 61–63, 67, 69, 70, 73, 77, 78, 81–83, 84 nt. 36, 94, 97, 101, 102, 105, 111, 126, 133, 134, 137, 139

Gogh, Rev. Theodorus van (father), 1, 83 nt. 32, 108, 113

Gogh, Vincent van (uncle: "Oom Cent")

Gogh, Vincent Willem van, son of Theo and Jo Bonger, 61

Gogh, Wil(lemien) van (sister), XVI, 23, 41, 60, 70, 79, 80, 83, 93, 109

gold, 49, 55, 85, 94, 115
golden beams, 57
golden light, 68
Good Samaritan, The, XV, 32, 45
Gospel, XV, 3, 5, 12, 15, 28, 31, 46, 79, 82, 109, 139, 140, 142
gospel of nature, 65
Goupil & Cie, 2, 31, 123
grain, 8, 53, 60, 64–67, 78, 95, 98, 139, 140
grainfields, 66, 67, 139
Granville, 116. *See* Jean Baptiste Loyer.
grass, 57, 67, 95, 96, 113, 115
graphic (artist; painting), XIII, 30, 76
Graphic, The, 17, 18, 21, 36, 39, 72, 131
greed, 48
Great Britain, 17
Great Lady, The, 19, 39
Great Light, 88, 94
Greek, 5, 9, 30, 64, 85,130
grief, 70, 83, 104, 138
Groningen School ("life more important that doctrine"), 2, 6, 42
Guild of St. Luke, 141. *See* Jan Toorop.
guillotine, 46, 47

Hague, the, XVII, 2, 13, 16–19, 32, 36, 39, 41, 44, 45, 49, 50, 61, 71–73, 87, 89, 95, 100, 109, 123–125, 133, 138
Hague school, XVII, the, 17, 87. *See* Anton Mauve, Jan Hendrik Weissenbruch
halo, 54, 66, 115
Hard Times, XV, 36, 39, 72 nt. 6, 75
harmony, harmonist, harmonious, XIII, 30, 42, 51, 98, 124
harmony of color, 30, 98
harmony of tones, 30
harvest, 54, 65, 77, 125, 138, 142
hatred, 76, 78
Haunted Man, The, 70, 71. *See* Charles Dickens.
heart disease, 103
heaven (ly), 4, 35, 48, 63, 113, 114, 116–18, 140–42
Helen of Troy, 36. *See* Homer.

Helvoirt, 2, 83 nt. 32
Her Firstborn, 18. *See* Frank Holl.
hieroglyphics, 9
hiddenness, 67
Hillen, Johannes, catechism teacher, 2
Hoogeveen, 113
Holl, Frank, 17, 18, 41, 131
holly oaks, 56
Holy City, 115
Holy Family, 72, 82
Holy family in the Evening, The, 72, 82
holy struggle, 84
Homer, 9
honest man, 9, 134
Hoornik, Clasina, 41, 111. *See* Sien.
horla, 129, 130
hospital, 18, 22, 23, 41, 45, 72, 93, 102, 108, 110, 132, 137
Houseless and Hungry, 18. *See* Luke Fildes.
humanity, XVI, 20, 44, 45, 50, 67, 88
humility, 2, 84
Hunt, William Holman, 39, 84, 85.*See Light of the World*.
hysteria, 103

ichtus, 130
Illustrated London News, The, XV, 17, 36, 38
illness (mental), 25, 26, 30, 55, 63, 65, 91, 93, 118, 130, 133, 135, 138
illustrator, 16, 17, 19, 30, 36, 39, 106, 115, 132. *See* George H. Boughton, Gustave Doré, Thomas Faed, Paul Gavarni, Lançon, *The Graphic, Illustrated London News*.
imagination, 51, 56, 67, 101, 106, 127
Imitation of Christ, 2, 30. *See* Thomas à Kempis.
immortals, immortality, 66, 91, 142
impressionistic, impressionism, XIII, 109, 127, 135, 136, 142
incredulity, 47
independence, 105
industrialism, 51
infinity, 72, 141

innocent, innocence, 43, 52, 84, 90, 112
insane, 33, 91, 100, 136, 137, 138, 142
invalids, 72,
Irises, The, 33
Isleworth, 4, 10, 130, 133
ivy, 65, 78, 85, 91–93

"Japonaiserie forever," 96 nt. 63
Japanese (art; prints), 87, 96, 97, 100, 101
Jerome, church father, 140
Jewish Bride, The, 86. *See* Hamens
    Rembrandt
Jewish quarter, 30, 40
Jesus, Christ, XV, XVI, XVII, 6, 7, 8, 12,
    24, 59, 64, 83, 88, 97, 1-7, 110,
    126, 130, 139
Joan of Arc, 27
Jodenbreestraat, 86. *See* Amsterdam
Jonas Daniël Meijerplein, 30, 85. *See*
    Mendes da Costa
journey, 4, 11, 23, 35, 50, 62, 88, 96, 114,
    116–18
joy(s), joyful, 6, 14, 36, 43, 61, 62 nt. 51,
    84, 93, 113, 116, 117, 136
Joy of Life, The, 80, 91, 92. *See* Émile
    Zola.
Jupiter, 95

Kate, Jan Lodewijk I, ten, 8, 64, 81
Kempis Thomas à, 2, 30, 28, 84, 126
Kerssemakers, Anton, 142
"kind of Bible," a, XV, 19

La Berceuse, 63, 128, 129
labor, 8, 14, 48, 65, 67, 75, 77, 118
labor, manual, 4, 53
labor pain, 14
laborer, 14, 48
laborer, Christian, 5
Lacerteux, Germenie, 55, 102, 103
lamp, 53, 54, 73, 75, 84, 85, 99, 100, 128,
    132
land, promised, 127
landscape, 19, 42, 51, 55, 58, 60, 66, 69,
    77, 87, 96, 103, 115, 119, 120,
Last Muster, The, 18. *See* Hubert von
    Herkomer.

"Last Supper," 53, 54
Latin, 5, 9, 10, 30, 64, 85
Laurillard, Eliza, 8, 64, 93
Lazarus, XV, 63
Lazarus, The Raising of, 15, 63,
leaf, leaves, 58, 91, 115, 120, 121
Leaving Home, 18. *See* Frank Holl.
legend, 24, 49, 128, 143
Leidsendam, 46
liberate, liberation, 43, 82, 118, 139
life, art of, 142
life, brevity of, 11
life above doctrine, 2. *See* Groningen
    School.
life, continuation of, 48. *See* resurrection
life, daily, 53
life, dilemmas, 110
life, every-day, 44
life, fruitful, 90
Life of a Horse, The, 67
life, human, 67, 112
life, idyllic, 58
life, image of, 121
life, joy of, 91, 92,
life, meaning of, XVI, 49
life, modern, 79
life, musical, 47
life, peasant, 54
life, practical, 3
life, private, 109
life, problem of, 108
life, real, 18
life, sad, 55, 103
life, salt of, 45
life, sober, 51
life, struggle for, 42, 138
life, symbol of, 92
life, true, 138,
life, utopian, 58
life, way of , 53
light, XV, XVII, 6, 8, 11, 21, 30, 41,
    45–47, 53, 54,55, 63, 64, 68–73,
    77, 78, 79, 80, 84, 86–88, 90, 93,
    94, 96, 99, 100, 115, 118–20, 132,
    133, 135, 139, 141–43
light, feast of light, 71. *See* star.

Light of the World, 39, 84, 85. *See* William Holman Hunt.
"Light on my path," 84
Light, painter of, 142. *See* Hamens Rembrandt, Jan Vermeer, Jan Hendrik Weissenbruch.
light of renewal, 46
lighthouse, 70
lightning, 48, 60, 138
lilies of the valley, 43
lion, 140
literature, literary, XVI, 2, 17, 24, 26, 27, 49, 50, 74, 77, 79, 81, 82, 84, 93, 125, 132, 139, 142
literature, christian, 142
lithograph(er), 55, 106
Little John, 88, 129. *See* Frederik van Eeden, show of light.
life, witness to, 82
living again, 61
living people, 142
London, 2, 3, 7, 13, 17, 36, 44, 82, 84 nt. 38, 87, 97, 106 nt. 2, 115, 116, 123
loneliness, XVII, 36, 67, 124, 139
looms, 51, 52
lottery, 49
love , XIV, XVII, 1, 2, 11, 14, 15, 19, 25, 28, 29, 37, 41, 46, 48, 50, 56, 57, 64, 67, 71, 72, 79, 82, 83, 89, 90, 98, 105, 107, 109, 112, 116, 118, 122, 133, 134, 135 nt. 74, 80, 91, 11, 121, 124, 131, 136, 138, 139, 141, 143
Loyer, Jean Baptiste, 116. *See* Granville.
Luke Painting the Virgin, 140

machine people, 52,
Madonna, the, (modern), 43, 128, 140. *See* Augustine Roulin.
madness, XVII, 129, 130, 136, 137, 138
magician, 86. *See* Hamens Rembrandt.
mammon, 48. *See* money.
man, 141 (symbol for Matthew), 141
manger, 72
mania, religious, 110

Manette Salomon, 102, 103. *See* Edmond and Jules Huot de Goncourt.
Marcasse, 75. *See* mine, miners.
margin poetry, 64
Marseille, 127, 136
Martha, sister of Lazarus, 63
Mary, sister of Lazarus, 63
Mary (the Virgin; the mother of Jesus), XV, XVII, 54, 55, 125, 128, 129
Mary Magdalene, 24, 43
Mary star of the sea, 125
Mask of an Egyptian Mummy, 65
Mater dolorosa, 55
materialism, 52
Matthew, XVII, 140, 141
Mauve, Anton, 17, 61, 98, 108, 123, 124. *See* the Hague School.
medicine, 137
Mediterranean coast, sea, world, 24, 95, 113
melancholy, 6, 9, 21, 43, 65, 89, 102, 103, 106, 113, 120, 133–35
Mennonite Church, 83 nt. 32
mercy, 44
metaphysical magic, 87. *See* Hamens Rembrandt.
Methodism, 118
Methodist Church, 4, 31, 116
Michelet, Jules, 33, 49, 51, 67, 70, 76, 103-6, 115, 131, 144, 163, 172, 179
Michelangelo, 54
Middle Ages, 24, 91, 110,
mineworkers, 50, 52, 53
miner, XVII, 10, 12–14, 19, 46, 52, 53, 75–79
minister (of the church), XVI, 1–5, 8, 9, 16, 21, 26, 28, 29, 35, 44, 51, 81, 83 nt. 32, 85,97, 107–09, 111, 123, 137
Misérables, Les, 80, 81. *See* Victor Hugo.
missionary, 3, 7, 11
mockery, 47
modern, modernity, 6, 20, 24, 46, 79, 80, 103
modern art, 103
modern Bible criticism, 7

modern Christians, 5, 7
modern city, 25
modern civilization, 80
modern devotion, 126
modern era, 79
modern factory, 52
modern French writers, 126, 132
modern insights, 7
modern life, 79, 82
modern literature, XVI, XVII, 74, 132
modern Madonna, 128
modern motif, 80
modern painters, 20, 83
modern people, XVI, 83
modern period, XVII, 74, 80, 103
modern pilgrims, 78
modern society, 43, 79, 81
modern soul, 80
modern time 82,
modern theological thinking, XV
modern time, 82
modern way, 79
modern woman, 74
modern world, 48, 49
money, 18, 19, 32, 33, 48, 53, 100
monks, 125. *See* Buddhist monks
Moody, Dwight Lyman 97. *See* Ira David
    Sankey, C.H. Spurgeon.
moon, 88, 96, 119
moonlight, 87
Mons, 10, 50
Montmajour, 56, 57
Montmatre, 77. *See* Paris.
Montpellier, 102, 136
morality, 42
mother of Jesus, 24
mother of Kee Vos-Stricker, 107
mother of Sien, 44
mother of Vincent, 1, 2, 3, 18, 21, 24, 35,
    61, 81, 107, 109, 111, 112
Mouret, Serge, 56, 57. *See* Émile Zola.
Multatuli, 107
Musée Fabre, 136. *See* Marseille.
music, musical, musicians, 11, 30, 62,
    130, 136
My religion, 47. *See* Leo Tolstoy
mysticism, 15

Nathan, prophet, 31. *See* David, parable
naturalists, French, (writers, school)), 25,
    80, 102, 103
nature, XIV, 1, 8, 9, 13, 20, 27, 42, 58, 64,
    66, 67, 76, 84, 87–91, 93, 95–98,
    110, 116, 120, 124, 137, 138, 140,
    141
nature, book of, XVII, 68
nature, Gospel of, 65
nature, the language of, 89
nature, cycle of, 66
neediness, 50
neighbor, love of, 15, 46
Netherlands, the, IX, XV, 4, 8, 21, 39, 95,
    110, 118, 120
neurosis, 129
New England, 115
Nieuwenhuis, Domela, 109
Night Café, 100, 101. *See L'Assomoir.*
note, high yellow, 143
non-violent, 48, Tolstoy
novel, novelist, 25, 36, 45, 51, 52,
    55–57, 69, 75, 77, 79, 80, 83, 100,
    102,103, 109, 118, 127, 128, 131
novel, French naturalist, 32, 80
novels, naturalist, 25, 80
Nuenen, 2, 19, 20, 21, 23, 32, 47, 49, 50,
    51, 73, 78, 83, 95, 99, 111–13,
    119, 120, 134, 142

oak trees, 91, 92, 93
obelisks, 95
Old Man with Head in his Hands, 71
Old Church Tower at Nuenen, The, 112
oleanders, 55, 91
olive (tree), XVII, 56, 58, 59, 60, 91, 95
oppressed, oppression, 6, 9, 43, 75, 77,
    136
orchard, 59, 60, 61
orphan(age), 18, 53
Osiris, 65, 92, 137
ox, 140
oxen (symbol for the painter Luke) 141
pain, 19, 41, 45, 65, 83, 93, 106
painful, 11
palette, 98, 99, 142

Pangloss, Father, 135. *See* Voltaire, Serge Mouret, Émile Zola.
parable, 30, 31, 62, 142
parable of the fig tree, 31
parable of the Good Samaritan, 32
parable of the lost coin, 31
parable of the lost son, 31,
parable of the mustard seed, 11, 31
parable of the rich man whose steals a poor man's ewe lamb, 31
parable of the sower, 31, 64, 77
parable of the unmerciful servant, 31
paradise, XVII, 37, 56, 57, 58, 95. *See* Paradou.
Paradou, La, 56, 57, 58. *See* Serge Mouret, paradise, Émile Zola.
paranoia, 129, 136
Paris, Parisian, XIII, XVII, 2, 17, 19, 21–23, 27, 28, 31–33, 40, 45, 50, 62, 64, 77, 80, 82, 83, 87, 88, 94, 96, 99, 109, 113, 125, 127, 129, 134, 135, 139
Paris Poor, Soup Distribution, 17. *See* Auguste André Lançon.
park, public, 55, 56, 57, 91, 95
Parthenon, 139
pastor, 5, 12, 16, 109, 113
pastor, village, 16
pastor, city, 16
patience, 62, 137, 138, 140,
patron god of graybeards, 95. *See* Zeus.
patron saint of the painters (Luke), 140. *See* Luke
patron saint (of fishermen), 128. *See* Mary.
Pâturages, 11. *See* the Borinage.
Paul, the apostle, 11, 29, 107, 115, 139, 142
Paul, letters of St., 139
peace(fully), 8, 9, 11, 26, 40, 42, 63, 105, 134
peace on earth, 12, 70
peace of mind, 137
peasant, 20, 36, 39, 53, 85, 113
peasant life, 19, 39, 40, 47, 54, 67, 125
peasant painter, 20. *See* Jean François Millet.

Peasant Woman in a Green Shawl, 78
pearl, precious, 4, 66, 122
Peat Diggers in the Dunes, 57, 58
Pêcheur d'Islande, 125, 127. *See* Pierre Loti.
peony, 93. *See* Georges Jeannin, Ernest Quost.
perspective, 14
Peter, the disciple, 59
Peter's, St., 54
Petites-Wasmes, 13. *See* the Borinage, Wasmes.
Petersham, 31
Petrarch, 55, 56. *See* Giovanni Boccaccio, Garden of the Poet.
Pharisees, pharisaism, 10, 16, 38
pietà, XV, 54, 55
Phryne before the Areopagus, 40. *See* Jean-Léon Gérôme.
Pilgrims" Progress, 4, 35, 37, 116, 117, 118. *See* John Bunyan.
pilgrimage, XVI, 24, 56, 113, 116, 118–21
Petrarch, 55, 56
philosophers, 9, 141. *See* Christ, first name? Michelet, Pangloss (Voltaire).
pine tree, 70, 92, 100, 119, 132, 140
pipe, 36, 132, 133, 134, 135
Place du Forum, 99. *See* Night Café, Arles.
Place Lamartine, 73, 99. *See* Arles, Café de la Gare, Madame Ginoux.
plant(ing), planters, 54, 66, 67, 91, 92, 93, 95, 96, 124, 141
plough(man), 8, 18, 19, 41, 48, 54, 66, 120
poet, XVII, 8, 28, 38, 56, 61, 62, 86, 93, 112, 113, 115 nt. 23, 120, 134
poet-painter, 50
"poet of creation," 8. *See* Eliza Laurillard.
poetry, 20, 38, 52, 64, 70, 72
poet"s garden, XVII, 55, 56
pollard willows, 45, 91, 95, 120
pomegranate trees, 56
poplars, 92, 119–21

poor, 3, 4, 6, 9, 17–19, 26, 28, 31, 35, 37–39, 41, 43–46, 49, 50, 51–53, 67, 70, 75, 76, 83, 85, 98, 108, 109

Poor and the Money, The, 19

portrait(s), 5, 29, 30, 40, 73, 79, 86, 99, 101, 102, 104, 128, 136

potatoes 19, 26, 45, 53, 54,

Potato Eaters, The, 19, 21, 53, 54, 73. *See* Last Supper.

Poverty, 12, 16, 18, 37, 41, 44

power, creative, 142

power, germinative, 64

power, intellectual, 38

power of love, 83

power, invisible, 65

power, miraculous, 85

power, priest's, 28

power of poetry, 56

power, sovereign, 14

powers, spiritual, 110

prayer, praying, prayer, 4, 66, 71, 88, 107, 112, 122, 128, 131

Prayer before the Meal, 71

preach, preacher, XVI, 3, 6, 11, 13, 28, 31, 35, 70, 116, 117

preacher poets, XVI, 8, 64, 124. *See* Petrus Augustus de Genestet; Jan Lodewijk I. ten Kate, Eliza Laurillard

pre-Raphaelites, 31, 84, 85. *See* William Holman Hunt, John Everett Millais, Dante Gabriel Rossetti

pride, 38, 39, 60, 76

priest, 28, 57, 82, 110, 116, 137, 140

priest, village, 57

priestess, 65

prophets, minor, 81 nt. 27

progress, idea of, 32, 41, 88, 94

prostitution, prostitutes, 15, 22, 41, 42, 100, 102

Protestants, Protestantism, 5, 51, 113, 37

Provence, Provençal, 24, 55, 56, 60

Psalm(s), 4, 6, 11, 52, 84, 93, 116

psychiatric asylum, hospital institution, 37, 106, 110, 136, 137

Public Soup Kitche, 44

Quelque chose la haut ("something above"), XVII, 15, 37. *See* Jean François Millet.

radiant, radiance, 30, 54, 61, 93

raft, 127

rain, rainy, 8, 18, 43, 44, 49, 50, 60, 113

Raising of Lazarus, The, 63,

Ramsgate, 3, 26

Rappard, Anthon van, 20, 21, 45, 75 nt. 12, 90, 114, 121, 122

Raveloe, 52. *See* George Eliot (*Silas Marner*).

ray, 88, 94, 96. *See* black and white ray.

ray, the black and white, 69. *See* Victor Hugo (*Ninety-Three*).

"ray from above," XVII, 69

"ray from on high," 139

Reading Farmer at a Hearth, 36. *See* Charles Dickens, Jozef Israels

Reaper, 65, 67

reform, 26, 51, 80

rejuvenation, 72

religion, religious, XVII, 25, 28, 47, 51, 71, 82, 96, 109-13, 118, 125, 134

Rembrandt Bible, XV, XVII, 14, 17, 30, 59, 60, 63, 64, 72,73, 85, 86, 87

Remonstrant Church, 83 nt. 32

Renaissance, 55, 56, 84

renewal in nature, 19

renewal, social, 46, 77, 80

resign(ation), 22, 107, 108, 138

rest, 6, 12, 28, 95, 101, 117, 128, 131

restless(ness), 38, 52, 61

resurrection, 26, 40, 47, 48, 63, 64, 67, 85, 117

revelation, 46, 98, 140

revelatory power of poetry, 56, 82

revival movement, 118

revolution, 48

Revolution, French (1793 and 1848), 9, 14, 26, 27,46, 47, 69, 102

revolution, industrial, 51, 75

rich, 2, 4, 31, 35, 49, 92, 125

Richmond, 4

Rijksmuseum (Amsterdam), 85

river, 4, 18,112, 122
Road with Pollard Willows, 120
Romanticism, 30
Romein-Verschoor, Annie, XVI, 50
rosary, 128, 129
Rouen, 63
Roulin, Augustine, 63, 127, 128. *See La Berceuse* (The Rocker).
Roulin, Joseph, 22, 127, 128

sabbath, 64
sacrificial animal, 140
sadness, sadly, XVII, 5, 12, 40, 41, 55, 61, 67, 68, 79, 88, 89, 93, 103, 104, 110, 116, 117, 131, 136, 138, 139
sailboat, 122
sailing, 4, 122, 127, 130,
sailor, 76, 125, 126, 127, 128, 129
Saintes-Maries with Cemetery, 24, 113
Saint Rémy, XVIII, 33, 37, 44, 45, 55, 60, 65, 67, 74, 87, 93, 95, 101, 106, 108, 110, 118, 128, 134, 135, 137, 138
Saint Paul de Mausole, 37, 106, 110, 137
Saintes-Maries-de-la-Mer, Les
Salles, Rev. Frédéric, 137
Sankey, Ira David, 97. *See* Dwight Lyman Moody, C.H. Spurgeon.
sacrament, 54
sarcophaguses, 92, 95, 121
Saturn, 95
Scenes of Clerical Life, 25, 26. *See* George Eliot.
Scheveningen, 139
Scrooge, 70. *See* Charles Dickens, Christmas story.
sculptor, 76
sea, XVII, 4, 22, 24, 27, 60, 67, 76, 122, 123, 125, 127–30
sea of reality, 121
seamstresses, 38, 40. *See* Charles Edouard Frère.
Seamastressess, The,
season, XVII, 3, 65, 66, 97, 98, 106, 128. *See* Dickens, *Tale of Two Cities*.
season of light, season of darkness, 47

"secular saint," 51. *See Felix Holt* (George Eliot).
self-confidence, 138
self-portrait, 45, 88, 89, 97, 132
Self-Portrait with Bandaged Ear, 132
Self-Portrait with Bandaged Ear and Pipe, 132
sensualist, 139
serenity, 43, 74, 141
sermon, 4, 64, 81, 108, 116, 122
serpent, 90
Several Figures on a Road with Trees, 119
Shakespeare, William, 24, 25, 91
sheaf of grain, 65
sheen, 128
sheep, 48, 52
shepherd, 16, 19, 30, 54
shine, 75, 76, 78, 93, 114, 115, 118, 119
show of light, 88. *See* Frederik van Eeden, *Little John.*
Sien, 15, 41–45, 58, 72, 100, 103, 109, 111, 114, 124. *See* Clasina Hoornik.
Siddhartha, 97
Silas Marner, 26, 27, 52, 53. *See* weaver.
sin, sinner, 42, 111
Sitting Woman, 103
skeptic(ism), 26, 47, 48
sketch, 26, 36, 45,
sketchbook,122,
sky, 27, 55, 58, 60, 65–67, 86, 87, 96, 97, 98, 99, 119, 120, 142
slavery, 79. *See* Harriet Beecher Stowe.
Small, William, 131
smile, 60, 65, 68, 78, 104, 117
smoke, smoking, 131, 133, 134
"social realists" *See* Luke Fildes, Frank Holl, Hubert von Herkomer
Socrates, 139
soldier, 6, 18, 60, 114, 117, 127
sorrow (ful), XV, XVII, 19, 26, 29, 30, 35, 36, 42, 43, 54, 58, 65, 83, 115, 116, 117, 120
sorrow, worship of, 42
soul, 9, 11, 21, 25, 26, 40, 41, 48, 49, 61, 85, 90, 91, 93, 95, 113, 130
soul, human, 28, 37, 65, 66

soup, 17, 44, 79

sower, XV, 8, 18, 20, 31, 45, 54, 63, 64, 66, 77, 142

"sower of the word," 5

space, 142

spinning, 30, 51

spring, 38, 43, 58, 60, 61, 72, 77, 80, 93, 97, 98, 105

Spurgeon, C H , 97

stable,12, 53, 70, 73, 76

star(s), starry, XVII, 62, 63, 86, 89, 99, 140

Star of the Sea, 125. *See* Mary.

Starry Night, 58, 6 nt. 51, 111, 112, 119. *See* Walt Whitman.

Starry Night over the Rhone, 112

starvation, 78

statues, 55, 141

steamboat, 52, 63

Still Life around a Plate of Onions, 132

Still Life: Vase of Oleanders and Books, 91

Still Life with Open Bible, 83,

storm (y), XVII, 4, 19, 28, 42, 46, 55, 65, 67, 106, 122, 124, 125, 128

stranger, 4, 6, 13, 116, 117, 129. *See* modern Bible criticism, Johannes Paulus Stricker.

Strauss, David Friedrich, 7

Stricker, Johannes Paulus, 2, 5, 6, 81, 108

strike, 77, 78

studio, 14, 50, 73, 87, 99, 124, 132,

studio of the South, 126

suffer(ing), XVII, 1, 7, 13, 21, 23, 40, 45, 48, 60, 65, 74, 77, 83, 108, 137, 138

suffering servant, 7, 83

suicide, suicidal, XV, 133, 134, 135

sun, 8, 20, 40, 53, 57, 63, 64, 65, 66, 68, 75, 86, 87, 88, 93, 94, 96, 97, 98, 103, 104, 115, 120, 136, 141, 142, 143

sun, worship of the, 96

sunflowers, XIV, 91, 93–95, 128

sunlight, 84

"sun of righteousness," 64

sunset, 88, 115, 116, 120, 142

sunshine, 66, 106

surf, 122

symbol(ize), XVII, 17, 43, 49, 58, 61, 64–66, 74, 77, 80, 85, 91, 92, 93, 95, 111, 119, 121, 130, 133, 139–41, 143

symbolism, 91

symbol of immortality, 66,

sympathy, XIV, 7, 14, 17, 21, 32, 45, 50, 75, 102, 107, 124, 125, 128

symphony of the yellow, 30

table, 54, 71, 73, 82, 94, 100, 102, 131, 133

Tale of Two Cities, A, 46, 47. *See* Charles Dickens.

Tanguy, Julien, 29. *See* Paris.

Tarascon, 63

Tasso in Prison, 136

tears, tearful, 39, 43, 67, 91, 114, 130, 131

temptation, 48, 118

textile industry, 52

Thames, 13, 18, 31,

Thebe, Thelui, 65, 137

Theo, brother of Vincent. *See* Theo van Gogh.

theologian, liberal, 6

theologians, 111

theology, 2, 8, 10,

third-class waiting room, 18, 44

"through a glass darkly," 35

tobacco, 36, 133, 134, 135

tolerance, 6

tomb, 38, 39, 121, 137

tragedy, 46, 58, 103

transform(ation, 48, 53, 54, 60

travelers, 44, 114, 119

Trippenhuis, 85, 86. *See* Rijksmuseum (Amsterdam).

Turnham Green, 3

twilight, 30, 36, 76, 86, 120

Uncle Tom's Cabin, 74, 79. *See* Harriet Beecher Stowe.

unemployed, 51

unrest, 35, 101

unrest, social, 77

"university of sorrow," 14,
Uriah, 31. *See* David.
Valenciennes, 50
Valjean Jean, 81. *See* Hugo (*Les Miserables*).
value(s), XIV, 32, 51, 59
Vente de Paris, 45. *See* Émile Zola.
Vermeer, Johannes, XVII, 87, 142
Virgin, the, XVII, 46, 74, 128, 129, 140
virgin birth, 46
Virgin of Lourdes, 110
vision, 42, 128
visionary, 27, 112
St. Vitus dance, 129
Voltaire, 135. *See* Pangloss.
Vondel, Joost van den, 141
Voorburg, 46
Vosges, 129
Vos-Stricker, Kee, 71, 107

Wagner, Richard, 130
walking, walker, 8, 44, 47, 50, 64, 101, 115, 118–21
walking with God, 19
Wasmes, 11, 12. *See* the Borinage, Pâturages.
watercolors, 76, 87, 124
Wayen Pieterszen, Rev. van der, 10
weaver, 27, 50, 51, 52, 73, 76
Weeping Tree on a Lawn, 55
whore, 111
widow(hood), 71, 101, 107, 120
Willemien, Wil, Vincent's sister, 70, 83
willows, 45, 56, 93, 95, 120
wind, 4, 50, 53, 67, 88, 89, 91, 120, 121, 122, 130
Windekind, ("Child of the Wind"), 88. *See* Frederik van Eeden, *Little John*.
wisdom, 41, 47, 137
woodcuts woodcutters, 17, 18, 36, 40
wolves, 48, 49
woman, women, XIV, 1, 18, 25, 26, 28, 31, 40–44, 49, 50–52, 54, 55, 59, 63, 72, 74–76, 78–80, 82, 86, 90, 95, 98, 100, 103, 107, 109, 111, 114, 115, 117, 120, 121, 127–29,

Woman Reading a Novel, 80
women miners, 13
"woman of sorrow," 83. *See* Émile Zola, *Joie de vivre*.
words, spoken, 142
workers, 50, 52, 85, 139. *See* laborers.
Worn Out, XIV, 19, 36, 37
worship of sorrow, 42, 43
worship the sun, 65, 96
yellow, 30, 58, 60, 64, 66, 67, 73, 79, 80, 94, 96, 98–100, 115, 119–21, 132, 142, 143. *See* light, note.
Yellow House, the, 22, 99, 73, 91, 101, 125, 126, 127, 128. *See* Paul Gauguin.
yew tree, 66
Young Citizen of the Year V, A, 46. *See* Jules Goupil.
Young man with a Pipe, 134
Zeus, 95. *See* Jupiter.
Zundert, 1, 2, 39, 40
Zweeloo, 30

INDEX OF BIBLICAL TEXTS AND CHARACTERS

N.B.: all quotations from the Bible, including those within quotations, are by the author.

Bible, biblical, XV, 3, 5, 7, 11, 15, 19, 25, 27, 28, 29, 31, 42, 59, 64, 72, 78, 79, 82, 83, 84, 97, 118, 140, 141
Old Testament, 29
New Testament, XVII
John the Baptist, 116, 140
John the Evangelist John, XVII, 26, 47, 54, 63, 64, 78, 82, 140, 141
Luke the Evangelist, XVII, 29, 139, 140, 142
Mark the Evangelist: XVII, 140
Matthew the Evangelist, XVII, 140, 141
Paul the Apostle, letters from, 142

Genesis 3:8	8
Genesis 3:19	7, 58
Genesis 4	48
Deuteronomy 4:21	22, 127
2 Samuel 12	31
Psalm 36:10	6
Psalm 77	11
Psalm 84:11	93
Psalm 86	11
Psalm 119:19	4, 116
Psalm 119:105	84
Psalm 130	52
Psalm 138	11
Isaiah 53	83
Isaiah 53:2	45
Zechariah	140
Matthew 5:16	115

Matthew 10:16	90
Matthew 10:42	49
Matthew 11:25	28
Matthew 12:1	64
Matthew 13	77
Matthew 13:31	32
Matthew 18:21–35	31
Matthew 21:13	112
Matthew 21:25	112 nt. 13
Matthew 23:27	38
Matthew 24:35	111
Mark 4	77
Mark 4:1–27	31
Mark 13:1	2, 31, 142
Luke 2	12
Luke 5:1–11	123
Luke 10:25–37	32
Luke 13:18	19
11	
Luke 13:1–9	31
Luke 13:19	31
Luke 15:8–10	31
Luke 18:16	1
Luke 22:43–44	59
John 1:5	78
John 11:1–5	23–25, 38–44, 63
John 11:25	26, 47
John 12:24	64
John 14:6	82
Acts of the Apostles	139
Romans 12:2	80
1 Corinthians 11:24	22
1 Corinthians 13	11

Index of Biblical Texts and Characters

1 Corinthians 13:12   35
2 Corinthians 6:10   2, 35, 65, 115
Revelation   140
Revelation 3:20   85
Revelation 4:7, 140

List of Artists and Writers

Aurier, Albert (1865–1892), art critic, 22, nt. 44, 93 nt. 57, 138, nt. 81, 142, 143, nt. 90

Balzac, Honoré de (1799–1850), French writer and novelist, 25, 26

Beecher Stowe, Harriet Elizabeth (1811–1896), American writer, 25, 74, 79, 81, 82

Bernard, Emile (1868–1941), French painter, 22, 29, 58, 59, 62, 126, 134, 140–42

Boccaccio, Giovanni (1313–1375), Italian poet, 56

Boch, Eugène (1855–1941), Belgian painter, 13, 33 nt. 67

Boughton, George H. (1833–1905), Anglo–American landscape and genre painter, illustrator and writer, 115

Boulenger, Hippolyte (1837–1874), Belgian landscape painter, 120

Braekeleer, Henri de (1840–1888), Belgian artist, etcher, 135

Breton, Jules (1827–1907), French poet and painter, 21, 50, 128

Brontë, Charlotte (1816–1855), British author, 51

Bruyas, Alfred (1821–1877), art collector and patron, 136

Bunyan, John (1648–1688), English writer, 35, 37, 117, 118, 121

Carlyle, Thomas (1795–1881), Scottish historian, 25, 42, 75 nt. 12, 79, 110

Conscience, Hendrik (1812–1883), Flemish novelist, 109, 118

Coppée, Francois J.E. (1842–1908), French poet, 120

Corot, Camille Jean Baptiste (1796–1875), French painter, 19, 69

Courbet, Gustave (1819–1877), French realist painter, 59

Daubigny, François (1817–1878), French painter, lived in Auvers, 19, 101

Daudet, Alphonse (1840–1897), French writer, 25

Delacroix, Eugène (1798–1863), French painter, 30, 45, 59, 68, 130, 136

Dickens, Charles (1812–1870), English author, XV, 9, 17, 25, 26, 36, 39, 46, 47, 70, 71, 72 nt. 6,73–75, 79, 86, 92, 131, 133, 134, 135, 151

Doré, Gustave (1832–1883), French artist and lithographer, 106, 120 nt. 39, 140

Dostoyevsky, Fyodor, 27

Dupré, Jules (1811–1889), French painter and engraver; painted landscapes and seascapes; member of the Barbizon school, 89, 135

Eeden, Frederik van (1860–1932), Dutch writer, physician, and psychiatrist, 88, 89, 129

Eliot, George (1819–1880), English author, pseudonym for Mary Ann Evans, XIV, 25–27, 51, 52, 53 nt. 34, 79, 101 nt. 72,

Faed, Thomas (1826–1900), Scottish illustrator, 36

Fildes, Luke (1843–1927), English artist, 17, 18, 131

Frère, Charles Edouard (1861–1897), French painter, 40

Gachet, Paul-Ferdinand (1828–1909), French physician and amateur painter, 101, 102, 103 nt. 82, 104

Gauguin, Paul (1848–1903), French painter, 21, 22, 23, 25, 32, 56, 58, 59, 71, 73, 74, 85, 111, 125–30, 132, 133, 136

Gavarni, Paul (1804–1866), French artist, illustrator and graphic artist, known for his illustrations of contemporary daily life, 30

Genestet, Petrus Augustus de (1829–1861), Dutch preacher-poet, 28, 124

Gérôme, Jean-Léon (1824–1904), French painter, 40

Goncourt, Edmond Huot de (1822–1896), French novelist, 25, 55, 96, 102, 126

Goncourt, Jules Huot de (1830–1870), French novelist, 25, 55, 96, 102, 103, 126

Goes, Hugo van der (ca 1440–1482), Flemish painter, 135, 136

Goupil, Jules-Adolphe (1839–1883), French painter (studied with Ary Scheffer), 46

Groux, Charles de (1825–1870), Belgian painter, 40

Heemskerck, Maarten van (1498–1574), Northern Dutch painter of religious and mythological scenes and portraits, 140

Herkomer, Hubert von (1849–1914), English artist, 17, 18, 131

Hood, Thomas (1799–1848), British poet and publisher, 38, 39 nt. 12

Holl, Frank (1845–1888), English illustrator and painter, 17, 18, 41, 131

Houghton, Arthur Boyd (1836–1875), English illustrator, 72

Hugo, Victor (1802–1885), French writer, 15, 24, 25, 69, 70, 80, 81, 111

Hunt, William Holman (1827–1910), British painter, one of the Pre-Raphaelites, 39, 84, 85,

Israëls, Jozef (1824–1911), one of the most important painters of The Hague School, 16, 17, 36, 40, 85

Jeannin, Georges (1841–1925), French painter of still lifes, 93

Kerssemakers, Anton (1846–1924), Dutch amateur painter, tanner, 142

Lançon, Auguste André (1836–1887), French illustrator, 17, 30

Loti, Pierre (1850–1923), French writer, was a naval officer, 97, 125, 127–29

Longfellow, Henry W (1807–1882), American poet, 42, 43

Maaten, Jacob Jan van der (1820–1879), Dutch painter, 64

Maupassant, Guy de (1850–1993), French painter, 25, 99, 129, 135

Mauve, Anton (1838–1888), painter of The Hague School, 17, 61, 89, 98, 108, 123, 124,

Meunier, Constantin Emile (1831–1905), Belgian sculptor, painter and graphicus, 76, 77

Millais, John Everett (1829–1896), one of the pre-Raphaelite painters, 31, 84 nt. 38, 85 nt. 42

Millet, Jean François (1814–1875), French painter, 15, 19, 20, 30, 40, 59, 66, 69, 73, 103, 134

Monticelli, Adolphe Joseph Thomas (1824–1886) French painter of Italian descent, 136

Pissarro, Camille (1830–1903), French painter, 102

Puvis de Chavannes, Pierre-Cécile (1824–1898), French painter and artist, 79

Quost, Ernest (1844–1931), French painter of still lifes, 93

Rappard, Anthon Gerhard Alexander van (1858–1892), Dutch artist,

painter and etcher, 20, 21, 45, 75
      nt. 12, 90, 114, 121, 122

Rembrandt, Harmens, son of Rijn
      (1606–1669), painter, XV, XVII,
      14, 17, 30, 59, 60, 63, 64, 72, 73,
      82, 85, 86, 87

Renan, Ernest (1823–1892), French
      Orientalist, *La Vie de Jésus,* 7, 28

Richepin, Jean (1849–1926) French poet
      and prosaist, 80

Rossetti, Christina G., 115 nt. 23

Rossetti, Dante Gabriel, 17, nt. 31 and
      32, 18, nt 33, 36, nt, 3, 4 and 6,
      84, nt. 38, 115, nt. 23, 154

Ruysdael, Jacob I van (1628–1682),
      Dutch landscape painter, 87

Scheffer, Ary (1795–1858), Dutch
      painter from Dordrecht,
      primarily well–known in France,
      3, 4, 5, 6, 8

Signac, Paul (1863–1935), French
      (Parisian) painter and graphicus,
      neo-Impressionist, 25, 137 nt. 79

Tasso, Torquato (1544–1595), Italian
      poet, 135, 136

Tolstoy, Leo (1828–1910), Russian
      writer, 47, 48, 103 nt. 82

Toorop, Jan (1858–1928), Dutch painter,
      artist, 141

Vermeer, Johannes (1632–1675), Dutch
      painter and art dealer from Delft,
      XVII, 87, 142

Wauters, Émile Charles (1846–1933),
      Belgian painter, 136

Weissenbruch, Jan Hendrik (1824–
      1903), Dutch painter of the
      Hague School, XVII, 42 nt. 15, 87

Whitman, Walt (1819–1892), American
      poet, 112

Zola, Émile (1840–1902), French writer,
      27, 56, 57, 62 nt. 51, 77, 80, 83,
      91, 100

www.ingramcontent.com/pod-product-compliance
Lightning Source LLC
Chambersburg PA
CBHW071426170526
45165CB00001B/411